The Political Foundations of Judicial Independence in Dictatorship and Democracy

The Political Foundations of Judicial Independence in Dictatorship and Democracy

BRAD EPPERLY

OXFORD
UNIVERSITY PRESS

OXFORD
UNIVERSITY PRESS

Great Clarendon Street, Oxford, OX2 6DP,
United Kingdom

Oxford University Press is a department of the University of Oxford. It furthers the University's objective of excellence in research, scholarship, and education by publishing worldwide. Oxford is a registered trade mark of Oxford University Press in the UK and in certain other countries

First Edition published in 2019

Published in the United States of America by Oxford University Press
198 Madison Avenue, New York, NY 10016, United States of America

British Library Cataloguing in Publication Data
Data available

Library of Congress Control Number: 2019934007

ISBN 978–0–19–884502–7

DOI: 10.1093/oso/9780198845027.001.0001

To my grandmother, Patricia Englert

Acknowledgments

As with any book, I am grateful to many. Numerous comparative courts scholars provided feedback on my ideas. Tom Ginsburg commented on the manuscript, and has provided time, advice, and good conversation since we met when I was only a graduate student. Maria Popova and I spoke on the competition/ independence question when the project was in its infancy, and her thoughts—like her work—were insightful; I am further grateful for her comments on the manuscript. Conference feedback was helpful at various points, and Paloma Aguilar and Julio Ríos-Figueroa were nice enough to invite me to a workshop on institutions of protection in autocracies where these ideas received helpful input from each, as well as from Abel Escribà-Folch, Tamir Moustafa, Jeff Staton, Milan Svolik, and Joe Wright. Jackie Sievert, whose friend-and-coauthorship are thanks to the workshop, has been a great sounding board since.

Fieldwork was funded by the Max Weber Programme at the European University Institute and the Provost's Office at South Carolina; the latter also funded helpful research assistance from Kimberly Pilatovsky and Yuleng Zeng. I owe thanks to Ramon Marimon, who as Director of the MWP supported me decamping from Florence to Budapest. Without the aid and advice of two people at the EUI and one at the Central European University, my research in Hungary would have been far less productive. Dániel Horn offered informal advice before the first trip, and World Cup camaraderie during the second. Next time we'll go curling. Laszlo Bruszt opened numerous doors in Budapest, most notably Renáta Uitz's. Chapter 4 would not have been possible without Renáta's gracious support and guidance. I am indebted. The list of Hungarian legal scholars, government officials, and justices to whom I owe gratitude is long. Though I am undoubtedly leaving someone(s) out, and advance apologies for it, much appreciation to: Károly Bárd, András Bozóki, András Bragyova, Nenad Dimitrijevic, Zoltan Fleck, Péter Hack, Gábor Halmai, Tünde Handó, András Jakab, András Kádár, Kriszta Kovács, Péter Kovács, Miklós Lévay, Zoltan Miklosi, Péter Paczolay, Pál Sonnevend, István Stumpf, and Gábor Tóth. And many thanks to those individuals who took the time to speak to me on background. Budapest would have been far less pleasant without my friend Maria Karagiannidou, who had the good sense to live not only on the Danube, but a few floors above the best Belgian beer bar in town (if only we had the good sense to not miss that flight).

Although work on this project really began while a post-doctoral fellow at the EUI, the foundation was laid while a graduate student at the University of Washington, where I was fortunate to have wonderful advisers and fellow graduate students. Bottomless gratitude to Margaret Levi, whose advice, when taken, has never steered me wrong. The first half of Chapter 2 is the result of many conversations with comparative courts scholars; the second a single question posed by Victor Menaldo, whose continued feedback and friendship are invaluable. Two post-communist scholars were instrumental in my education: I would not have gone to UW were it not for Steve Hanson, and I would never have gone to grad school period were it not for Mike Urban. Thanks to Daniel Berliner and Stephan Hamberg for the earliest thoughts on the earliest iterations of my ideas, and to Nimah Mazaheri for sharing his expertise on oil. At South Carolina, colleagues (current and former) have given feedback on these ideas, knowingly or otherwise. Thanks to Toby Heinrich, Kirk Randazzo, Lee Walker, and Chris Witko. Barbara Barnes, an able and friendly a staff member as there ever was, helped clear roadblocks laid down by others.

Three anonymous reviewers at Oxford offered impressively engaged and incisive comments on the manuscript, and integrating (almost) all of them made for a far better book. My thanks to them, and to Dominic Byatt at OUP—as responsible and responsive an editor as any author could hope for—for soliciting them. Part of Chapter 2 draws on elements of my paper, "The Provision of Insurance? Judicial Independence and the Post-Tenure Fate of Leaders" (*Journal of Law and Courts*).[1] Hats off to the Law and Courts Section of the American Political Science Association for establishing a journal with decent authors' rights, and choosing such a superb founding editor in David Klein.

The bulk of this book was written in a comical apartment on Piazza S. Lucia in Siracusa, in the company of two friends. Cheers to Greg Wynne, perhaps the only man to go to Sicily that summer with neither shorts nor short-sleeved shirts, and Adam Bower. Both made the writing of the manuscript all the more pleasurable, and Adam was kind enough to read it all once I finished.

Of course, this would not have been possible without my family. I will be forever grateful for the support of my parents, Sue and Dale, and my grandparents, Don and Pat. The most important person in my life was thousands of miles away when most every word was written. So while I guess I can imagine the book without her, I cannot imagine my life: many thanks to my wife, Katherine. Who demands I also thank my dog, Bug.

Finally, I would like to acknowledge a group invisible, silent, and grossly underrepresented in the professoriate, which neither academia in general nor our disciplinary organizations in particular offer support. To my fellow first-generation college students, past, present, and future who—somehow—ended up professional political scientists.

Contents

List of Figures

List of Tables

Introduction

Since Federalist No. 78, the notion of the weakness of the judiciary vis-à-vis the executive and legislative branches has been widely accepted. Having "neither force nor will, but merely judgment," Hamilton famously argued that a judiciary is unable to realize even mere judgment without the aid of the branches wielding the powers of the sword and purse. While focused primarily on the relative risks posed to individual liberty by the three branches of government, in reframing Montesquieu's famous dictum in *The Spirit of the Laws* that the "judiciary is next to nothing," Hamilton makes plain that the judiciary is not only reliant upon the other two branches for its efficacy, but as importantly "all possible care" is necessary to defend the prerogatives and power of the courts from encroachment by the executive and legislature.

Federalist No. 78 forcefully argues for the importance of life tenure for federal judges as a safeguard against such encroachments. Recast in the language of the contemporary study of law and politics, Hamilton is simply arguing that without de jure, constitutional protections for judicial independence, courts will be unable to be effective, de facto independent protectors of individual liberty; the US experience is of course far from unique in this respect, as all political regimes face variations on these fundamental dynamics. The precise determinants of the constitutional assurances for independent courts and the fundamental question of under what conditions the judiciary is able to exert de facto behavioral independence remain contested questions in the literature on comparative constitutional politics. The continued vital importance of this question is illustrated both by the increasing scholarly attention paid to constitutional matters in autocratic regimes, as well as by systematic attacks on judicial independence and the separation of powers in consolidated democratic states.

Recent developments in Hungary, for example, call into question not only the role of its judiciary, but also more generally the fabric of the rule of law within the European Union and our very ideas about the stability of democratic consolidation. Although the "constitutional coup" originating with the center-right Fidesz party winning 53% of the vote and 68% of the seats in 2010 involved undermining independent state institutions of all stripes—from electoral commissions to media boards to the central bank—perhaps its most worrying developments involved systematic and sustained attacks on the power and autonomy of the Constitutional Court and judiciary more generally. In its yearly Nations in Transit review of

The Political Foundations of Judicial Independence in Dictatorship and Democracy. Brad Epperly, Oxford University Press (2019).
DOI: 10.1093/oso/9780198845027.001.0001

political changes in the post-communist states of Eastern Europe and the former Soviet Union, Freedom House (2012) summarized the constitutional and statutory changes to the status of Hungarian courts that occurred in 2010 and 2011, trenchant in its observation that "the changes cleared the way for more direct political manipulation of the courts, which had represented one of the last state institutions outside the government's control." While the Hungarian case has generated significant attention and concern on the part of civil society organizations, scholars, and policymakers in Europe and beyond, a central argument of this book is that the dynamics of the Hungarian case are both far more complicated and much more widely applicable than often appreciated.

In addition to the many normatively important cases of fluctuating judicial independence around the world—of which Hungary is but one among many, as subsequent developments in Romania and Poland illustrate—this work is also motivated by three questions fundamental to our understanding of judicial independence, questions to which existing answers are either incomplete or entirely missing. While the content of the book is product of an attempt to unify our understanding of judicial independence across both regime type and form of independence, its form flows from tackling these questions. In briefest summary, I have two simple goals: to convince the reader that there is significantly more evidence supporting the "insurance" model of judicial independence than is arrayed opposite it, and more importantly that the logic of the framework allows us to understand judicial independence across regime type and form of judicial independence. To make the case in the most convincing manner possible, I use a mixed-methods approach. Quantitatively, I employ descriptive statistics, panel regressions, and instrumental variables analysis to show that the data are consistent with my arguments concerning the insurance framework. In developing an explanation for variation in the form of judicial independence affected by competition, I rely on an in-depth case study of the status of the Hungarian judiciary under the Orbán government including extensive expert interviews with governmental officials, legal scholars, and sitting Constitutional Court judges. This mixed-methods approach offers a thorough account for the utility of strategic models focusing on the importance of electoral competition, and one which not only unifies the explanation across regime type but also across de jure and de facto independence. It is my hope that the reader will be persuaded not only of the continued and indeed expanded relevance of the insurance framework, but also that I have provided convincing resolutions to these questions, each important and lacking adequate answers.

So what are these three unanswered questions that limit our understanding of judicial independence, and which dictate the manner in which the book unfolds? The first is how regime type affects the way competition matters for judicial independence. Despite popular perceptions otherwise, elections are the name of the game in most non-democratic regimes throughout the world. In such contexts, elections are the means by which autocrats rule, and while in some instances these elections are severely restricted and uncompetitive, in many others they are both contested and meaningful. Indeed, the study of comparative politics has focused significant attention on the fact that elections are increasingly the *dominant* method by which autocrats rule. While elections may not be entirely free and fair in autocratic regimes, they have for the past quarter century been contested in more regimes than not, with autocrats fearing their results. Despite this fact, our understanding of how this common facet of contemporary autocratic regimes affects the independence of the judicial branch—whether and how political competition affects judicial independence across regime type—remains unaddressed at worst and unresolved at best. Strategic models of judicial independence that consider how competitive electoral environments induce leaders to desire independent courts as a form of insurance are at heart predicated on an expected utility calculation on the part of those leaders: the costs of losing office (which courts mitigate) conditional on the likelihood of that being the case. Law and courts scholars advocating strategic insurance explanations have to date focused entirely on the likelihood of losing office, holding the costs of such constant, and furthermore arguing that the logic applies only to the democratic context.[1] If it is the case that judicial independence is in no small part the result of calculations on the part of political leaders about the uncertainty of their future in office and what happens if removed, then a full understanding of the phenomenon necessitates understanding both components of the cost benefit analysis, and under what conditions the analysis obtains in both democratic and autocratic regimes.

The second unanswered question is whether or not incoming leaders respect the integrity and autonomy of a judiciary, and the judiciary's concomitant ability to constrain a leader's freedom of action. If incoming leaders are free to run roughshod over the courts they inherit, then the ability of those courts to provide any insurance is severely attenuated. There has, however, been no attempt to systematically assess the issue of how newly empowered leaders treat the independence of the judicial institutions they inherit. While this is an important question in its own right, it is also important because the result of its being unanswered is that whether or not the mechanisms by which the insurance model of independence is purported to work are actually working remains unexamined. In fact, despite dozens of monographs and articles advancing the insurance explanation of independence, there has been no attention to the twin questions of whether courts *can* provide any insurance to leaders once they are no longer in office and whether they in fact *do* provide such insurance. And if articles by and conversations with comparative law and courts scholars are any indication,

[1] A handful of critics, on the other hand, have in case studies of a small number of autocratic regimes argued that electoral effects differ depending on regime type. This is discussed at length in the Chapter 1.

this inattention has resulted in widespread discomfort concerning the insurance model's descriptive accuracy, based in no small part on the belief that—absent analysis otherwise—incoming leaders are not bound by the decisions of those no longer in power. In other words, the skeptical position is that new leaders can and will run roughshod over the judicial branch if they so desire, and since those formerly in power can thus never collect on an insurance policy they would not pay its premiums when in power. There exists to my knowledge no work that attempts to assess the mechanisms by which the insurance model does or does not function as supposed. Given the prominence of the insurance framework in qualitative accounts of judicial independence, it is troubling that these critical factors have remained unexamined both within these works themselves and more generally.

Rather than being long-standing and unanswered, the final question that calls for an answer is the result of my attempts to address the previous two questions. In Chapters 1–3 I show that not only does the insurance framework's focus on expected utility calculations mean that competition matters in non-democratic contexts, but in fact the salience of electoral competition—when it is present—is far greater for understanding judicial independence in non-democracies. This produces the final question: why does competition seem comparably unimportant in democratic contexts, especially considering the fact that the insurance framework does so much heavy lifting in qualitative accounts of judicial independence from case studies all around the globe?

The outline of this book tracks closely to these open questions, in turn presenting answers to each. In doing so, I offer not only answers to issues of great importance to advocates and critics of the insurance framework, but also a unified theoretical account of judicial independence in democracies and dictatorships and the ways in which electoral competition induces changes in de facto and de jure independence across regime type. Chapter 1 revisits the insurance framework for explaining judicial independence. After a brief discussion of existing work that forwards and responds to the insurance framework I offer a theoretical account to address the first question, arguing that once one focuses on the relative utility provided by more independent judiciaries as well as the probability of losing office to electoral challengers, the insurance framework provides clear expectations about the relative importance of competition across regime type. After developing this argument I formalize it with a simple expected utility model that produces clear implications for understanding insurance in autocratic regimes.

Chapter 2 addresses the causal logic underlying insurance theory, focusing on the two related but distinct questions concerning whether courts can and do provide insurance for those formerly in power. Drawing on multiple measures capturing attacks on the judicial branch as well as general measures of de facto independence, it shows persuasively that there is no evidence to support the criticism that, all else being equal, new leaders are more likely to attack or undermine the judiciary. I argue that the best way to ascertain whether courts in fact do provide insurance is to look at the personal fates of leaders once they are no longer in power, and show that independent judiciaries are strongly associated with improved post-tenure fate for former leaders; by examining multiple empirical implications of this relationship, the results provide solid evidence that not only are courts associated with better outcomes, but that the reasons they do so are highly consistent with the logic of the insurance framework. The overall result of Chapter 2 is the first-ever examination of the foundations underlying the insurance framework, which provides overwhelming support for the framework's descriptive accuracy.

Chapter 3 returns to the first question: how does political competition affect judicial independence across regime type? Rather than focusing on it at the theoretical level, it instead examines the relationship between electoral competition and de facto judicial independence, conditional on regime type, from a cross-national perspective. Statistical models of the key explanatory variables and a number of potential confounders are presented, with results showing a strong and consistent relationship between levels of electoral competition and the independence of the judiciary. Furthermore, this relationship between competition and independence is conditional on regime type: while competition is important across regimes, its substantive importance is small in democracies but large in non-democracies. These results are robust to a host of alternative model specifications, hold under different ways of measuring de facto independence, and have high out-of-sample predictive accuracy, all of which are presented in Chapter 3's appendix. Beyond these purely associational results, the chapter also offers a first attempt to take steps towards a causal interpretation of judicial independence. I argue that measures capturing salient economic conditions and non-tax sources of state revenues are convincing instruments for political competition, as the only ways they should affect levels of judicial independence are via the causal logic of the insurance framework. As evidence shows both factors increase support for incumbents—democratic or otherwise—they should thus decrease the fear those in office have of losing elections, dampening the need for more expensive insurance policies. The results of instrumental variables analyses provide further evidence that competition is of great import in non-democratic contexts, and in doing so present a first step in the comparative law and politics literature to determine whether the relationship is causal.

The results of Chapter 3 raise the empirical question that motivates Chapter 4: why do cross-national empirical results diverge from the myriad existing case studies of democratic polities, with the former showing that competition is of minimal substantive importance in such contexts? To offer a compelling answer, I move back from the empirical analyses that occupy Chapters 2 and 3 and return to the matter of theory development. In developing my answer, I theorize that while competition is critical across regime type, when observing large changes in the level of competitiveness in democratic contexts the result is not a large shock to the level of de facto judicial independence, but instead changes to the formal, de jure protections enjoyed by courts (not infrequently the focus of scholars examining specific cases). I argue that this is because more liberal political environments impose variable constraints on the behavior of leaders, such that manipulating the specifics of often esoteric formal rules regarding things like nomination and jurisdiction have far less popular political salience than blatant de facto attacks. In other words, while competition is important in both democracies and dictatorships, in the former its effects on judicial independence are on the formal, de jure rules rather than de facto behavior. This theoretical insight is developed by way of a case study of the changing judicial environment in Hungary after Fidesz won a constitutional majority (the two-thirds share of seats required to engage in unilateral constitutional change) in the 2010 parliamentary elections. An examination of the changing formal rules surrounding the Constitutional Court and the "normal" judiciary is bolstered by interviews with dozens of legal experts and judges of the Hungarian Constitutional Court. To determine its generalizability both in other democracies and in non-democratic contexts, Chapter 4 ends with a cross-national examination of the theoretical account developed in the Hungarian case.

In the concluding Chapter 5 I lay out the contributions of the book, as well as the implications of my findings for future research in comparative law and courts. In brief, there are three key contributions to the study of judicial independence specifically—and comparative law and courts more broadly—that are worth noting at this early stage. First, I offer a unified understanding of judicial independence across regime type, showing that rather than being associated with positive outcomes in consolidated democracies and negative outcomes elsewhere, competition is rather associated with higher levels of judicial independence in both, and that in fact, for reasons inherent in the logic of the insurance framework, competition's salience is heightened in autocracies. In doing so I present not only the first cross-national analyses that explicitly address questions of conceptualization of the key phenomena and the proper operationalization of these conceptualizations, but also the first attempt to leverage methods of causal inference to better understand judicial independence.

Second, even for those who might continue to question the salience of competition in non-democratic regimes, the thorough examination of the mechanisms foundational to how the insurance framework operates is in itself an important contribution. To date, neither advocates nor skeptics have presented any systematic attempt to determine the descriptive accuracy of these mechanisms, and most importantly whether or not new leaders freely run roughshod over independent judiciaries and thus invalidate any potential insurance function they may offer. I present exhaustive evidence to show that the skeptical take is incorrect, providing significant support for the insurance framework. While hardly a settled issue, future debate over this question will now be informed by data rather than intuition.

The third signal contribution offered stems from the question raised by the empirical analyses: rather than dismiss or ignore the disparity between findings from existing case-study research and the cross-national research I present, I instead return to the key factor of regime type to develop an explanation for this disparity. The result is a preliminary theoretical account that unifies insurance-based explanations of both de jure and de facto independence across regime type.

Combined, these three key contributions challenge existing theoretical arguments developed in single-country case studies or comparisons of a handful of states. Furthermore, throughout the book I demonstrate why constraining the analysis to one of the four potential contexts limits not only the empirical conclusions scholars are able to make, but also constrains theorizing about (i) the role played by political competition, (ii) its relationship to both de jure and de facto independence, and (iii) the importance of regime type as a mediating factor, interacting with political competition to affect the independence of the judicial branch. The central argument of this book is that to better understand the relationship between political competition and judicial independence, one must consider the critical mediating role played by democratic institutions (or lack thereof). In contrast to nearly all recent work on judicial independence, I argue that political competition matters for judicial independence in democratic and non-democratic regimes alike, but that changes in the competitiveness of the electoral arena produce differing results depending on the regime context in which they occur.

1
The Expected Utility of Insurance

Boris Yeltsin's re-election in 1996 included shocking reversals between the first and second round of voting, and his campaign was in part funded by the diversion of significant resources away from the state as part of the "loans for shares" scheme, in the process undermining the legitimacy of post-communist privatization in the country (Goldman 2004, Myagkov & Ordeshook 2008). Less than a decade later, his hand-picked successor used the might of the tax police against Mikhail Khodorkovsky—believed the richest person in the country, and who secured much of his wealth through the very loans for shares programs that helped Yeltsin remain in office—after he began financing nascent opposition groups (Elder 2010). Khodhorkovsky found himself on trial for his alleged misdeeds—many of which were not in fact crimes when committed—only after the 2003 legislative elections in which the "party of power" secured its political dominance (winning three times as many votes as the second-place party, and more than four times the number of seats) and the 2004 presidential elections in which Putin increased his vote share from a bare majority (in 2000) to over 70%. The result was conviction, which outside observers saw as predictable as it was flimsy (Gessen 2012). A decade after Khodorkovsky was arrested, a Russian court convicted Alexei Navalny, a leader of the still-incipient opposition, of embezzlement, the same charge previously leveled against the (then) still-imprisoned Khodorkovsky as the date of his possible parole neared (Herszenhorn 2013);[1] importantly, Navalny's conviction in his retrial disqualifies him from running in the 2018 presidential elections. All the while, Russian elections have been plagued with serious electoral fraud, consistently ensuring increased levels of support for Vladimir Putin individually and his party United Russia in general (Myagkov, Ordeshook, & Shakin 2005, Rundlett & Svolik 2016, White 2016).

These examples from Russia's post-communist experience are well-known to those familiar with the manipulation of elections and the electoral arena typical of competitive or electoral authoritarian regimes, those states where autocrats rule

[1] Gessen (2012) notes that "If the first set of charges [against Khodorkovsky] was thin, the second was absurd." Noteworthy is the fact that like the case against Navalny this second, far more fantastical and politicized prosecution occurred only after the subsequent legislative elections in which Putin's United Russia party nearly doubled its already dominant vote share, winning six times more votes and seats than the second-place Communist party and burying the idea of a credible electoral threat to those in power.

The Political Foundations of Judicial Independence in Dictatorship and Democracy. Brad Epperly, Oxford University Press (2019). © Brad Epperly
DOI: 10.1093/oso/9780198845027.001.0001

through elections that are neither entirely free nor fair, using the "administrative resources" of the state to tilt the playing field in their favor (Levitsky & Way 2002, Schedler 2002). Indeed, the use of elections in autocratic regimes has become the norm rather than the exception: as a recent Freedom House report on the mechanisms of autocratic governance points out, an "obligation to hold some form of multiparty balloting is felt by nearly all governments" (Puddington 2017, 10). And recognizing this electoral nature of autocratic rule has serious implications for conceptualizing and understanding non-democratic regimes and their dynamics (Lindberg 2009, Roessler & Howard 2009, Levitsky & Way 2010).

While the details of competition that is neither free nor fair is likely familiar to comparative politics scholars (especially those focused on autocratic regimes), these details are potentially less familiar to others, including legal scholars. What do such contexts look like, exactly? While there is no inarguably definitive case, common aspects can be highlighted via example. Key to understanding how elections look different in autocratic regimes—especially those where elections "matter"—is in understanding the ways in which these elections are neither free nor fair. And the ways in which the freedom and fairness of elections are undermined hinge on the choices and strategies those in power make to decrease the possibility of unwanted electoral outcomes. To understand but one way in which competition looks fundamentally different in autocratic regimes, and in which elections are fundamentally unfair, we can look to actions taken by Hugo Chávez in Venezuela in the run up to the 2012 elections. Beyond outright vote-buying and ballot box-stuffing (both common activities for rulers in competitive and non-competitive authoritarian regimes), a key aspect of unfair elections is a playing field tilted heavily in favor of incumbent autocrats. In Venezuela this included rules mandating both that presidential speeches must take precedence over normal television and radio programming, and that stations must broadcast ten 30-second state messages daily. While potentially neutral on face, such mandates are classic examples of the administrative resources possessed by illiberal leaders, who wield them as weapons with which to bludgeon the opposition.[2] A Venezuelan NGO estimated that, in the run up to elections, the 100 hours of broadcast presidential speeches and the highly politicized state messages utilized by Chávez produced a combined value of over $2 billion of free advertising for the incumbent regime (Puddington 2017). All told, in combination of paid and unpaid advertising, the result was an opposition with access to only 4% of the incumbent's airtime.

Despite the fact that elections are ubiquitous in autocratic regimes, there has been little focus in the study of courts in non-democracies on how elections

[2] Of course, there are carrots as well as sticks. The same analyst estimated that during the 2012 elections the state oil company handed out approximately $20 billion worth of gifts in various forms (including cash) to voters.

might affect the judiciary; this is in no small sense a fundamental contradiction in the popular strategic insurance account of judicial independence, and the inattention presents barriers to bridging significant strands of research. Resolving this contradiction thus promises not only a better understanding of electoral theories of judicial independence, but also a greater synthesis between comparative constitutional research on democratic as opposed to autocratic systems, and between law and courts research and comparative politics more generally.

This contradiction arises from, first, the logic of the insurance accounts of judicial independence used to explain democratic contexts and, second, the self-imposed barriers to its use under conditions of authoritarianism. The logic of the insurance account, to which I subsequently turn, is that to protect against the costs associated with losing elections and office, incumbents further an independent judiciary as a means of constraining those in power in the future. This contradiction is puzzling, because even the insurance account's largest proponents in democratic contexts reject its applicability to autocracies, treating as self-evident the idea that while elections are the main driver in democracies, they induce none of the same preferences in non-democracies despite the far greater risks associated with autocrats losing power. In the introduction to their seminal volume on courts in authoritarian regimes, Ginsburg & Moustafa (2008, 28) contend that "the electoral logic of judicialization in democracies clearly does not apply in authoritarian settings," though they offer no evidence or argument for why this is the case. In this chapter I lay out the case for why this assumption on the part of insurance theorists is incorrect, ignoring the fact that elections in non-democratic regimes, be they of the competitive authoritarian or hegemonic variant, are meaningful (Lust-Okar 2009), and "incumbents are forced to sweat" (Levitsky & Way 2010, 10).

Taking this understanding of the importance of electoral politics in non-democratic systems, I argue rather that electoral competition—when present—is of even greater salience in authoritarian settings. In making this case I proceed as follows. In Section 1.1 I offer a tour of the insurance explanation of judicial independence in democracies, with a detour along the way to examine the conceptualization of de jure and de facto independence (I beg the reader to put questions concerning this conceptualization on hold until this detour). Those steeped in the literature on the insurance framework might want to move directly to Section 1.2, which begins rather than ends with a detour to discuss precisely how I conceptualize democracy and autocracy.[3] After this, I briefly discuss how existing research assesses the relationship between competition and independence

[3] An important note on terminology is in order. As is common among comparative politics scholars working on non-democratic politics (see, for example, the work of Jennifer Gandhi or Milan Svolik), for reasons of readability I use terms like non-democracy, dictatorship, autocracy, and authoritarianism interchangeably. Similarly, in discussing the insurance model of judicial independence, I use terms like model, framework, explanation, and account as equivalents.

in autocratic regimes, including that of scholars like Popova (2012) who formulate arguments whose scope and implications differ from mine. After this groundwork is laid, I then present my argument: that the logic of the existing insurance model, predicated as it is on intertemporal uncertainty and electoral competition, should have not only great salience in the autocratic context, but greater salience than in the democratic. In other words, competition matters, but it matters far more in non-democratic regimes. After laying out the details of the argument, I develop a simple expected utility model to illustrate the argument's implications.

Before moving on to these theoretical concerns, however, I want to first convince the skeptical reader of the relevance of the matter at hand, thus answering the question of whether this is actually a subject worthy of attention. Stated directly: is either electoral competition or judicial independence actually of relevance in the autocratic regimes of the world? Asked independently of one another, the answer to these questions for scholars of comparative politics and law and courts is undoubtedly 'yes'. Significant attention is paid to elections in non-democratic regimes (Levitsky & Way 2002, Schedler 2002, Lindberg 2009), and courts as well are the subject of much work (Helmke 2005, Moustafa 2007, Ginsburg & Simpser 2013).

Figure 1.1 further illustrates this point. It plots the distribution of political competition and de facto judicial independence in non-democratic regimes from 1960 to 2006.[4] Plot (a) illustrates quite clearly that in the large minority of

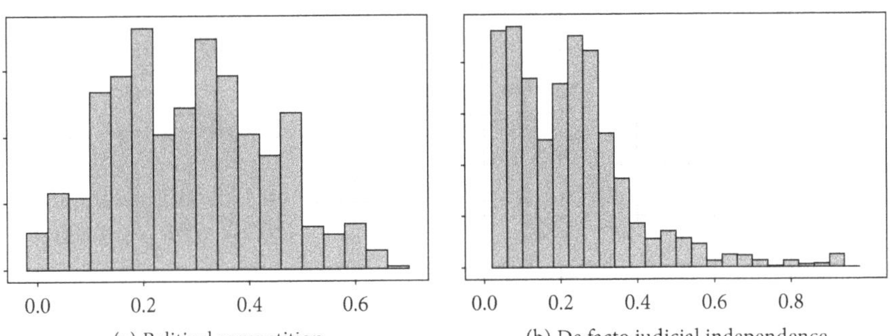

Figure 1.1 Political competition and de facto independence in autocracies. Two histograms showing the distribution of political competition and de facto judicial independence in non-democratic regimes from 1960 to 2006 (each measure ranges from 0 to 1). Plot (a) shows non-zero levels of competition to better visualize the variation in the more than 20% of autocratic country-years where this is the case; plot (b) shows judicial independence in all autocratic country-years.

[4] The specific measures used here are the Henisz (2000) measure of legislative constraints on the executive and the Linzer & Staton (2015) latent judicial independence measure. These will be discussed at greater length in subsequent chapters.

non-democratic regimes that witness electoral competition there is marked variation, and also that competitive or electoral authoritarian regimes are far from rare. This is even more the case if one were to consider only the post-Cold War era that Levitsky & Way (2010) focus on in their comprehensive treatment of the phenomenon: a full 40% of autocratic country-years after 1991 show some degree of electoral competition, suggesting that this analysis is even more important in the contemporary era.

Recent attention by some comparative law and courts scholars notwithstanding, the idea that judicial independence exists in autocracies is likely a more contentious claim than that of electoral competition. If one moves away from a dichotomous conceptualization of the phenomenon—are courts independent or not?—to one in which variation is the issue, however, it quickly becomes clear that such variation must exist. Not all autocracies, after all, are able to so adroitly employ the "telephone justice" for which the Soviet Union was famous (Pepys 2003, Hendley 2009), and more than a few autocrats inherit democratic institutions, clamping down on their independence with varying degrees of success. The histogram in plot (b) of Figure 1.1 conveys this visually, plotting the popular Linzer & Staton measure of de facto judicial independence for all autocratic country-years from 1960 to 2006, where 1 is a more independent judiciary. While the bulk of the observations cluster to the left side of the x-axis representing lower levels of independence (to be expected, considering these are autocratic regimes), a large minority demonstrate meaningful levels of independence, and a not insignificant minority demonstrate levels that can only be called high.

The two plots in Figure 1.1 echo the literature on competitive authoritarianism and authoritarian constitutionalism and courts, respectively: in some sense, plot (a) visualizes the distribution of the competitive or electoral authoritarian regimes analyzed by those such as Levitsky & Way (2010) and Schedler (2006). Similarly, like the many contributors to the influential volume on judicial independence in non-democracies edited by Ginsburg & Moustafa (2008), plot (b) illustrates that there exist many autocracies where judiciaries exercise meaningful levels of independence. Of course, neither plot demonstrates that these two ought be studied in autocracies *together*, merely that each is itself relevant. Making a convincing case that competition matters for explaining independence matters in non-democracies is my goal in this chapter. But first, let me turn to the important work on this relationship in democracies.

1.1 Competition and Independence in Democracies

Fundamental to any explanation of judicial independence is the question of why political leaders—be they parties or individuals, democrats or dictators—would establish, maintain, or expand an institution with independent power and the ability to check their policies and prerogatives. As such, positive theories of judicial independence seeking to answer this question typically focus on the benefits that independent judiciaries can offer the political branches, and thus why these branches would delegate these powers to courts.

1.1.1 Delegative Explanations

One of the earliest and most influential delegative accounts focuses on the ability of courts to solve the time inconsistency problems that plague government actors, especially legislatures. For Landes & Posner (1975), the crux of the matter is the fact that while legislatures desire to maximize their campaign contributions and support from interest groups at time *t*, there exists nothing to constrain the legislature—even if comprised of the very same individuals—from reneging on campaign promises and policies enacted in exchange for support in future time periods. An independent judiciary can thus solve, or more accurately mitigate, this problem by making it more difficult to renege. As with all credible commitment and time inconsistency problems, the obvious analogy is that of Odysseus and the Sirens: legislators know that in the future their short-term interest will be to offer new deals to new groups to maximize contributions, but that doing so will attenuate the value of their promises. Here, an independent judiciary plays the role of the crew, binding the legislature to the mast of its previous commitments.

There are two other direct benefits that have been argued to induce the political branches to tolerate judicial checks on their authority worth mentioning before moving on to those directly concerned with political competition. Both focus on the informational benefits independent courts provide. First, courts that are independent of the executive and legislature are able to provide the benefit of effective and cheap "fire alarm" oversight of the bureaucracy (McCubbins & Schwartz 1984). As routinized "police patrol" forms of oversight are costly, establishing fire alarm mechanisms is critical. An independent judiciary helps solve principal-agent problems, allowing for significant monitoring costs to be offloaded to non-state actors: private citizens, firms, and non-governmental organizations who bring suit against state agents, signaling when these agents require sanctioning for failing to comply with the mandates of their government principals.

Second, independent courts with judicial review powers help resolve issues surrounding the uncertainty of the specific outcomes of state policies, allowing courts to identify problematic policies ex post whose ill effects were unexpected ex ante (Rogers 2001, Whittington 2003).[5] For two reasons, both informational

[5] Developed by scholars of American courts, both explanations have clear cognates in judicial systems lacking diffused judicial review powers in ordinary courts: constitutional complaint and abstract review. The former allows agents to be monitored and sanctioned by the public, while the

benefits rely not just on courts, but on *independent* courts. First, as both state agents and policies can be beholden to or preferred by either the executive or the legislature, an impartial adjudicator is necessary; in instances where the judiciary is dependent on one or the other, any information it provides is thus suspect.[6] Second, because many policies are examined ex post, and many agents were appointed by different actors, a dependent judiciary cannot effectively solve the intertemporal dimensions of these problem across successive governments, as any decisions it made would be suspect due to its dependence on political actors with preferences often dissimilar to those enacting the policies or appointing the agents.

Although summarized only briefly, these three explanations highlight the importance of looking at the benefits that an independent judiciary can provide for political actors, thus answering to some degree the vital question of why these actors would tolerate an institution able to tell them 'no'.[7] These three explanations also highlight a problem for explanations that focus solely on the direct benefits independent courts provide, and one that is of far greater import in the comparative rather than American study of courts and constitutionalism. This is the fact that they are far less able to adequately explain variation in levels of independence. If time inconsistency problems are as ubiquitous for legislatures as Landes & Posner (1975) suggest, then surely the need to mitigate them is as ubiquitous. Principal-agent problems similarly abound, and deciphering ex ante how policies might fail ex post is always costly. At their core, these explanations emphasize the benefits independent courts provide, but have far less emphasis on why these benefits might be seen to vary temporally or cross-sectionally. It is for this reason that I now turn to an explanation focused on how variation in political conditions should help us better understand variation in judicial independence.

1.1.2 The Insurance Model

The insurance explanation of judicial independence, focused on the salience of political competition and uncertainty, is a direct outgrowth of the delegative explanations presented above. In arguably its first articulation, Ramseyer (1994) details the ways in which neither the interest-group nor bureaucratic oversight perspective is able to adequately explain the dissimilarities between post-war Japan

latter offloads the cost of assessing the legality of legislation to a dedicated institution, lowering the costs for both the legislature and executive.

[6] This is related to the benefits courts can provide due to competition among different levels in federal systems. See, for example, Vanberg (2000) and Whittington (2005).

[7] A fourth explanation, notably advocated for by Vanberg (2005) and Staton (2010), focuses on the role of public support for the court and the threat of backlash against democratic actors who attack a popular judiciary. This perspective will be addressed at length in Chapter 4.

and the United States. Ramseyer demonstrates that despite having highly similar constitutional arrangements, a result of US occupation after the war, the degree of behavioral independence varies markedly. He argues that this variation is a result of decades-long, uninterrupted rule by the Liberal Democratic Party in Japan. The security in office and expectations of future rule created far different incentive structures for those holding the executive and legislature than the conditions of uncertainty observed in the American case.

The basic logic of the political insurance framework is that when those in power have expectations that they will in the near or intermediate future be out of power, their fear of majority encroachment on minority interests drives them to establish or maintain independent judiciaries as a form of insurance against untrammeled majority rule. In such circumstances, political leaders will make the calculated trade-off to pay costs today to be secure if things go poorly in the future, and thus induce those holding the reins of power to transfer some of this power to the judiciary. Key here is the degree of competition within the electoral arena: it is only when incumbents fear that an opposition party is able to present itself as a credible alternative that they will pay the costs of insurance.

Although rarely framed explicitly, the insurance framework is one in which leaders face an expected utility calculation, the product of the costs of losing office (minus the costs of independent courts) and the probability that such an event might occur. Focusing as it does on democratic contexts, the existing literature conceives of the costs of losing office as fundamentally policy-based, and thus the *form* of insurance courts offer is the continuation of preferred policies after losing power.[8] In the insurance framework, courts provide policy stability not by solving the time inconsistency problem, but instead by ensuring that the opposition, after taking power, is unable to engage in wholesale revision or reversal of its predecessor's policies (Ramseyer 1994); this insurance is thus analogous to the insurance function provided by independent central banks (Horn 1995, Boylan 2001) or impartial bureaucracies (Geddes 1994). It is not that those in power are unable to infringe on judicial independence to reverse their predecessor's policies if the judiciary upholds them. Rather, what matters in the insurance logic is that expectations of being out of office themselves in the not-too-distant future "keeps them honest": parties in power respect independence and forgo some policy objectives that could be gained through its violation so that their opponents do the same once they take power. Lacking an opposition able to credibly threaten incumbents, however, there is no incentive for incumbents to acquiesce to the independence of an institution capable of checking their preferred policies (legal

[8] Implicitly, existing work assesses only changes in the probability of losing office, i.e. the competitiveness of the electoral arena, holding the costs of losing office constant. In Section 1.2 I present an argument about when we should consider changes in the costs of losing office.

or otherwise). Judicial independence is thus, essentially, a "risk-reduction device," offering electoral losers insurance (Ginsburg 2003, 32).[9]

The electoral logic of the insurance model has been widely applied to understand judicial independence in case studies of states in Europe (Magalhaes 1999, Halmai 2002), Latin America (Chavez 2004, Finkel 2005, Ríos-Figueroa 2007), and East Asia (Ginsburg 2003), as well as the United States (Whittington 2003). Stephenson (2003) explicitly formalizes the logic, and the clarity of his presentation warrants further discussion.[10] He presents a game theoretic model, analyzing changes in five parameters that affect the payoffs for political parties to accept or violate judicial independence, and testing an empirical implication. Two of these parameters—the judiciary's deference and policy slant—involve the judiciary as an actor, and Stephenson shows that courts that desire to maintain independence should not stray too far in either direction with regards to the (two) political actors (but especially not towards a consistently politically weak pole): too much deference to one or a policy slant too far in one direction bodes ill for the court, conditional on the degree of political competition. Testing this empirical implication would be highly difficult, given the issues confronting work on comparative judicial behavior (Ginsburg 2008, Epperly & Lineberger 2017). Two further parameters, while doubtlessly of vital importance to a complete understanding, involve the subjective mental states of political leaders. While one might possibly attempt to ascertain the risk aversion of the apex leader(s) of a given political party or regime, as well as their discount rate with regards to future payoffs, determining either of these in a comparative manner is likely impossible; as such, and completely justifiably, Stephenson develops the theoretical implications of these parameters without testing their empirical implications.

The critical parameter for Stephenson (2003) is, not surprisingly given the focus, the competitiveness of the electoral system, and it is here that his model and its implications are most fully examined. His formal results demonstrate strong support for the critical nature of a competitive political arena, as without one maintaining judicial independence is unlikely. Empirically, Stephenson presents one of the handful of quantitative examinations of the insurance framework. Like Aydın (2013), he averages the key variables for a cross-section of countries, finding that past executive turnover is strongly associated with de facto judicial independence.

Another key contribution of Stephenson's (2003) formal treatment of the insurance model is that it stresses the need for continued political competition in the

[9] Critical to this logic is the assumption that independent courts are in fact capable of and do offer effective insurance, as without it there is no reason for incumbents to pay the costs associated with judicial independence; although this assumption has remained untested, the Chapter 2 demonstrates that courts are both capable of and do provide insurance for those formerly in power.

[10] I refrain from examining the formal implications of Stephenson's (2003), as his presentation is straightforward and it is further examined in depth by Vanberg (2015).

maintenance of de facto judicial independence. As Vanberg (2015, 175) notes, it thus "underscores the importance of clearly distinguishing between explanations for the creation of independent courts and explanations for ongoing judicial authority." Vanberg contrasts this with those formulations of the insurance framework that focus instead on the distribution of political power among parties during the constitution-drafting stage, the most notable being Ginsburg (2003), whose agenda-setting work popularized the term 'insurance model'.[11] On a theoretical level, Vanberg is correct that we must carefully distinguish explanations for the establishment of institutional arrangements and explanations for their continued salience, as many institutionalists have long stressed. While Ginsburg's treatment is explicitly about electoral uncertainty when constitutions are being drafted and its effects on de jure independence, the role of continued political competition implicitly plays a significant role in how this de jure independence is realized behaviorally, both immediately after new constitutions are in force and in the proceeding decade(s).[12]

Nonetheless, I highlight this distinction here because it is of great importance in going forward, as it is specifically *changes* in the degree of judicial independence that I seek to explain, rather than the adoption of formal rules during times of constitutional development and adoption. There are three reasons for this. First, comparative constitutional research offers significant insights into the dynamics of this stage, as the many examples cited above and countless others attest, and reinventing the wheel is needless.[13] More important is the second reason, which is that if one considers political factors to be vital, then looking solely at moments of constitution-drafting offers little purchase in understanding behavioral, de facto independence if political conditions change after constitutions are adopted; given a key premise of insurance accounts is conditions of uncertainty, it seems safe to consider changing conditions is the rule rather than exception. Third, it is also the case that de jure independence is far from static, and as a result change in the de jure constitutional provisions for judicial independence is worthy of examination, and such would also be ignored if we restricted our analysis to adoption. For these three reasons, the theoretical account in Section 1.2 and 1.3 (and the analyses presented in subsequent chapters) focus not on formal provisions set during moments of constitution-drafting, but rather as changes in the level of judicial independence over the many years a regime is in existence.[14]

[11] Hirschl (2000, 2004) offers an important account related to the insurance framework, arguing that hegemonic decline that is key, with formerly dominant elites adopting judicial independence to ward against what they see as the writing on the wall.

[12] For a thorough cross-national examination of the association between competition and the adoption of formal judicial review powers, see Ginsburg & Versteeg (2013).

[13] For overviews, see Ginsburg (2008) and Hirschl (2014).

[14] In these subsequent chapters, the analysis of change is conducted both by fixed effect "within" models that allow me to analyze absolute levels but capture their change within a given country over time as well as models explicitly using a measure of the change in independence from preceding years.

1.1.3 De Jure and De Facto Independence

At the beginning of this chapter I implored the reader to set aside for a while questions concerning the conceptualization of judicial independence, not because they are unimportant but precisely because they very much are, and thus warrant a detour. Now that a number of important distinctions have been made concerning the nature of the insurance model(s) and how it relates to different forms of judicial independence, it is time for just such a detour. Unsurprisingly, given my focus on the empirical examination of judicial independence, I reject the argument that the supposedly "essentially contested" nature of judicial independence prevents its analytic usefulness (Kornhauser 2002). Beyond conflating empirical and theoretical issues surrounding our understanding of judicial independence, such claims also conflate an inability to reach a complete and settled consensus definition with an inability to understand what others mean when using the concept. This extreme position offers few solutions, other than abandoning attempts to reach consensus or engage in parallel avenues of research employing differing definitions and measures (Staton 2017). Such a position seems not only problematic but also incorrect, given that consensus seemingly does exist on many of the basic principles of the concept and how to measure it (Tate & Keith 2007, Ríos-Figueroa & Staton 2012).

At the most basic level, the distinction between de facto and de jure independence is the distinction between formal rules and actual behavior, with all that implies about any potential relationship (or lack thereof) between the two. While some debate remains about what specific constitutional provisions should be considered critical for assessing the degree to which a given system protects formal de jure independence, consensus exists that what is important are the rules of the game as laid out formally by the constitutional structure.[15] Such a scholarly consensus is aided by a global consensus on the desirability of constitutional structures ensuring independence, as evidenced by the United Nation's *Basic Principles on the Independence of the Judiciary*. The sorts of provisions assessed by various authors as important include formal statements of independence and review, guaranteed term length, the separation of powers, selection procedures,

[15] A case can be made that in some systems many of the formal rules providing for judicial independence are statutory, not constitutional (Epperly & Sievert 2018). While it might be argued that statutory rather than constitutional provisions are weaker, it is more difficult to argue that statutory provisions *should* be entirely ignored. Many constitutions leave the specific articulation of the provisions considered important to statute, and even if these protections are weaker than the constitutional variety, variation can still exist, and rules can be respected. If one considers, for example, a constitutional provision of twelve years for judicial tenure to better protect judges than six years, then it follows that a statutory provision of twelve years better protects than a statutory provision for six. The United States is illustrative of this point, with significant provisions empowering the federal judiciary adopted by Congressional statute (especially after the Civil War) and many state constitutions calling for statutory enumeration of judicial powers and prerogatives. Unfortunately, compiling such statutory data for even the US federal judiciary, let alone a broad selection of cases, remains extremely difficult and an avenue for promising future research.

hierarchy, and removal procedures (Finkel, Pérez-Liñán, Seligson, & Tate 2008, Melton & Ginsburg 2014). As noted previously, significant attention has been paid to how changing levels of competition might affect de jure protections during eras of both constitution-drafting (Ginsburg 2003, Ginsburg & Versteeg 2013) and hegemonic decline (Hirschl 2000), as well as the relationship more generally (Ramos 2006).

Despite the normatively appealing idea that de jure provisions "matter," and that incorporating the proper text into constitutions can better ensure a judiciary that is independent in a practical, de facto sense, the empirical results on the matter are mixed, with significant evidence to suggest that they are mere parchment barriers (Smithey & Ishiyama 2002, Helmke & Levitsky 2006, Aydın 2013). This is, naturally, somewhat troubling: while few would contend that the only things that matter are formal rules, with actual behavior being entirely disconnected, the opposite extreme is similarly counterintuitive. What is thus more likely is that the rules matter, but only conditional on some other factor. That is, whether de jure independence is associated with behavioral independence is likely a matter of when, not if. In a recent analysis of de jure independence, Melton & Ginsburg (2014) raise the potential for de jure independence to matter only when such independence is self-enforcing. Unfortunately, while appealing and promising, their empirical results remain mixed, and the jury is still out on whether de jure judicial independence "matters" for de facto.

The fact that as a phenomenon de facto judicial independence is latent and not directly observable would lead one to expect that it would be far more difficult to reach a consensus on how to best conceptualize and measure the phenomenon. Thankfully, despite these hurdles such a consensus is being reached. Ríos-Figueroa & Staton (2012) illustrate this development in their analysis of the concept and the most popular ways to operationalize it, and in the intervening years consensus on measurement in empirical work has improved even more markedly, a function of Linzer & Staton (2015) developing an important measure.[16] When conceptualizing de facto independence, a distinction is sometimes drawn between the twin components of autonomy and power (Burbank & Friedman 2002). Judicial systems are autonomous when judges are the "authors of their own opinions." That is, when the decisions handed down by courts are the result of judicial decision-making unadulterated by undue outside influence. Outside actors able to unduly influence courts are in practice limited to those with power: executives, legislatures, and the agents of both, often have the ability to violate the independence of the judicial branch, as do powerful non-state actors. Inappropriate influence can take a variety

[16] In fact, it might be the case that the past few years have observed greater consensus on measurement of judicial independence than democracy. This general consensus might, however, be reversed due to the development of a similar measure by the Varieties of Democracy project. Both will be discussed at length in the Chapter 2.

of guises, from intimidation and threats to corruption and bribery. In less dramatic variations, courts can become accomplices in violations of their own autonomy, with individual actors within the judicial branch engaging in actions undermining their corporate interests.

On the other hand, judiciaries have power when other actors listen to what they say. When the rulings of courts are routinely ignored by state actors, or the required enforcement fails to materialize, courts cannot be said to be powerful. Lacking as they do the powers of the purse or sword, courts must rely on other branches to support their decisions. This support may be in the form of modifying or rescinding governmental policies when courts rule against the government, or exacting punishment when courts rule against non-state actors. Regardless of the target of judicial rulings, when support by the executive and legislature does not exist, regardless of the level of autonomy the courts may enjoy, they lack power, and are therefore not independent in the de facto sense.

Drawing a clear distinction between these two aspects of independence is of little utility to those interested in discerning empirical patterns, especially with regards to de facto independence, as the degree to which the two are so analytically distinct remains unclear (Epperly & Sievert 2018). It means little, after all, to say that a court is de facto independent if it possesses significant autonomy but its decisions regularly go unenforced, or if a court has the power to affect outcomes via its rulings but those rulings are not the result of autonomous decision-making. In some part, this attempt to draw clear analytical boundaries between these interrelated components is likely a result of a focus on a clear dichotomy between those judiciaries that are either powerful or not, autonomous or not (as well as a focus on formal provisions rather than observed behavior). A focus on variation, however, illustrates that different judiciaries can be more or less powerful, and the same judiciary's power can fluctuate over time (Whittington 2003). Furthermore, given the latent nature of the phenomenon, attempting in practice to ascertain change in only one component independent of the other is difficult at best. As such, following standard practice in the comparative study of judicial independence (Epperly 2013, Epperly 2017, Escribà-Folch & Wright 2015, Linzer & Staton 2015, Randazzo, Gibler, & Reid 2016), I consider these interrelated components together.

One final note on the nature of judicial independence is necessary before turning to the logic of the insurance model in non-democratic regimes, concerning the question of which courts' independence are at issue in the subsequent chapters. Following standard practice in the literature (Melton & Ginsburg 2014), I focus on the independence of high courts (be they constitutional tribunals like the German Federal Constitutional Court or the court of last resort like the US Supreme Court). There are both practical and theoretical reasons for doing so. Practically, it is routine practice precisely because it is feasible both with regards to issues of the reasonableness of data collection and comparability across cases (e.g. federal and non-federal). Theoretically, there is reason to believe that the independence of the highest court is meaningful for the entire judiciary, as it is either the court of last resort or the sole body tasked with interpreting the constitutionality of state action. Indeed, if one is particularly interested in the *political* determinants of judicial independence, the independence of the court with the only or final say on the constitutionality of government action is critical: if only constitutional tribunals are able to rule against governments, then their independence is critical, and in systems where judicial review is diffused throughout the judiciary, if a government captures the highest appellate court it has effectively neutralized lower courts due to the nature of judicial hierarchies and precedent. Empirically, recent data collection efforts and research suggest that this focus on the independence of high courts also captures the independence of the judiciary writ large: in surveys of legal experts in over a hundred countries, the World Justice Project (Agrast, Botero, & Ponce 2011) asks for separate assessments of the degree to which national and local courts are free from political influence. As Voigt, Gutmann, & Feld (2015) note, the fact that these assessments are correlated at 0.98 suggests that—even absent theoretical reasons for privileging high court independence—there is little reason for practical concern about serious divergence between the highest court and the ordinary judiciary.

1.2 Competition and Independence in Non-democracies

In Section 1.1 I recapitulate the key insights of the insurance framework and highlight the logic as it has been applied to democratic regimes. One of my main goals in this book, however, is to offer a persuasive argument that the mechanisms underpinning the insurance model should apply to non-democratic states as well, and in fact that competition should be of even more salience—when it is present—in non-democracies. At the beginning of this chapter I demonstrated that both electoral competition and judicial independence vary in autocratic regimes; the rest of this chapter makes the case for why these two phenomena are related. Before doing so, however, I turn my attention to two important issues: how to conceptualize regime type and existing research looking at competition and independence in non-democracies.

1.2.1 Democracy vs. Dictatorship

One of the most fundamental questions concerning the conceptualization—and subsequently the measurement—of democracy is whether it should be conceived of as a categorical or continuous phenomenon. Our chosen answer to this question has significant implications for our understanding not only of democracy itself but also other related phenomena (Cheibub, Gandhi, & Vreeland 2010), not least of all judicial independence. If conceptualized as a constellation of different categories, closely following on the heels is the second question of the nature and proper number of categories. While no small amount of ink has been spilled on this question,[17] it is Collier & Adcock (1999) who propose what is perhaps the most pragmatic solution to the debate over the proper concept and measure of democracy. Pointing out that most advocates of a given approach make assumptions concerning the self-evident nature of their preferred concept and that are persuasive arguments for various alternatives, they suggest that the nature of the research question being asked should dictate the appropriateness of alternative conceptualizations. It is my opinion that for the purposes of understanding whether and how the relationship between political competition and judicial independence is conditional on regime type, a categorical conceptualization of democracy is most appropriate, and that this categorical approach should be fundamentally dichotomous. This is the case for at least two key reasons.

First, on a conceptual level, if one's goal is to understand the differences between regime *types* (i.e. categories), a continuous measure is fundamentally problematic. For example, if one uses the popular Polity measure to assess the relationship between competition and independence like Randazzo, Gibler, & Reid (2016), it makes little sense to speak of how competition differs across the type of regime, as one is instead conceptualizing regime in a manner consistent with Polity's 21-point scale ranging from complete autocracy to complete democracy.[18] On the one hand, this is because there is no conceptually grounded reason for any set of given cut-points to convert Polity's 21-point scale into (any number of) regime categories; this holds true if one instead uses a different continuous measure of democracy. Continuing with the Polity example, there is no conceptually motivated reason to make a distinction between regime types when a given state moves from a score of 5 to 6 (where a state is classified as a democracy), as the score for a given state at any point in time is the aggregation of disparate components, none of which is a "'necessary condition' for characterizing a political system as democratic" (Marshall, Jaggers, & Gurr 2015, 15). On the other hand, the nature of aggregating these disparate components means that one is unable to consider two states with the same score as comparable (save for those scoring perfectly autocratic or democratic, i.e. −10 or 10) unless one makes the conceptually unexamined assumption that aggregating diverse categorical components and applying to

[17] See, for example, Dahl (1971), Sartori (1987), Alvarez, Cheibub, Limongi, & Przeworski (1996), Collier & Levitsky (1997), Elkins (2000), and Wilson (2014); the list could go on, with scholars arguing for unidimensional continuous conceptualizations, multidimensional, or categorical with categories ranging from two to double digits.

[18] Aydın (2013), on the other hand, uses a cut-point derived from aggregation multiple Freedom House components. For a discussion of the problem with the arbitrary use of cut-points, see Bogaards (2010).

them arbitrary numerical values is appropriate. This is further the case if there are no well-defined reasons for how scores on components are determined or aggregated (Munck & Verkuilen 2002), or if these scales are inconsistently applied (Gleditsch & Ward 1997).

Even if one considers these conceptual issues unproblematic, a final serious issue arises from the fact that continuous measures of democracy by definition attempt to operationalize conceptions of democracy that are more than minimal. Therefore, they include a variety of other things that conceptually either travel along with or are conditions of being "fully" democratic. This is a severe problem, because the commonly-used continuous measures of democracy such as Polity and Freedom House explicitly include an independent judiciary in their concepts and measure. The result is that scholars interested in democracy and independence have two options. First, to include a measure of judicial independence as both an explanatory and outcome variable on both sides of the equation, regressing judicial independence on itself (the option taken by, e.g. Stephenson 2003 and Randazzo, Gibler, & Reid 2016). Second, to remove the component measures that include but are not limited to judicial independence (in Polity, for example, independence is part of the important executive constraints component), thus invalidating the very operationalization they prefer (the option taken by, e.g. Aydın 2013 and Herron & Randazzo 2013).

While it could be the case that one would prefer an explicitly categorical (as opposed to continuous) conceptualization of democracy with more than only two categories, nearly all such conceptualizations proceed in doing so in a two-step manner: first determining whether a country is democratic or non-democratic, and only then deciding what kind of democratic or non-democratic regime it is.[19] This is at heart the process Collier & Levitsky (1997) discuss when thinking about democracies with adjectives and concept-stretching, and what scholars of autocracy such as Geddes (1999), Levitsky & Way (2002), and Lindberg (2009) do when conceptualizing varying forms of autocracy. As Sartori (1987, 156, emphasis original) notes, however, "what makes democracy *possible* should not be mixed up with what makes democracy *more democratic*."

Specifically for the research question here, these second-order categories are either unrelated to the nature of competition (e.g. "classic" subtypes of democracy such as parliamentary vs. presidential), and thus the proliferation of regime types provides little to no value-added, or they are explicitly related to the concept of competition and thereby make understanding its role impossible. This is most clear when one considers the dominant competitive or electoral authoritarian

[19] Indeed, even most continuous measures like Polity or Freedom House categorize regimes based on continuous scores in this manner, either considering "partial" as opposed to "full" democracies or creating a residual category (e.g. "anocracies") that is explicitly not conceptualized as a separate type of regime.

concepts advanced by Levitsky & Way (2002) and Schedler (2002), in which the presence or absence of electoral competition is a defining regime characteristic. Employing a polytomous concept in which one considers competition a defining characteristic of a specific type of non-democratic regime therefore makes examining the effects of competition in autocracies impossible. This impossibility is even more pronounced when one recognizes that Levitsky & Way specifically consider the judiciary one of the arenas of democratic contestation in competitive authoritarian states.

Second, on a methodological level, tying interpretation of empirical results to the underlying concept becomes nigh impossible when interacting a continuous measure of democracy with something like competition, itself fundamentally continuous.[20] Even were one to think there is a conceptually meaningful difference between scoring 4 vs. 5 on Polity (or that this difference is identical to the difference between 6 and 7, let alone −8 and −9), it does not follow that one can understand the interaction between these different scores and differing levels of competition.[21] What inferences should one draw the fact that the interaction of a Polity score of 4 and a 0.5 score on any given competitiveness measure (e.g. % of seats) would be identical to a Polity score of 5 and a competitiveness measure of 0.4? To make this even more extreme, the methodological decision to interact these two continuous measures means that a regime with a Polity score of 2 and a "perfect" score on competition of 1 is observationally equivalent to a regime scoring 4 on Polity with a 0.5 score for competition, as well as a regime scoring a perfect 10 on Polity with a 0.2 competition score.[22] Thus, even if one were to contend that there was a conceptually meaningful difference between how competition operates in a regime scoring differently on a continuous democracy measure, it does not follow that one can empirically assess such differences.

The use of a dichotomous conceptualization of democracy, on the other hand, allows for clearly conceptualizing—and then measuring—the theorized difference that, on balance, the nature of the expected utility calculation varies between democratic and non-democratic regimes, with the potential costs of losing office vastly higher in the latter. This is not to say that there are not specific examples from democratic regimes where the costs of losing elections are remarkably high (or low in autocracies), but rather there exists a general pattern across regime type. Following Sartori's (1987) conceptualization above that there might often exist a second-order conceptualization, further developed by Collier & Adcock

[20] While one could potentially argue that competition is categorical rather than continuous, it is certainly no less continuous than democracy; thus if one were to advocate for a continuous measure of democracy it would be incoherent to simultaneously advocate for a categorical measure of electoral competition.

[21] I refer to Polity here simply because it remains the most widely used continuous measure of democracy. These issues would apply similarly to other continuous measures.

[22] The effects of the constituent terms would of course vary in these situations, but if one is interested specifically in the conditional relationship between the two, as is the case here, the problem remains.

(1999), it is entirely possible that there exists some amount of sub-type variation within the broader categories of democracy and autocracy; establishing such is first, however, predicated on establishing the relationship between the broader conceptual categories, which is the goal of this book.

1.2.2 Existing Arguments looking at Competition in Autocracies

In the existing literature on the relationship between political competition and judicial independence, the question of regime type is rarely addressed, despite burgeoning interest in the role courts play outside the democratic context (Ginsburg & Moustafa 2008). The manner in which existing studies deal with how the insurance model might extend to non-democracies can be said to fall into one of three categories, which I will briefly sketch below, starting with the most common approach and ending with the rarest.

Most commonly, those studying judiciaries in non-democracies assume that competition plays no role in explaining levels of behavioral independence, even if it thought relevant in explaining whether constitutions formally grant review powers to the judiciary (Ginsburg & Versteeg 2013). While on occasion this irrelevance of competition for judicial independence in non-democracies is expressed explicitly (Ginsburg & Moustafa 2008), it is more often implicit. In his important early formulation, Ramseyer (1994) does not address how regime type might matter, even in the context of clearly autocratic Imperial Japan, and Ginsburg's (2003) focus on competition after authoritarian collapse implicitly assumes competition prior to this point is irrelevant. Similarly, Moustafa (2007, 2008) argues that a number of factors allowed Egyptian courts more independence after reforms initiated by Anwar Sadat in the late 1970s, including the need to effectively monitor the bureaucracy as envisioned by McCubbins & Schwartz (1984). Despite the shift from a one-party regime in Egypt during this time, competition is not considered as a possible explanation.

The second approach to the role of competition in non-democratic regimes looks at transitions from authoritarian rule. In case studies of Mexico, Finkel (2005), Ríos-Figueroa (2007), and Magaloni (2008) argue that as the Partido Revolucionario Institucional's electoral dominance waned in the 1990s, the degree of independence of Mexico's judiciary increased as a result. A similar account is offered to explain variation in independence in Argentina: as incumbents' dominance waned, judicial "defection" increased (Helmke 2005). Here, the contention is reminiscent of Hirschl (2004): when elites are fragmented and a transition to democracy (or hegemonic decline) is a fait accompli, then incentives are structured in a way that political actors who would otherwise prefer to keep power centralized devolve some of it to the judiciary (or judicial actors expecting diminished chances of punishment defect and rule against incumbents). Here, the account is forwarded not in contexts of consolidated or new democracies but instead states emerging from authoritarianism, and autocracies not undergoing transition to democracy are not considered.

The third approach focuses not on non-democracies per se, but on those states that many conceive of as falling somewhere between democracy and non-democracy. Such states have many names, including "new," "electoral" or "emerging" democracies (Lindberg 2009). Both VonDoepp's (2009) analysis of three Southern African states and Popova's (2010) work on Russia and Ukraine restrict analysis to these states (the time period examined by Popova predating Putin's authoritarian re-entrenchment).[23] Each argues that given the nature of the political environment, competition can impede rather than further judicial independence.[24] Like in the political insurance explanation developed in democracies, VonDoepp and Popova focus on the risks and benefits of independent or non-independent courts, suggesting that benefits accruing to incumbents by limiting judicial independence outweigh the risks. It should be noted that both authors stress that their analyses are limited to emerging or electoral democracies, and that they do not aim to explain independence in cases of "full-blown authoritarianism" (Popova 2012, 42). Nonetheless, while recognizing neither Popova nor VonDoepp's perspective necessitates doing so, one could potentially extend their logics to a wider variety of non-democratic contexts. If this were the case, we would plausibly expect the exact opposite empirical relationship from the one I hypothesize, instead seeing a negative correlation between competition and independence.

Each of the above approaches has much to recommend it, and the varying approaches to competition and regime type is a function of the specific phenomenon it seeks to explain. If one is interested in hegemonic decline and regime transition, focusing on "stable" autocratic regimes might be ill-advised.[25] Similarly, if one is interested in how electoral authoritarian regimes differ from one another (e.g. Russia and Ukraine) or democratic states, then a narrower focus is warranted. I highlight these approaches precisely because they have offered us much insight into their objects of study, and because their arguments complement or contradict the broader argument I seek to make about the nature of competition in autocratic regimes writ large. It is to this I now turn.

[23] For a perspective on this time that treats Russia as autocratic rather than a liminal category, see Trochev (2004), who examining federal units of Russia argues against the utility of competitiveness during moments of constitutional adoption. Unfortunately, however, Trochev leaves unexplored how dynamics might differ at the sub-national level, or why insurance would be so critical in these contexts.

[24] While Popova's strategic pressure theory differs in a few key ways from VonDoepp's framework, it shares logics, producing similar empirical predictions.

[25] But see Roessler & Howard (2009) and Levitsky & Way (2010), among others, on the difficulty of predicting the timing of autocratic collapse.

1.2.3 Autocratic Insurance

The electoral logic of the political insurance account of judicial independence is fundamentally about the downside risk of no longer being in power, and expectations about the probability of losing power. Put in the simplest terms, if (1) autocrats and not just democrats pay costs of no longer being in power, and (2) they fear losing power through elections, then (3) absent some mitigating factors that derail the insurance logic, it follows that this logic should obtain.[26]

When opposition political groups present credible electoral threats, rational actors in power will establish or maintain independent judiciaries because they are an effective and inexpensive minoritarian institution.[27] Political leaders in autocracies face a similar expected utility calculation, a product of the risks of losing office and the probability that such an event might occur. Obviously, under a "classic" non-democratic situation like a one-party regime, when the level of competition is non-existent and the risks of losing power electorally are similarly minimal, the expectation would be that courts are weak and lack independence. When competition does exist, however, and opposition parties are able to provide credible alternatives to those in power, the risk of losing elections becomes an issue.

The focus here, as with political insurance explanations in the democratic context, is on the benefits courts can provide to incumbents who fear the risks associated with losing office. If courts provide such benefits (which I will show in the Chapter 2), then the empirical implication is that electoral competition in autocracies—the rise of which is well documented by Roessler & Howard (2009)—should be associated with more judicial independence.[28] This highlights the two things I need to demonstrate to make a compelling preliminary case for autocratic

[26] Few who reject the insurance logic in non-democratic contexts articulate precisely what is different about autocracies with electoral competition that should make them different. One exception to this is Popova (2010, 2012), whose compelling argument will be addressed subsequently.

[27] As Ginsburg (2008) notes, what is less developed is the reason why courts would be the specific risk-reduction device chosen. Discussing in particular constitutional creation, Ginsburg (2008, 10) makes a salient point: it is indeed an important question in the comparative constitutionalism literature, which needs to better understand "the institutional tradeoffs in the process of constitutional design." This is less a problem, however, for empirical studies interested in variation in behavioral independence, as there need not be an institutional trade-off being made, and also because we are looking at this in a probabilistic sense. In instances of high competition, political actors should be more likely to pursue policies—formal or otherwise—that allow for judicial independence. That dictators might on occasion pursue different institutional insurance options rather than courts when faced with credible electoral threats—it is entirely plausible that they are in a sense laboratories of non-democracy—does not undermine the argument, but simply makes finding a relationship more difficult empirically.

[28] The question of *why* autocrats allow elections is beyond the scope of this inquiry. Prominent explanations consider the need to co-opt key players in politics (Magaloni 2006, Boix & Svolik 2013, Wright 2008), signal dominance and discourage opponents (Simpser 2013), and strengthen the cadres of the ruling regime (Magaloni 2008). For a review, see Gandhi & Lust-Okar (2009).

insurance: that conditions of electoral competition produce uncertainty regarding their continued hold on office, and that autocrats face risks if they lose power.

The answer to the first question, of whether autocratic rulers ever fear losing power as a result of electoral defeat, is undoubtedly 'yes'. As Levitsky & Way (2010, 12) explain in their thorough examination of non-democracies with electoral competition, incumbents cannot rest easy in such circumstances, as "[g]overnment officials fear a possible opposition victory (and must work hard to thwart it), and opposition leaders believe they have at least some chance of victory." Thompson & Kuntz (2006, 113) go so far as to argue that the possibility of unexpected electoral loss is an "existential threat" to autocratic rule in electoral authoritarian regimes (and perhaps even hegemonic regimes, see Lust-Okar 2009), highlighting the fact that levels of electoral competition that would be considered of little threat to democratic incumbents might very well pose significantly larger threats to autocrats.

The Color Revolutions in the post-communist world are some of the most striking examples of autocrats losing power as a result of elections (Way 2008). And as Schedler (2006) illustrates, this unease can extend to more hegemonic variants of electoral authoritarianism (Brownlee 2009). In fact, the collapse of communism provides similar and perhaps surprising examples of how competition can bring down even the most powerful-seeming regimes, as it was in many ways the opening of the electoral space to those not hand-picked by the party that led to many of the constituent Republics being controlled by anti-Union forces (Lieven 1994, Pabriks & Purs 2001, Smith 2001); this electoral pattern was also present in multiple Soviet satellite states, most notably Poland, where Solidarity's unexpected sweep of the final communist-era elections precipitated the regime's collapse (Friedheim 1993).

A second factor that demonstrates that autocrats consider electoral risk a real possibility and a threat to their continued hold on power is the careful attention they pay to elections in neighboring autocracies. The collapse of communism in Eastern Europe and the Soviet Union and the Arab Spring both illustrate how opposition can diffuse across borders and imperil regimes. Electoral defeats like those in the Color Revolutions are no different, and caused autocrats in neighboring countries to perceive the significant possibility of electoral defeat in the face of robust political competition (Myagkov, Ordeshook, & Shakin 2005).[29] As Finkel & Brudny (2012, 7) note, these events create an "acute feeling of threat among authoritarian elites" in not only neighboring autocratic regimes, but also in more distant autocratic regimes with entirely different bases of rule (Tezcür 2012). Indeed, the increased attention paid to civil society organizations and policies

[29] Suffice to say, in hindsight the Russian provinces were not the most advisable place for an American political scientist in the run-up to Russia's first post-Orange Revolution election.

aimed at constraining their ability to mobilize support are often attributed to autocrats in electoral authoritarian regimes observing the removal from power—or threat thereof—of neighboring autocrats (Polese & Beacháin 2011). Even when riddled with fraud and abuses of power, elections in non-democracies can have serious consequences (Case 2006, Levitsky, & Way 2010), and competition clearly affects the expected utility calculus of those in power.

If the possibility of losing office is real and well recognized by those in power, the next issue is the other half of the calculation: are the risks of losing office also real? That is, if the costs associated with losing power in democracies are worth insuring against, the question is whether the costs of losing power in autocracies are similarly so. The answer to such a question is patently obvious. Consider policy reversals, the main risk of losing office that insurance research focuses on in the democratic world. Even if we assume an autocrat's primary goal is the perquisites of power and they therefore care less about policy than a committed democrat, it does not mean they care not at all about policy, as the long incumbency and policy focus of Lee Kuan Yew demonstrates. Specific examples from post-Orange Revolution Ukraine demonstrate clearly the degree to which previous policies can be reversed after losing elections, and how those policies are not meaningless to prior incumbents or their successors. After the defeat of his hand-picked successor, former President Leonid Kuchma saw some of his most critical policies reversed: his successor Victor Yushchenko shifted Ukraine's foreign policy, focusing more on relations with the European Union and the United States, as well as aligning Ukraine against Russia during its conflict with Georgia over South Ossetia. Similarly, linguistic policies in the country were vastly transformed (Olszański 2012), with Ukrainian implemented as the state language, removing Russian from a place of equality, a conflict with lasting volatility (Polityuk 2012).

The literature in comparative politics examining autocratic regimes makes clear that elections matter in autocracies, especially but not only the competitive authoritarian/electoral autocratic variety. The threat of electoral removal is real. It is similarly the case that there are real risks to losing office for these leaders. Policy reversals can and do occur after autocrats lose power, and the fact that these policy reversals are often fundamental should make up for any lessened interest in policy continuity on the part of autocrats. This contention that autocrats care little for the stability of policy after they leave office, however, is predicated on the idea that what autocrats truly care about is the power that comes with office and the ability to direct its spoils to their friends, families, and personal bank accounts abroad. This idea, of course, implies that the desire to hold office for such perquisites is greater than for democrats. Not only does this undercut the contention that they do not want insurance against being out of power, it leads us to the reasons autocrats face significantly greater costs of losing power than leaders of democratic regimes.

1.2.4 The Greater Need for Insurance in Autocracies

The reason that political competition should be more salient in autocracies than in democracies is the fact that courts provide insurance against risks beyond just policy reversals.[30] The insurance function of policy continuity that more independent courts can play is an impersonal form of insurance, focused as it is on broader questions of public policy. More independent judiciaries can also, however, offer more *personal* protections to autocrats who fear the possibility of losing power. Such protections can have the gloss of an impersonal character—for example, securing against the redistribution of property or lustration policies—but they nevertheless secure the former autocrat (and his or her co-partisans, associates, etc.) in a personal rather than policy sense. These types of personalized insurance can protect against three potential infringements that should be of vital importance to autocrats who hope their life after losing power is not poor, nasty, brutish, and short. These are protections of property, political rights, and physical security.

One important attribute of more independent judiciaries is their ability to guard against the violation of property rights. This is a key reason why many political economists consider them one of if not the most critical component in the law-growth nexus (Feld & Voigt 2003, La Porta, Lopezde Silanes, Pop-Eleches, & Shleifer 2004, Haggard, MacIntyre, & Tiede 2008). Even in emerging democracies, control of the state can mean control of significant economic resources, as Gryzmala-Busse (2007) illustrates in her study of Eastern Europe; this control is an even more lucrative business in non-democratic systems (Levin & Satarov 2000). When courts are weak and justice is politicized, who owns what is a function of who holds the reins of power, not a result of rules and procedures established by and codified in law (Dawisha 2014). Many observers of the Russian political scene attribute the significant political battles among the elite that arose during the transition from the first presidency of Vladimir Putin to Dmitri Medvedev to the uncertainty surrounding the property rights of assets accumulated during the early and mid-2000s (Whitmore 2007).

A focus on the ways in which judiciaries with greater independence from political actors and a less biased legal system can ensure economic rights are protected foregrounds not only the benefits that an independent judiciary can provide to autocrats after losing power, but also the costs of such while in power. This further illustrates why, absent political conditions that induce leaders—democratic or autocratic—to respect judicial independence, we should not expect those in power to embrace independent judiciaries. The risks associated with the expropriation of property rights after losing power, however, are much greater in autocratic

[30] Although not developed, the potential for insurance to be of a non-policy nature in emerging democracies is raised by Ginsburg (2003).

regimes. In autocracies, those who acquire state power also secure substantial economic assets and power to a degree (usually) unsurpassed in democracies (Tullock 1986, Robison 1988, Coolidge & Rose-Ackerman 1997, Levin & Satarov 2000, Dawisha 2014). The nigh unfettered access to economic resources that power typically grants to autocratic rulers raises the stakes of losing power to opposition groups even higher than they would be otherwise, as it also likely that those taking power will attempt to gain control of those resources for themselves, making the need for depoliticized justice all the greater. Thus, all else being equal, in those autocratic systems where electoral competition develops, the risks it poses to autocrats far outstrip any comparable risks faced by democratic leaders.

The second personalized form of insurance that more independent judiciaries can provide is insurance against expropriation of political rights. Even in consolidated democracies, incumbents have access to resources that those out of power do not, and can use legal means to tilt the playing field in their favor. In the US context, this is demonstrated by the continued attempts in some states controlled by Republicans to pass laws designed to protect against "voter fraud," requiring forms of identification that groups that consistently vote Democratic systematically possess at lower levels (Bentele & O'Brien 2013). The phenomenon is more prevalent in consolidating democracies, where policies such as lustration laws are often instituted as systematic mechanisms to expropriate the political rights of those previously in power. Courts that are independent can and often do rule against governments, striking down such lustration laws as unconstitutional (Cienski 2007, Horne 2009, Dimovski 2012). In non-democracies, such expropriation is ubiquitous, including outright removal of opposition leaders from electoral lists, lawsuits challenging opposition party registration procedures, and the use of other "administrative resources" against challengers (Colton & McFaul 2003, Popova 2012).

The costs of independent courts providing the benefit of preventing such issues are costs paid by democrats and autocrats alike in the form of decreased control over political outcomes (Popova 2010). The benefits, however, should accrue disproportionately to autocrats in systems where electoral competition develops, as it often does long before regime change itself (Roessler & Howard 2009). Here, shifts to more independent courts can be an effective way to allow these autocrats to possess more significant political rights if they lose power, which can make easier the protection of economic rights and personal security. Compounding this is the fact that the access to administrative resources and electoral fraud ubiquitous in autocracies (and distressingly far from rare in emerging democracies) means that if the opposition is successful in taking power, the chances of prior incumbents returning to power are lessened. This translates into a situation where, if an autocrat loses power as a result of one of the "well-known 'stunning elections' phenomenon," their successors likely not only get access to their economic resources, but also control over the administrative resources that make incumbent losses stunning in the first place (Thompson & Kuntz 2006, 113). And, as the Color Revolutions throughout the post-communist space have demonstrated, the opposition that topples autocrats often establishes a playing field tilted markedly in their own favor. To the degree that an independent judiciary is able to mitigate against these developments, it thus insures against risks that autocrats disproportionately face.

The third form of personalized insurance that independence courts can provide is insurance against the risk of personal, targeted punishment. Why might independent courts provide more protection to former leaders than dependent courts? Simplified, the two typical situations facing a former leader are courts that have been independent—that is, courts possessing autonomy and the ability to make judgments free from undue political influence—and those that have been dependent, where the previous conditions do not hold. At first it might seem that departing leaders would prefer the reins of justice to be held by those they appointed (especially with regard to apex courts), in the expectation that these individuals will side with them should they find themselves the target of legal action. However, this is very much not the case: in instances where attacks on the judiciary and purges were common before a transfer of power, they will remain so afterwards, and those newly in power will replace high-ranking officials—including and especially judges—with their own people (Helmke 2005). And the expectation of this replacement being possible is likely to incentivize dependent judges appointed under the old government to defect, siding with their new bosses over their old (Helmke 2002). As a result, the real situation typically faced by those formerly in power is not between independent and dependent courts but between independent courts and courts dependent on those newly in power.

Given that dependent courts should be expected to side with those newly in power, the question of whether independent or dependent courts should be of greater protection against politicized prosecutions becomes clear. If a former leader is free from the taint of corruption or criminality, an independent judiciary effectively insures an unpunished post-tenure fate, almost by definition: in instances in which accusations are baseless, prosecutions of former leaders are politicized by their very nature. And if the judiciary is in fact independent of political actors, attempts to politicize prosecution and punish former leaders should be constrained by the courts and, thus, unsuccessful. If, however, a former leader were under genuine suspicion for actions committed while in office, an independent court increases the likelihood of legal rules being applied fairly and judges ruling without bias. This, however, is not the case when courts are lacking independence. In such situations, it is unclear whether even innocence of wrongdoing is enough to secure an unpunished post-tenure fate in all instances: neither the use of fabricated charges nor the criminalization of questionable administrative decisions are rare. In this context, the question of post-tenure punishment instead relies on the discretion of those in power and the degree to which they are able to influence the judiciary.

Similarly, any extrajudicial punishments of former leaders when courts lack independence are far less likely to be constrained by the judicial branch, and the actions of those in power are far more likely to be upheld as permissible. Contrast this to a situation in which independent courts serve as effective arenas for redress of grievances, better allowing individuals to contest state actions. In such a context, even extrajudicial punishments of former leaders should be less likely because those in power are aware that their actions can be nullified by judicial decisions. As a result, independent courts can serve to block both politicized prosecutions and extrajudicial forms of punishment. But perhaps more important, we should expect independent courts to serve as a deterrent mechanism, inducing leaders to refrain from pursuing such activities in the first place, knowing that the chances of success are limited.

This third form of personalized insurance should be especially salient for autocrats, because of the significantly greater risks to the physical security of former leaders in autocratic regimes. Put simply: it is a lot riskier to be a former leader of a non-democracy. Figure 1.2 charts four types of post-tenure fate a state leader can experience after leaving office, showing what percentage of leaders from each type of regime experienced these four possible outcomes: being unpunished, exiled, imprisoned, or killed.[31] Comparing the relative frequencies of these outcomes across plots (a) and (b) reveals that former leaders of autocratic states are seven times more likely than former leaders of democracies to be punished after leaving

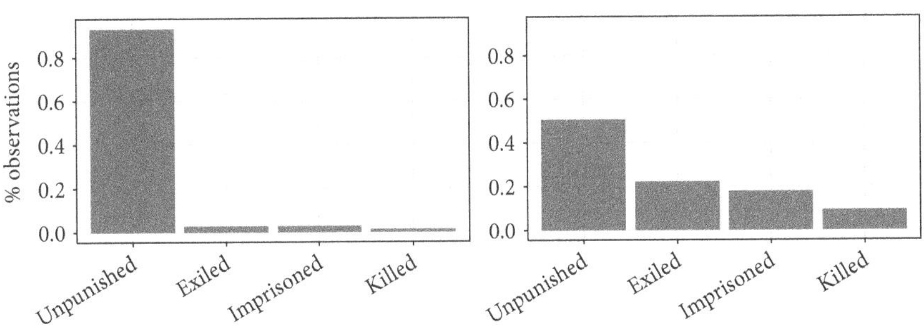

(a) Democrats (b) Autocrats

Figure 1.2 Post-tenure fate by regime type. Two histograms showing the proportional distribution of post-tenure fate. Plot (a) shows democrats, plot (b) autocrats.

[31] For the reason that transitions mean regime type can change after a leader leaves office, data consider the form of regime when the leader left office. These are created using the Archigos (Goemans, Gleditsch, & Chiozza 2009) data, which will be discussed further in the Chapter 2.

office, with less than 8% of democratic leaders facing punishment.[32] Being a non-democratic leader, however, is quite dangerous. Almost 50% of former leaders in autocratic states were punished after leaving office. And the majority of the time the punishment is not exile to a friendly state and a comfortable retirement: over 55% of these punished leaders were either imprisoned or killed, which is the fate of over 25% of all—punished and unpunished—former autocrats.

Unsurprisingly, autocrats who lose power as a part of democratic transitions are less likely to be punished than former autocrats in states that remain non-democratic. That being said, however, the rate is still high: nearly one out of five find themselves punished. This contrasts sharply with former democratic rulers in democracies, where only one in twenty suffer punishment after losing power. It is clear that the physical integrity of former autocrats is significantly more at risk when compared to their democratic counterparts. This, the most basic of securities and the most significant of risks to a former leader, suggests strongly that the logic of the insurance model should be of even more salience outside the democratic context. Risk is of vital importance in assessing the potential benefits of independent courts (Epperly 2018), and risk is significantly greater in the non-democratic context.

There is one final reason why competition should be more critical in inducing leaders to respect de facto judicial independence in autocracies as compared to democracies. Uncertainty is critical for strategic electoral explanations—including but not exclusively insurance explanations—because it affects the probability of, and risks associated with, losing office (VonDoepp & Ellet 2011). And electorally competitive non-democracies are polities that, due to the nature of public support for parties and lack of trust, exhibit higher levels of uncertainty than consolidated democracies (Popova 2010). Compounding this is the fact that in non-democracies, competition signals a greater degree of uncertainty than in democracies; as many scholars of competitive or electoral authoritarianism observe, autocratic elections face a form of uncertainty not typically found in democracies, as the level of popular support for the opposition is not only less easy to ascertain than in democracies, but it also translates less directly into electoral outcomes (Thompson & Kuntz 2006, Levitsky & Way 2010). Because of the inhibited nature of electoral competition, uncertainty exists around how credible the opposition truly is at any given level of electoral success: it is unclear whether an opposition party gaining 20% of the vote signals a party commanding the support of only one out of every five voters, or in reality a party with significantly more support. This is due not only to problems like outright fraud (the distorting effects of which an autocrat could theoretically ascertain), but also due to the distorted

[32] These figures, in fact, *underreport* the security that democracy offers, as the plot is by the type of regime in the previous year. As such, a significant portion of the democratic leaders experiencing problematic fates are due to a collapse of democracy.

electoral arena found in non-democracies with electoral competition (Schedler 2006). As a result, an autocrat's ability to determine the true amount of support for the opposition—and potential performance in the next election—is inhibited, increasing the uncertainty around the possible results of electoral competition. The result is significantly higher levels of uncertainty, recognized as a hallmark of the need for insurance since at least the Code of Hammurabi nearly four millennia ago.

A focus on the personal security that courts can provide leaders offers a final compelling benefit: it allows us to easily use expected utility theory to develop implications about the conditions under which autocrats and democrats would prefer to pay the costs associated with an independent judiciary. It is to the development of this I now turn.

1.3 The Expected Utility of Insurance

As typically formulated in the literature on democratic insurance, the benefits that independent courts provide are policy stability; it is difficult to ascertain how one might go about trying to input this into an expected utility calculation, given the difficulty of measuring policy continuity. For this reason, democratic insurance work focuses exclusively on the changing probability of the outcome, measured by the competitiveness of the electoral system. Focusing on both democracies and dictatorships allows us to consider both the the risks associated with losing office and the probability that these risks might be realized, and in this section I develop an expected utility model that, despite its simplicity, has important implications for the theory of autocratic insurance advocated here. For those readers disinclined to read such things, I will stress that the insights of the expected utility model are developed both visually and with numerical examples, and I carefully lay out the implications of the results in a separate subsection. For those with a taste for formal models, on the other hand, the chapter appendix develops the model conventionally via a proof and comparative statics results.[33]

The nature of judicial independence and electoral competition under autocratic rule suggests that the issue for an autocrat is not to determine the best strategy conditional on another player's strategy, but conditional on their expectations of the future and the uncertainty over how different actions map onto different outcomes. Thinking about the nature of Stephenson's (2003) formal model of

[33] To summarize this here for more formally-inclined readers: while I develop one specification of the model below with various parameters defined at set values, for the implications of this specific iteration of the expected utility model to generalize requires only two minimal assumptions. First, that the utilities of being removed from office and punished as opposed to remaining in office are minimal and maximal, respectively (in the terms of the model, $z = 0$ and $x = 1$). Second, that the probability of a leader being punished after leaving office is greater when courts are not independent (in the terms of the model, that $a > b$).

democratic insurance and Popova's (2010, 2012) argument concerning strategic pressure (where competition incentivizes less independence in emerging democracies) highlights this fact. For Stephenson, both the government and the opposition are players, competition is conceptualized as alternation in power, and his measurement strategy for the empirical test of his model operationalizes the role of alternation in power. Doing so makes sense in the context of democratic regimes (although similar to other empirical work, in his examination of the implications of his game theoretic model the role of any actor save those in power disappears). It makes far less sense, however, in autocracies, especially considering that one of the most common conceptualizations of regime type explicitly considers alternation in power a defining trait of democracies (Alvarez et al. 1996, Cheibub, Gandhi, & Vreeland 2010).

Similarly, in Popova's (2010, 2012) strategic pressure theory (strategic in the sense that autocrats are rational actors pressuring the courts for gain rather than strategic in the sense of strategic interaction), focused as it is on quasi-autocrats, neither the actions chosen by the judiciary nor the opposition influence the choices these leaders make concerning judicial independence. Instead, what matters are the incentives facing leaders as structured by the competitiveness of the electoral arena. For Popova, competitiveness should mean weaker courts because of the benefits weak courts can provide. With regard to influences (but not their direction) on autocratic decision-making, my formulation is in complete agreement with Popova's: what matters is focusing on the preferences of leaders and the uncertainty surrounding the actions they might take to achieve their preferences. This is *not* to say that autocrats are not strategic actors who take into account the strategies of other actors. Rather, with regards to judicial independence there is not strategic *interaction*: autocratic decision-making is conditioned by structural factors, namely their expectations of the future of electoral competition and the possibility of losing office.[34] This is, in fact, how autocratic decision-making with regards to the courts is modeled by others, even if the logic is implicit rather than explicit: beyond Popova's argument articulated above, Moustafa (2003), for example, focuses on how the need for foreign investment induces autocratic preferences. In other words, the more appropriate way to model autocratic insurance is via decision theory as opposed to game theory. For this reason, in Section 1.3.1 I work out the expected utility of pursuing insurance (or not) for autocrats, conditional on a number of relevant parameters. The exercise has important implications for how we think about autocratic insurance, and allows us to adjudicate formally between the empirical implications of autocratic insurance and strategic pressure.

[34] The strategic decisions of autocrats are, of course, highly relevant for decisions made on other issues, especially interactions between the autocrat and his or her regime supporters. See, for example, Geddes (1999), Albertus & Menaldo (2012), and Svolik (2012).

Unlike policy stability, the personal security of former leaders is both easily measured—as Figure 1.2 illustrates—and fairly obvious. Being unpunished is better than being exiled, imprisoned, or killed. These observed patterns of what happens to democrats and autocrats after they leave office can be used in an expected utility calculation to provide empirical probabilities of the various possible outcomes. To simplify, consider there being three possible outcomes for a leader, with preferences for all leaders strictly ordered such that $x > y > z$. These three outcomes are, respectively, remaining in power until a leader chooses to retire (or die of natural causes), being removed from office but not being punished after power, and being removed from office and then punished. Pursuant with the logic of the insurance framework, leaders can pursue one of two actions, *A* and *B*, to affect the probability of what happens to them after leaving office: ensuring high levels of judicial independence to insure against the future or refraining from doing such so they can avoid paying the costs associated with independent judiciaries while in power.[35] These choices should affect the relative probabilities of outcomes y and z, while leaving unaffected the likelihood of x (remaining in office).

1.3.1 Autocrats

For autocrats, define the utility of: remaining in office, $u(x) = 1$; being removed from office but not punished, $u(y) = 0.5$; and being removed and punished, $u(z) = 0$. These are reasonable approximations of the utility autocrats should obtain from each outcome. Normalizing the utilities to the 0–1 range as is standard, it is neither contentious that autocrats would derive maximum utility from remaining in power ($u(x)$), nor the minimum amount of utility from being punished after leaving office ($u(z)$); consider the fact that many autocrats attempt to trade their power for personal security when things go south.[36] Setting the utility of being removed from office but unpunished ($u(y)$) is less obvious, but setting it midway between remaining in power and being exiled, imprisoned, or killed seems appropriate and is in fact a highly conservative approach that is more challenging for my model. Setting $y = 0.5$ is appropriate because there is no reason to expect autocratic preferences regarding being removed from office but unpunished are closer to removal and punishment than to remaining in power, given the extreme downside of punishment. That is, the difference between the utilities of y and z should be greater than y and x. Setting the utility to 0.5 is therefore likely the

[35] Like judicial independence itself, this choice is not in reality dichotomous, and there are options for judicial independence beyond low and high. For the sake of clarity here, however, I will restrict the analysis to these two general actions.

[36] While the utility of different forms of punishment would likely vary (for most, better to be exiled than killed) I refrain from considering this in the calculation, both for reasons of simplification as well as the inability to adequately predict what form of punishment might occur.

minimum reasonable value for the utility of removal without punishment. This a conservative decision that is a more stringent test of my argument, as setting this parameter to a higher value—as is justifiable—only produces stronger results for autocratic insurance than those below due to the fact that given losing power independent courts increase the likelihood of not being punished (for a proof of this, see the chapter appendix).

The utility function for autocrats has four parameters: l, the probability of losing office; a, the probability of escaping punishment if one is removed from office with an independent judiciary; b, the probability of escaping punishment if one is removed from office with a judiciary lacking meaningful judicial independence; and c, the cost of an independent judiciary that must be paid regardless of the outcome if an autocrat chooses insurance, here operationalized as the "cents on the dollar" cost of insurance, that is the percentage penalty (i.e. a tax) to their utility function that autocrats pay regardless of outcome if they choose option A. Table 1.1 briefly summarizes these various parameters for ease of reference. If an autocrat chooses option A, high judicial independence, then the parameters to determine the probability of each outcome are as follows:

$$Pr_A(x) = (1 - l); \quad Pr_A(y) = la; \quad Pr_A(z) = l(1 - a)$$

If an autocrat pursues option B, low judicial independence, then the parameters to determine the probability of each outcome are as follows:

$$Pr_B(x) = (1 - l); \quad Pr_B(y) = lb; \quad Pr_B(z) = l(1 - b)$$

These parameters are inserted into the utility function for the autocrats for each action, which are as follows:

$$E(UA) = (1 - c)[Pr_A(x) * u(x) + Pr_A(y) * u(y) + Pr_A(z) * u(z)] \tag{1.1}$$

$$E(UB) = (1 - c)[Pr_B(x) * u(x) + Pr_B(y) * u(y) + Pr_B(z) * u(z)] \tag{1.2}$$

Table 1.1 Parameters of the model. Notation of the various parameters of the model.

Parameter	Notation	Definition
Outcomes	x	Remain in office
	y	Removal, unpunished
	z	Removal, punished
Choices	A	Higher independence (insurance)
	B	Lower independence
Pr(unpunished)	a	With higher independence
	b	With lower independence
Other	l	Pr(losing office)
	c	Cost of independence/insurance

Note that although in both equations the total expected utility of the various options is modified by $1 - c$, the costs that leaders are faced to pay when courts are more independent, for equation 1.2, $c = 0$, as there are no costs being paid due to choosing B, and therefore the equation is multiplied by 1 ($1 - c$ when $c = 0$), i.e. unchanged.[37] To determine if insurance against just threats to personal security (i.e. not counting the benefits of policy continuity, property rights, or political rights) is worth the cost of independent courts, all that needs to be done is determine if $E(UA) > E(UB)$; if this is the case, then the expected utility is such that insurance is net beneficial, and autocrats choose high(er) levels of judicial independence.

Whether or not paying for insurance is net beneficial depends on the values of the parameters l, a, b, and c. The values of a and b, the likelihood of being unpunished when judicial independence is high and low, respectively, are the first parameters to analyze. Recall that the relative probabilities of whether or not an autocrat is punished if they are removed from office, i.e. y and z, should be affected by whether or not they have access to the insurance provided by an independent judiciary. Note that this is not just an assumption made for the sake of convenience, but rather a result that follows from empirical work. In previous work I show that more independent courts are strongly associated with a lower likelihood of former leaders being punished be they autocratic or democratic (an extension of this analysis is presented in Chapter 2).

The results of these empirical models can be used to determine the probability of being punished under the two options of high and low independence. I calculate the results of models of post-tenure fate from Epperly (2013) to generate predicted probabilities. I then set the value of independence at one standard deviation below and above its mean value in autocratic regimes (the mean and median values are 0.25 and 0.24).[38] This allows me to generate point estimates for the probability of punishment under conditions of low and high judicial independence (one standard deviation below and above, respectively). For autocrats, the point prediction for the probability of not facing punishment after leaving office when judicial independence is high (one standard deviation above the mean) is 0.61, therefore let $a = 0.61$. When low, the point prediction is 0.39, therefore let $b = 0.39$.[39]

[37] One minor aspect of the expected utility model worth noting is that for ease of explication, these expected utility calculations assume risk neutrality (as demonstrated by the fact that the utility functions shown in Figure 1.3 are neither concave nor convex). This is important because even with such an assumption, under conditions of threat of being removed from office insurance is net beneficial; this is even more the case assuming risk aversion on the part of leaders, as is standard (Hirschl 2013).

[38] This is a conservative estimate, as many focus not on these first differences but on the difference between observed minimums and maximums. Were I to do this, results would be even more markedly in favor of autocratic insurance.

[39] That these sum to 1 is chance; when discussing democrats the differences are far smaller and do not sum to 1.

Unfortunately, unlike the probability of being punished after leaving office, the value of c, the costs paid by leaders for tolerating judicial independence while in office, cannot be determined via reference to existing research, and intuition must take the place of empirics. As independent courts are costly, we know that $c > 0$; this is effectively the premium paid for insurance, and setting this at 10% of total utility seems a reasonable approximation of cost. Therefore let $c = 0.1$.

To reach a conclusion concerning the utility of autocratic insurance now only requires determining the value of l, the likelihood of losing office, which is the key parameter for studies of insurance (Stephenson 2003). The parameter l here captures the expectation about losing office held by an autocrat, itself a function of the underlying levels of electoral competition, and can be conceptualized as such.[40] The benefit of this exercise, however, is that this value does not need to be set, but rather can be allowed to vary so that the difference in the expected utility of each action A and B can be determined conditional on the autocrat's perceived risk of losing office. Determining the expected utility for each option at every level of probability of losing office is trivial, and can easily be visualized.

Figure 1.3 does just this, plotting the expected utility of options A and B as l, the probability of losing office, is allowed to vary from 0 to 1. Recall that action A is the strategy of paying the premium c to achieve higher levels of judicial independence to decrease the probability of being punished if losing office. The gray line thus shows the expected utility of pursuing this strategy as the chance of losing office changes. The black line, on the other hand, shows the expected utility of action B, where an autocrat declines to pay the insurance premium and is able to retain low levels of judicial independence.

Naturally, the overall expected utility decreases as the chances of losing power increase independent of the strategy. This is due to the fact that autocrats always prefer to remain in power rather than lose power (that is, $x > y > z$). This can be observed most readily when there is zero chance of losing office (0 on the x-axis). Here, the expected utility for autocrats is 1, unless they unwisely chose to pay the premium for insurance, c, in which case their expected utility is 0.9. The vital takeaway from Figure 1.3 is the expected utility of a strategy compared to the other as the likelihood of losing power increases, or in other words the relationship between the two lines as one travels right along the x-axis: once there is a reasonable expectation of losing office, the benefits of a more independent judiciary outweigh the costs.

[40] It should be noted that there are certainly other reasons why an autocrat might fear losing office, from angering key regime supporters to rebel groups. Note, however, that in these cases it is not clear that the threats should produce any inducement to insurance via independent courts. There are two reasons for this. First, these should lack the clearer signals that electoral competition provides, making the inducement—irrespective of any benefit—less salient. Second, as I demonstrate in Chapter 2, unlike with regards to electoral outcomes these non-normal means of leaving office are not in fact associated with incentives to increase the independence of the judiciary.

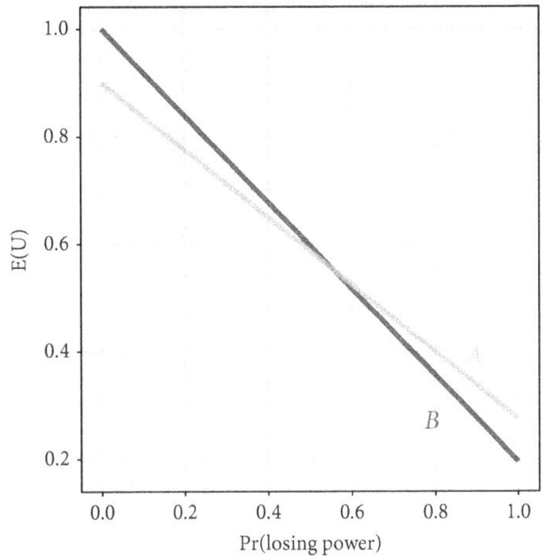

Figure 1.3 Expected utility of insurance in autocracies. The expected utility of each option as l, the probability of losing office, is allowed to vary from 0 to 1. The gray line is the expected utility of option A, buying insurance, that is paying the costs associated with higher judicial independence to reap the decreased likelihood of punishment if one loses office. The black line is the expected utility of B, low levels of judicial independence.

1.3.2 Implications

Figure 1.3 clarifies the first of three important implications of the simple expected utility model I present: for an autocrat to prefer to pay the cost and pursue higher levels of judicial independence to be the action that provides the most utility requires at least a moderate fear of losing elections. With the parameters used above, it is only when autocrats suspect there is a better than even chance of losing elections that they should opt for insurance.

The second important implication of the model that Figure 1.3 illustrates concerns the costs of insurance and how these affect an autocrat's expected utility. The model makes clear that as the cost of independence rises (i.e. as the specific 0–1 numeric value of c increases) the utility decreases, such that it requires higher levels of competitiveness to be the option that maximizes expected utility. This is important, not only because the model produces interesting implications about how much a court can push back against an autocrat before its benefits are no longer worth its costs, but also because it can help adjudicate between the polar expectations of my autocratic insurance argument and Popova's (2010, 2012) strategic pressure theory. Recall that c is the costs that an independent court imposes on an autocrat. It is therefore also the benefits that a dependent court can provide for an autocrat. This implication is then clear: if Popova is correct and dependent courts provide significant benefits under conditions of competition, then the expected utility of dependent courts relative to independent courts should increase as the likelihood of losing office increases. That is, the black line in Figure 1.3 should be lower than the gray line along the left side of the x-axis and higher than the gray along the right side. On the other hand, if my autocratic insurance argument is correct and the benefits independent courts can provide in insuring the future outweigh any costs, then the exact opposite relationship should be observed. Looking at Figure 1.3, it is clear that the relative value of independent courts is greater when the chances of losing elections are higher. This corresponds exactly to my autocratic insurance argument, and is the opposite of what is predicted by the strategic pressure theory. [41]

Third, this exercise demonstrates that under conditions of moderate competition, insurance by itself is enough to induce autocrats to opt for higher levels of judicial independence.[42] Thus, even assuming autocrats care little to nothing for policy continuity and are unwilling to pay the costs associated with courts for this purpose, there is still reason to believe that autocrats should desire the insurances provided by independent courts. This has an important second-order implication: if protection against punishment is enough to induce autocrats to prefer higher levels of judicial independence, then looking at how independence relates to the post-tenure fate of autocrats is an important way to assess the assumptions and mechanics of the insurance logic. This is precisely the focus of the second half of Chapter 2.

1.3.3 Democratic Leaders

In briefly sketching the expected utility functions of democratic leaders, I will note only where the utilities and parameters of the model change from those above. Like autocrats, democratic leaders naturally prefer remaining in office to being removed, which in turn is preferred to being removed and punished.[43] Therefore, as above, $x > y > z$. The utility for these options differs for autocrats, however. While $u(x) = 1$ and $u(z) = 0$ like autocrats, the fact that democratic leaders can more easily continue to contest elections after leaving office means that the utility of removal from office without punishment should be greater for democrats.

[41] Of course, the two are not necessarily competing theoretical frameworks. While she presents her strategic pressure framework as a complication of the general insurance account, Popova's empirical focus is not on high courts and general levels of independence, but rather on the decisions made by ordinary courts in specific disputes. Put more concretely: at the end of the day, both countries had low levels of independence in the early 2000s, and assessing general/apex court independence for each could very well produce results in line with my framework. Popova's more granular focus, on the other hand, examines differences within these two countries when it comes to specific manifestations of judicial behavior by low-level judges in particular types of cases. Many thanks to Maria for raising this important point.

[42] Figure 1.3 shows this by using point estimates for + / − one standard deviation of independence; increasing the differential levels of independence to the minimum and maximum values, for example, only illustrates a greater expected utility of choosing option A, insurance.

[43] It is worth further noting at the outset that unlike with autocrats, democratic leaders are likely engaged in strategic interaction with the opposition (Stephenson 2003), thus suggesting the decision theoretical framework here is incomplete. Nevertheless, the results have interesting implications for my argument about the greater salience of competition in autocratic as opposed to democratic contexts.

Therefore, let $u(y) = 0.7$. The predicted point estimates for the probability of being unpunished after leaving office conditional on high and low levels of independence also differ markedly, unsurprising given few democrats are punished after leaving office as opposed to roughly half of autocrats. Therefore, the predicted probabilities based on one standard deviation above and below the mean for high and low levels are 0.97 and 0.91, respectively. Therefore $a = 0.97$ and $b = 0.91$. Given the fact that autocratic courts can be a unique source of constraint on rulers, and their existence precludes the greater benefits of dependent courts, relax the cost of independent courts in democracies such that $c = 0.05$. The expected utility calculations are therefore identical to equations 1.1 and 1.2, save for the input values of the parameters varying as described.

Figure 1.4 plots the expected utility of options A and B for democratic leaders as l, the probability of losing office, which is allowed to vary from 0 to 1. The gray line shows the expected utility of A, the black B. Figure 1.4 illustrates two important implications about the expected utility model for democrats. First, the salience of competition—here the expectations about losing office—is lower for democrats. It is only when expectations of losing office reach levels of almost near certainty that the high independence is the utility maximizing option for democratic leaders (this is, of course, usually the norm in highly competitive consolidated democracies). This differential effect follows perfectly with the argument I forward concerning the greater salience of competition, when present, in autocratic regimes. The second important implication is that this suggests it is less personal security that drives democratic insurance, but rather more the reasons more commonly articulated by scholars advancing insurance arguments in democratic contexts. In other words, Figure 1.4 does not imply that there is

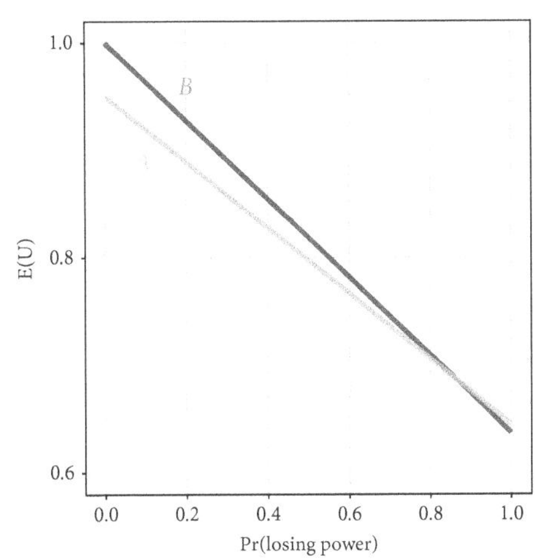

Figure 1.4 Expected utility of insurance in democracies. The expected utility of each option as l, the probability of losing office, is allowed to vary from 0 to 1. The gray line is the expected utility of option A, buying insurance, that is paying the costs associated with higher judicial independence to reap the decreased likelihood of punishment if one loses office. The black line is the expected utility of B, low levels of judicial independence.

no utility to more independent courts for democratic leaders, but rather that we cannot as easily observe the utility of more independent courts outweighing the alternative of less independent courts based solely on their ability to insure against punishment after leaving office. This is in some sense unsurprising given the fact that so few democrats are punished after leaving office. It is homeowners in floodplains, after all, for whom flood insurance is particularly attractive. The attractiveness of insurance against this threat to one's home, however, does not speak to the utility of insurance against fire or some other disaster.

1.4 Conclusion

The logic of insurance explanations in democracies—be they focused on constitutional provisions protecting the judiciary (Ginsburg & Versteeg 2013, Stroh & Heyl 2015) or its de facto power (Ramseyer 1994, Aydın 2013)—hinges on the risks of losing power and the uncertainty around such an event happening. When the possibility of losing power is real, rational leaders will establish or maintain minoritarian institutions capable of protecting those in the political minority from being trampled by the majority. Judicial independence is an inexpensive and effective minoritarian institution, and as a result when this possibility is higher we should expect higher levels of judicial independence. Political competition signals to those in power that the possibility of losing office is real. When an opposition party is able to control a significant portion of the electoral space, political leaders face the real threat of finding themselves out of office. This logic is in no way restricted to democratic contexts:[44] competition—when it exists—in autocracies should produce the same fears and incentives for those in power.

In non-democracies, the risks of losing office are significant, and typically much higher than in democracies. And as the literature on competitive authoritarian regimes makes clear, autocrats in electorally competitive systems routinely fear losing power as a result of, and at times do lose, elections. I demonstrate formal support for this theory using a simple expected utility model illustrating how more and less independent courts can maximize the utility of autocrats who fear losing elections. The results show that "buying" insurance in the form of a more independent judiciary is a preferable strategy for autocrats facing moderate levels of electoral competition, but not those fully secure in office. These results hold even if we assume that independent courts mean greater costs paid by autocrats when in office. That is, absent any other ill outcomes independent courts might insure against (policy, economic, or political), pursuing a strategy of independence outweighs its associated costs.

[44] Or, in the case of autocracies, solely to formal constitutional review powers (Ginsburg & Versteeg 2013).

At its simplest, the argument of this chapter is that, given that so much of the insurance model's force flows from the risks faced by leaders after leaving office, the model should be of even more explanatory value in the non-democratic context: competition in non-democracies should be of more salience for judicial independence than competition in democracies, because the insurance offered by independent courts should be more valuable. Whether or not independent courts provide insurance is the topic of the Chapter 2.

1.5 Appendix

The problem:

$$E(UA) = (1-c)[Pr_A(x) * u(x) + Pr_A(y) * u(y) + Pr_A(z) * u(z)]$$
$$E(UB) = [Pr_B(x) * u(x) + Pr_B(y) * u(y) + Pr_B(z) * u(z)]$$

Also,

$$Pr_A(x) = 1 - l;\ Pr_A(y) = la;\ Pr_A(z) = l(1-a)$$
$$Pr_B(x) = 1 - l;\ Pr_B(y) = lb;\ Pr_B(z) = l(1-b)$$

For simplicity, omit the notation for utility. That is, write $u(x)$ as x, $u(y)$ as y, $u(z)$ as z. Then the utility maximization problem can be rewritten as

$$\begin{aligned} E &\equiv E(UA) - E(UB) \\ &= -c(1-l)x + ((1-c)a - b)\,ly + ((1-c)(1-a) - (1-b))\,lz \\ &= l\big((a - ca - b)(y - z) - cz + cx\big) - cx \end{aligned}$$

Taking the derivative with respect to l, we have

$$\frac{\partial E}{\partial l} = (a - ca - b)(y - z) - cz + cx$$

In terms of which choice is optimal, there are two possible scenarios:

Scenario 1. If $(a - ca - b)(y - z) - cz + cx > 0$, then as l increases, E also increases. When $l > cx/\big((a - ca - b)(y - z) - cz + cx\big)$, choice A is optimal. Otherwise, choice B is optimal.

Scenario 2. If $(a - ca - b)(y - z) - cz + cx < 0$, then as l increases, E decreases. Since $l > 0 > cx/\big((a - ca - b)(y - z) - cz + cx\big)$, one should always choose A.

In terms of whether $E(UA)$ and $E(UB)$ is increasing with l or not, theoretically there are two possible scenarios as well. Taking the derivative of $E(UB)$ with respect to l, we have

$$\frac{\partial E(UB)}{\partial l} = ay + (1-b)z - x$$

Therefore, when $ay + (1 - b)z < x$, $E(UA)$ and $E(UB)$ decrease as l rises. When $ay + (1 - b)z > x$, $E(UA)$ and $E(UB)$ increase as l rises.

1.5.1 Possible Further Simplifications:

There are two assumptions that can make the model more general:

1. If we assume $z = 0$ and $x = 1$, then $ay + (1 - b)z < x$ is always supported, i.e., $E(UA)$ and $E(UB)$ always decrease as l rises.
2. If we further assume $a > b$, then only Scenario 1 can be supported. That is, the relationship will always be similar to Figures 1.3 and 1.4: $E(UB) > E(UA)$ is for lower values of l and $E(UB) < E(UA)$ is for higher values of l. This is because if $a > b$, then $a - ca - b > -bc$, which means $(a - ca - b)y + cx > -bcy + cx > c(x - y) > 0$. From assumption 1, we have $(a - ca - b)(y - z) - cz + cx = (a - ca - b)y + cx$, which, as has just been derived, is always positive. Hence, only *Scenario 1* will be supported.

1.5.2 What are the Effects of Democracy?

Write $l^* \equiv cx/\left((a - ca - b)(y - z) - cz + cx\right)$. The question is: how do changes in a, b, c affect l^*? The affects for a and b are straightforward: if a increase then l^* decreases while the opposite is true for b.

Taking the derivative of l^* with respective to c, we have (assuming the previous two assumptions)

$$\frac{\partial l^*}{\partial c} = \frac{(a - b)xy}{\left(((a - ca - b)(y - z) - cz + cx)\right)^2}$$

which is always positive. That is, if democracy decreases c, then it raises that bar for option A to be attractive.

1.5.3 Proof

The two utility functions are reproduced as follows:

$$E(UA) = (1 - c)[Pr_A(x) * u(x) + Pr_A(y) * u(y) + Pr_A(z) * u(z)]$$
$$E(UB) = Pr_B(x) * u(x) + Pr_B(y) * u(y) + Pr_B(z) * u(z)$$

We also know that

$$Pr_A(x) = 1 - l;\ Pr_A(y) = la;\ Pr_A(z) = l(1 - a)$$
$$Pr_B(x) = 1 - l;\ Pr_B(y) = lb;\ Pr_B(z) = l(1 - b)$$

To examine which choice is better, we define $E(UAB)$ as the difference between the two utility functions:

$$\begin{aligned} E(UAB) &\equiv E(UA) - E(UB) \\ &= -c(1-l)u(x) + ((1-c)a - b)\,lu(y) + ((1-c)(1-a) - (1-b))\,lu(z) \\ &= l\big((a - ca - b)(u(y) - u(z)) - cu(z) + cu(x)\big) - cu(x) \end{aligned}$$

I make two assumptions:

Assumption 1. *$u(z) = 0$ and $u(x) = 1$.*

Assumption 2. *$a > b$.*

Under these two assumptions, we can obtain the following results.

Lemma 1 *As l increases, both $E(UA)$ and $E(UB)$ decrease.*

Proof Taking the derivative of $E(UA)$ with respect to l, we have

$$\frac{\partial E(UA)}{\partial l} = (1-c)\big(au(y) + (1-a)u(z) - u(x)\big) = (1-c)(au(y) - 1)$$

which is always negative, since $a < 1$ and $u(y) < u(x) = 1$. Analogously, taking the derivative of $E(UB)$ with respect to l, we have

$$\frac{\partial E(UB)}{\partial l} = bu(y) + (1-b)u(z) - u(x) = bu(y) - 1$$

which is always negative, since $b < 1$ and $u(y) < u(x) = 1$. □

Lemma 2 *As l increases, $E(UAB)$ always increases. For lower values of l (i.e., when $l < c/\big((a - ca - b)u(y) + c\big)$), choice B is optimal. Otherwise, choice A is optimal.*

Proof Taking the derivative of $E(UAB)$ with respect to l, we have

$$\frac{\partial E(UAB)}{\partial l} = (a - ca - b)(u(y) - u(z)) - cu(z) + cu(x) = (a - ca - b)u(y) + c$$

If $a > b$, then $a - ca - b > -bc$, which means $(a - ca - b)u(y) + c > -bcu(y) + c > c(1 - u(y)) > 0$. Hence, $E(UAB)$ increases as l increases. Note that under assumption 1, we know $E(UAB) = l\big((a - ca - b)u(y) + c\big) - c$. That is, when $l > c/\big((a - ca - b)u(y) + c\big)$, $E(UAB) > 0$. □

Lemma 3 *Write $l^* \equiv c/\big((a - ca - b)u(y) + c\big)$. As c increases, l^* increases.*

Proof Taking the derivative of l^* with respective to c, we have

$$\frac{\partial l^*}{\partial c} = \frac{(a-b)u(y)}{\big(((a - ca - b)u(y) + c)\big)^2}$$

which is always positive, since $a > b$ and $u(y) > 0$. □

2
The Mechanisms of Insurance

After winning the Presidency of Argentina in 1946, Juan Perón immediately turned his sights on the membership of the Supreme Court. The Peronists sought impeachment of four of the five sitting justices on fifteen counts of misconduct, beginning a process by which every change in regime meant a wholesale attack on and replacement of judges, a process that lasted until the final year of the twentieth century (and even then which returned again in 2002). In the case of the military dictatorships that plagued Argentina throughout the Cold War, this replacement meant removal by decree of the junta (Snow 1975). Such replacements were not limited to the incidence of military dictatorship, however: changes in leadership arising from both transition to democracy and normal democratic elections produced a similar process of replacement.

After Raúl Alfonsín's Radical Party defeated the Peronists in the return to free elections in 1983, one of the first questions was the remaking of the judiciary, and while there was debate on how to cleanse lower courts of those judges associated with the dictatorship, that the Supreme Court would be entirely replaced produced little dissent (Helmke 2005). Similarly, only three months after Carlos Menem returned the Peronists to power in 1989, a proposal was sent to Congress to increase the number of seats on the Supreme Court from five to nine. Despite significant criticism—including from those sitting on the Court at the time—the proposal passed and was successful in reshaping the composition of the court. That the reshaping of the judiciary by incoming governments was commonplace in Argentina in the second half of the twentieth century is borne out by the numbers: as Helmke notes, across the eight decades before Perón took power, thirty-five judges served an average of eleven years each, whereas in only the five that followed, fifty-seven judges served less than five years apiece.

Despite widespread attention to strategic accounts of judicial independence focused on the incentives for rational political actors that electoral competition structures, and the preferences it can induce, there remains significant doubt among many of the veracity of the insurance framework for understanding judicial independence. The historical experience of Argentina under democracy and dictatorship in the latter half of the twentieth century typifies the first of two major criticisms of the insurance explanation of judicial independence: that it rests on shaky assumptions about the ability of courts to provide insurance and more vitally the likelihood of those assuming power after turnover respecting the

The Political Foundations of Judicial Independence in Dictatorship and Democracy. Brad Epperly, Oxford University Press (2019).
DOI: 10.1093/oso/9780198845027.001.0001

independence of the judiciary (Helmke & Rosenbluth 2009, Aydın 2013). In the second critique, the relationship between competition and independence is argued to be opposite the standard insurance account in some subset of states, such as unconsolidated democracies or electoral authoritarian regimes (VonDoepp 2009, Popova 2012).

To at least some degree, each of these critiques can be settled by reference to the empirical expectations it produces when compared to the insurance model. Despite this fact, there has been little attempt to do so, with scholars making general claims about the salience of various institutional or regime characteristics by way of introducing a new case or reinterpreting the details of an individual country's experiences with courts growing stronger or weaker. This is *not* to say that these are not important contributions to our understanding of comparative law and courts, but rather that they are inadequate foundations upon which to build our understanding of either the insurance framework or one of its alternatives. If a key aim of this book is to construct a full edifice of the insurance framework, the aim of this chapter is to ensure that it is built on solid foundations—foundations which to date have been asserted or assumed, but never examined.

With this goal in mind, the focus of this chapter addresses the first of the above critiques.[1] The goal is to determine whether the remarkable degree of attention paid to the spectacle of leaders newly in power purging the judiciary of its sitting justices and appointing in their place new judges presumably loyal to those recently empowered, typified by the Argentine experience, is justified. Because such attention calls into question the causal logic of the insurance account of judicial independence, it is vital to determine whether examples like those found in Argentina are commonplace or in fact outliers. After more fully engaging the critique, I systematically examine whether judicial independence is able to withstand turnover in office, partisan replacement, and regime transition. I then assess to what degree courts are in fact able to provide the insurance against future risk that is critical to the descriptive accuracy of the insurance framework. The conclusions of this chapter are consistent and clear, and for those readers who are *not* skeptics of the descriptive accuracy of the mechanisms upon which the insurance framework is built, my exhaustive treatment of the skeptical take is likely to be a long journey. As such, I will offer a brief account of the conclusions upfront.

First, and put simply, the story of Argentina told above proves the exception rather than the rule. Judicial independence is highly robust to transitions in power, with new leaders respecting the autonomy of the judiciary at rates far higher than criticisms of the insurance framework can justify. Regardless of how one measures turnover or regime transition, or how one assesses the scope conditions concerning democracy vs. dictatorship, new leaders do not uniquely undermine

[1] The second critique, suggesting that the relationship between competition and independence is reversed in non-democratic regimes, is addressed in both the previous and subsequent chapters.

the judiciary. This null relationship is robust across specifications and is assessed by means more rigorous than by simply showing statistical non-significance (Rainey 2014). Not only does the level of independence not suffer from transitions, but we do not see increased attacks on the judiciary in the first years of new leadership, unless that new leadership is the result of the collapse of a competitive electoral environment. I show that the descriptive reality of how executive turnover and regime collapse are related to judicial independence is invariably consistent with the underlying mechanisms of the insurance framework.

Second, I show that independent courts provide significant insurance against the most severe risk that comes with losing office: personal attacks on the former leader. Existing research demonstrates a robust relationship between de facto judicial independence and post-tenure fate (Epperly 2013). Going beyond this analysis, I show that *how* leaders are replaced and *who* replaces them are thoroughly consistent with the empirical implications of the insurance account, but inconsistent with any other existing explanatory frameworks.

2.1 The Mechanisms of the Insurance Model

For the insurance framework to be an accurate explanation of variation in levels of judicial independence around the world and over time, regardless of whether one views it as restricted to democracies or of more broad use, the two key mechanisms presented above must be correct. Both are related to the core causal logic of the insurance model, that competition induces those in power to pursue policies that they otherwise would not, absent the likelihood of losing power. They are essential precisely because they are the mechanisms by which we might expect the strategies of political leaders to be supportive of high levels of judicial independence. First, that maintaining or strengthening the judiciary is likely to serve as a binding constraint on others who come to power, and that such a judiciary is unlikely to face attacks or see its independence restricted, absent the demise of competition. If it were to come under the undue political influence of those next in power, its ability to provide insurance—policy-wise or personally—would be minimal. Second, that courts do in fact provide such insurance, given they have the power to do so.

As noted, despite these being critical to the overall insurance framework, theorized as they are to be the reason why those in power would countenance increased constraints on their abilities to realize their aims, these two components remain assumed rather than examined. This general lack of attention, and the resulting lack of evidence supporting these requisite mechanisms, is undoubtedly a key reason that many remain unpersuaded of the plausibility of the insurance framework. If the ubiquitous questions at conference panels and conversations with comparative law and courts scholars are any indication, this lack of persuasion is widespread. That these criticisms of the insurance framework only occasionally see publication (e.g. Helmke & Rosenbluth 2009, Aydın 2013) is predictable for two reasons. First, because it ought be incumbent on those advancing the insurance argument to persuade skeptics of the veracity of the mechanisms underlying it; without having done so, skepticism is warranted and entirely reasonable. Second, because such a situation will remain given the nature of the arguments: advocates of the insurance framework assume something should *not* matter, skeptics consider such a shaky assumption, and knowledge fails to advance because of the disinclination for researchers and journals to pursue null results (Franco, Malhotra, & Simonovits 2014). Nonetheless, the reality remains that many question the descriptive accuracy and key components that do much of the heavy lifting for insurance accounts of judicial independence, as Helmke & Rosenbluth's review of explanations of judicial independence indicates. And for good reason: that those assuming office would respect the efforts of previous office holders to establish or maintain judicial constraints on their authority should not be treated as self-evident.

Although the fact that it remains questionable and any settling of the question is at heart an empirical matter, absent empirics intuition has free reign to determine outcomes. The intuition articulated by many skeptics is that inasmuch as courts are able to serve as even moderately effective veto points limiting the actions of the political branch, required as it is for the insurance framework, then incoming leaders facing a high court or general judiciary stocked with appointees presumed to support the individual or party formerly in power would have no incentive to respect any independence possessed by the judicial branch. This should be the case even if the judiciary's limitations on those in power are only modest, as they nonetheless can inhibit the desired policies of those newly in power.

There are various empirical implications of this skeptical view, multiple of which are examined in Section 2.2. Here, however, it is imperative to note a more general perspective on global trends that each view articulates and the empirical implications thereof. The skeptical view, whereby those newly in power are free to and regularly do undermine the judiciary, suggests that we should see little to no secular temporal trend in judicial independence in a given country or globally. This is the case because each time executive turnover occurs—be it regularly via elections or via regime change—we should as often as not see a lowering of judicial independence. The empirical expectation is therefore either a series of reversions from the gains made over the course of one party's tenure in power at best, to the sequential erosion of a court's independence each time executive turnover happens at worst; the story of judicial independence is thus either Sisyphean or death by a thousand cuts. If it is the case that incoming leaders regularly scale back judicial autonomy, then any trends we see in improved judicial independence within a country over time or globally not only have to be unrelated

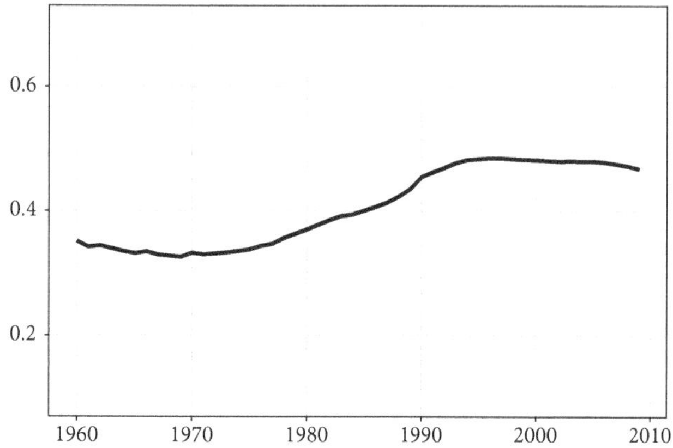

Figure 2.1 Yearly global mean of de facto judicial independence. The yearly global mean of Linzer & Staton's (2015) measure of latent de facto judicial independence.

to the electoral arena, but they must additionally override the assumed negative effects of executive turnover on judicial independence.[2]

The view of insurance proponents, on the other hand, is that barring the collapse of a competitive electoral arena, incoming leaders will respect the level of judicial independence they inherit. Thus, the expected patterns are ones of stability and slow positive change, inasmuch as reversions should be rare phenomena and there are of course other factors—the corporate interests of judges not least of all—that positively affect judicial independence. Unlike the skeptical account, the insurance framework *also* implies the conditions under which we should expect to see such reversions: those times and places where political competition breaks down and political leaders perceive far lower levels of uncertainty regarding their futures in office.

As many have observed, there is a general trend globally towards the increasing role for, and power of, the judicial branch in politics (Tate & Vallinder 1995, Hirschl 2004, 2008); Figure 2.1 shows one way of illustrating this trend in the increasing relevance of the judiciary. It shows the yearly global mean of the measure of latent (de facto) judicial independence developed by Linzer & Staton (2015). Working through the implications of the skeptical argument regarding how those newly in power should attack courts, it becomes clear that this view is difficult to square with the observed reality of the new constitutionalism and the global expansion of judicial power, given that the era has not simultaneously

[2] Skeptics might attempt to salvage the criticism by saying that only *some* incoming leaders inhibit independence, and even then do so only rarely. But then the skepticism reduces to something like "there exist rare exceptions to the rule," which is hardly a persuasive indictment of probabilistic social science.

observed a decline in executive turnover. This is merely one general implication about one observed aspect of global politics that the skeptical view implies about the world. As such, it offers merely the most preliminary of evidence to suggest that this view does not comport with what we can observe by thinking about its implication as compared to those of the insurance framework and marshaling the relevant data to test these implications. It is to far more specific implications that I now turn.

2.2 Binding Future Rulers: Examining the Unexamined

If the decision to establish, maintain, or further judicial independence does not bind future leaders to respect the judiciary, then it is a poor form of insurance, and the mechanisms within the insurance framework that are purported to produce equilibria of higher levels of judicial independence are invalid. If, on the other hand, new leaders do not attempt to subvert the courts, and instead respect the levels of independence existing when they take office, we have solid evidence suggesting that courts are able to provide insurance (though whether they *do* will be addressed subsequently).

This logic highlights an important fact of what is being examined here: if the insurance framework is correct, the empirical implication is that a thorough assessment of the data should produce no discernible relationship between new leaders taking power and weakening of the position of the judiciary. In other words, the expectation is a null effect. The bias in social science being what is is, favoring significant positive results rather than findings showing no relationship (Franco, Malhotra, & Simonovits 2014), a reader might wonder why time and effort should be devoted to such an endeavor. Put simply, the reason is because without properly constructing the foundations of the argument, the resulting edifice will be weak, susceptible like existing work in the insurance framework to the contention that there is little reason to believe that new leaders will respect their predecessors' decisions to undermine the judiciary.

This contention is, as noted previously, not without warrant. But this contention underscores the fact that the empirical expectation of no relationship between new leaders and judiciaries under attack is perhaps *not* the null hypothesis, despite being a null finding; the well-established preference against null findings also underscores a likely reason why there are not existing published examples defending and developing the mechanisms undergirding the insurance framework. This puts advocates of the insurance framework in a difficult position: assume or assert that a relationship does not exist and leave significant doubt as to the accuracy of the assertion, or dedicate the time and energy to marshaling evidence and hope for an audience sympathetic to an extensive treatment of a null relationship. As I find the former untenable for the reasons articulated, it is my hope that the reader is sympathetic towards the coming effort.

2.2.1 Conceptualizing and Measuring the Outcome

Incoming leaders and those newly in power can undermine the judiciary in a variety of ways, ranging from attacking the integrity of judges in comments to the press and speeches to supporters to waging all-out war against the court by means such as the open refusal to comply with judicial decisions, court-packing, or judicial purges. Of course, subverting the independence of the judiciary need not be by such openly public, let alone dramatic, courses of action. New executives are able to influence the judiciary via the selective use of carrots and sticks such as reappointment and promotion, in the case of the former, or transfer to less desirable posts or disciplinary proceedings, in the latter.

Although a well-developed typology of methods for undermining the judiciary and exerting undue influence is beyond the scope of this discussion, two broad forms of attack, naturally far from mutually exclusive, can be easily identified. The first form is public attacks on the judiciary and its members, accusing them of partisan bias, political rather than legal motivation, corruption, or the like. Examples of such attacks abound, and are observed in liberal and illiberal democratic regimes as well as autocracies: two decades ago, a judge of the High Court of Australia decried the phenomenon of increasing attacks on the judiciary and individual senior judges in common-law countries, which an out-going President of the American Bar Association suggested was the biggest challenge to the American justice system (Kirby 1998). The actions of the current and previous US Presidents provide more recent examples, with Obama heavily criticized for his 2010 State of the Union attack—"with all due deference to separation of powers"—on a recent decision, and Trump infamously questioning the legitimacy of federal judges handing down unfavorable decisions. Similarly, in 2016 a member of the Irish cabinet publicly advocated for a public register of judges to highlight potential conflicts of interests, suggesting that lacking such judges could not be trusted (Clarke 2016).

The degree to which such attacks actually undermine judicial independence per se, however, is an open question: while some might contend that decorum and the separation of powers means the branches with the powers of the sword and purse refrain from excoriating judges, others might with very good justification argue that judges do in fact overstep their bounds, and often themselves impugn the motives and actions of executives. If, however, public support for the judiciary is a critical component of judicial independence (Gibson, Caldeira, & Baird 1998, Vanberg 2005), then one can view sustained attacks on the branch as potentially part of a broader strategy to undermine the judiciary. Such was the case in Poland in recent years, where public criticism of the judiciary expanded into parliamentary investigations into the appointment of specific judges (Strzelecki 2017). Criticism of "unelected" or "so-called" judges, however, need not be coupled with more direct attacks on the independence of the judicial branch, and by itself such criticism likely remains the lowest bar with regards to the severity of possible actions.

A second, fairly common way executives are able to undermine the independence of the judicial branch is through the refusal to respect its decisions. Like the first method, this technique to minimize the relevance of the judicial branch is potentially easy to observe. The ease of observation varies on the nature of the non-compliance. At one end of the spectrum there are actions such as those taken by the PiS government in Poland in 2016, who promised ex ante not to respect the decision of the Constitutional Court on a number of issues were the court to rule against the government. Even at the other end of the spectrum, however, government non-compliance with court decisions—especially regular or systematic non-compliance—is fairly easy for legal experts to monitor: even if the court itself is disinterested in monitoring compliance, there are litigants invested in the outcome of the case and the resolution of the dispute, and often opposition parties happy to publicize governmental non-compliance and malfeasance.

These prior examples are all easily observed and obvious means by which the government can strip courts of the power to be independent entities with meaningful authority. Judicial independence, however, is often rightly conceived of as a latent concept, not only hard to measure but also hard to observe (Linzer & Staton 2015); while sacking judges appointed by the previous government is obvious, more subtle forms of pressure ranging from making expectations known to directly instructing judges how to rule are private rather than public forms of undue influence (Ledeneva 2008, Hendley 2009). As such, most law and courts scholars interested in de facto judicial independence rely on measures aiming not to capture just one aspect of potential improprieties in the executive–judicial relationship, but a more general sense of the degree to which courts (usually the high court) operate free from pressure, including the above public actions but also reports and evidence of the less obvious private means available to the government.

If assessing the degree to which the specific actions above and the general level of de facto judicial independence are associated with changes in the executive is the goal, data are required that enable an effective assessment. Thankfully, two such resources have (in only the past few years) become available to scholars. The first of these resources, the Varieties of Democracy (V-Dem) project, has—unlike with so many data projects focused on democracy and state institutions more broadly—put significant effort into measuring not only the usual suspects of executive, legislative, and electoral variables, but also a host of factors related to the judicial branch. This effort allows for not only an assessment of perceptions of broader levels of judicial independence, but also the frequency and significance of specific forms of state action that inhibit the proper functioning of an independent judiciary. Increasingly common in comparative studies of institutional phenomena, the V-Dem measures use Bayesian item-response theory (IRT). Developed in psychometrics, IRT models are employed to assess the relationship between observed performance on an item (e.g. a question on an exam or survey) and the underlying ability or trait the item is designed to measure; practically, rather than assuming each component is of equal weight or importance (or, on a test, equally difficult), IRT approaches explicitly model this relationship. For the V-Dem measures, the use of IRT models allows for the tackling of issues of scale inconsistency across questions, inter-coder reliability, and the ordinal nature of the assessments made by their multiple country experts for each question, as well as cross-national comparability. Put crudely, rather than providing a value for a latent concept like judicial independence by either aggregating across different components or averaging across different experts, the IRT approach used by V-Dem models the relationship among the expert raters and the component questions; for an extensive treatment of the conceptual scheme, data collection, and measurement process, see Coppedge, Gerring, Lindberg, Skaaning, Teorell, Andersson, Marquardt, Mechkova, Miri, Pemstein, et al. (2016*b*).

The second resource, the Linzer & Staton latent judicial independence (LJI) measure, also uses an IRT model, but instead of using it to leverage the use of multiple expert coders for country-years, uses it to leverage agreement between (and varying temporal coverage among) eight existing measures of de facto judicial independence (Linzer & Staton 2015).[3] The LJI measure has become increasingly popular in empirical studies of the phenomenon, such that by the time the paper introducing the dataset was published it was able to reference a dozen published works already making use of its contribution. Both the LJI measure and the measures produced by the V-Dem project are ideal for my purposes due to their careful creation and attention to problems of estimation and agreement among data sources rather than crude aggregation. In addition, the V-Dem project has further utility because the project asks various questions concerning not only broad levels of judicial independence but also specific actions of the government towards the judicial branch.

Table 2.1 reports the correlation among four relevant factors drawn from the V-Dem data (attacks on the integrity of the judiciary, compliance with decisions against the government, and general high court independence) as well as the LJI measure.

It is worth nothing that although the V-Dem dataset also contains measures for court-packing and purges of judges, I refrain from including them in the results presented here. There are two reasons for this. First, as the questionnaire for expert

[3] These eight measures include five directly attempting to measure de facto judicial independence and three doing so indirectly. The former include three measures constructed with US State Department *Country Reports on Human Rights Practices* (Howard & Carey 2004, Cingranelli & Richards 2010, Keith 2012), the Feld & Voigt (2003) measure developed by a survey of country experts, and the Global Competitiveness Report produced by the Fraser Institute (Gwartney & Lawson 2007). The latter three include the the executive constraints measure from the Polity project (Marshall, Jaggers, & Gurr 2012), the contract-intensive money measure developed by Clague, Keefer, Knack, & Olson (1999), and the Political Risk Services law and order measure (Group 2012).

Table 2.1 Interference with the judiciary. Correlation matrix of four factors relevant to government influence on the judicial branch. The first three are drawn from V-Dem, while LJI is Linzer & Staton's (2015) latent judicial independence measure.

	Attacks	Compliance	High court ind.	LJI
Attacks	1			
Compliance	0.41	1		
High court ind.	0.32	0.7	1	
LJI	0.36	0.7	0.67	1

coders that V-Dem uses to create its measures does not make a distinction between changes of membership that follow constitutional rules and those that do not, it is unclear to me the degree to which changing the composition of the court is always a de facto rather than de jure phenomenon.[4] The second is simply for the sake of brevity, as it would increase the presented results by 50%. More importantly, it would do so with little in the way of gain: not only are these two V-Dem measures well-correlated with the others (in the 0.4–0.6 range), but the results that follow in this section are effectively identical if also including purges and packing, with results substantively consistent with the four measures that are both analyzed and presented.

Table 2.1 illustrates something quite important: although they are drawn from completely different data sources, the V-Dem high court independence and the LJI measure are highly correlated, both with each other and similarly with the other V-Dem factors. This provides additional comfort that comparative law and courts scholars have reached a general agreement on how we ought to go about conceptualizing and measuring judicial independence (Ríos-Figueroa & Staton 2012). At the same time, although there are correlations among the various specific types of actions, as should probably be expected, Table 2.1 suggests that they are tapping into different phenomena: government attacks questioning the integrity of the judiciary, for example, are correlated with compliance and high court independence at fairly low levels, considering the data sources.

2.2.2 Infringements on the Judiciary before and after Turnover

There are two primary types of comparison the V-Dem and LJI measures make possible in assessing whether incoming leaders commonly ignore the decisions of their predecessors and attack the judiciary, which would thus undermine an

[4] This raises the issue of how to distinguish between "constitutional coups" and less formal, legalized attacks on judicial independence. This will be discussed in detail when examining the Hungarian case in Chapter 4.

important mechanism of the insurance framework. The first of these are within-country comparisons, looking at whether we observe far higher levels of "bad" outcomes (for judicial independence) immediately after there has occurred a change in state leadership. Such a comparison offers, in effect, a baseline means to determine whether new leaders respect prior decisions to allow for judicial independence or whether they target the courts after assuming power. According to the insurance logic, leaders have little to no incentive to target courts before elections and the possibility of leaving office, but instead have incentives to if anything strengthens the independence of the judiciary to insure their policies and persons in case they end up out of power. On the other hand, suspicion of the veracity of this logic rests on the idea that incoming leaders should not be expected to be constrained by any decisions of the prior government concerning the independence of the judicial branch. Thus, to start with we have two clear empirical expectations concerning the prevalence of actions that infringe on the judiciary before as opposed to after a turnover in leadership: to the degree that things look similar before and after leader turnover, we have preliminary evidence against the suspicion that new leaders are not bound by prior decisions.

Figure 2.2 plots the distribution of the four measures assessing some aspect of the potential to infringe on judicial independence listed in Table 2.1, with the V-Dem measures each normalized to a 0–1 scale for comparability with Linzer & Staton's latent judicial independence (LJI) measure. To assess whether previous commitments to judicial independence bind future leaders, each plots the distribution for the year before (dotted lines), year of (solid), and year after (dashed) an executive is replaced by someone from a *different* party. Replacement by leaders of different parties is critical if executives pursue judicial independence as means to ensure policy continuity, as we should expect far less likelihood of policy reversals when executives are followed by those of the same party. While it is also a far more difficult test than replacement of the same party, it is irrelevant, as the distributions appear almost identical, and the same patterns repeat themselves if one plots the distributions when replacement occurs by a co-partisan.

Looking at the distributions plotted in sub-figures *a–d* of Figure 2.2, it is at most points difficult to differentiate between the solid, dashed, and dotted lines: the distributions are so similar that it is difficult to discern their differences. Indeed, Kolmogorov-Smirnov tests (used to assess the equality of distributions) further demonstrate that there is no reason to think that the distribution of any of the four measures assessing aspects of infringements of judicial independence are different before and after the executive's replacement by another party. For attacks on the judiciary, for example, the p-values for the Kolmogorov-Smirnov tests between the pairs of distributions are 0.94, 0.99, and 0.75. Typically, to reject the null hypothesis that the two samples (here the values for the years before, during, and after executive turnover) are drawn from the same distribution requires a standard p-value of $p < 0.05$. Clearly, this is nowhere near close to rejecting the null. In other

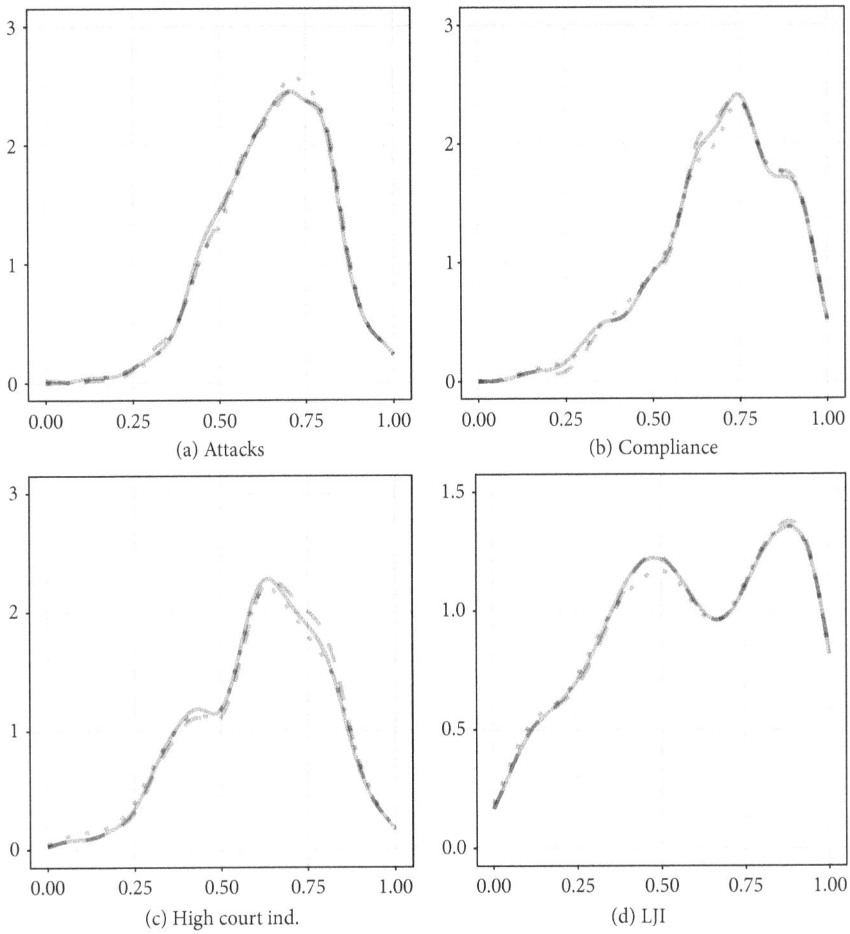

Figure 2.2 Distributions of factors after replacement by a different party. Each sub-figure plots the distribution of the listed factor assessing infringements of judicial independence in the year before (dotted), the year of (solid), and the year after (dashed) an incumbent executive is replaced by someone from a different party. V-Dem measures are normalized to the 0–1 scale for comparability with the Linzer & Staton LJI measure.

words, this provides strong preliminary evidence against the contention that new leaders are not bound by past respect for the independence of the judiciary.

The evidence presented in Figure 2.2 is pooled across space and time, and looks solely at the distribution of each measure. Such pooling means that not only are the longest-standing, firmly consolidated democracies considered alongside the newest and most fledgling, but in fact democracies are considered alongside dictatorships, and the poorest states alongside the richest. A skeptical reader should likely question whether the similarities illustrated in Figure 2.2 hold up once one takes such factors into account. An incumbent losing an election in an autocracy, after all, is typically considered to be qualitatively different from in a democratic regime, and conflating turnover across the democracy/dictatorship divide might be highly problematic. Furthermore, to the degree that economic development is inextricably linked to the factors being examined, it too has the potential to confound the relationship. Therefore, a more careful approach that disaggregates change and examines potential confounders is called for.

2.2.3 Disaggregating Change

The second type of comparisons these exhaustive data make possible are not simple baseline distributions before and after executive turnover, but comparisons between types of change that take into account other important factors that might confound the relationship. To take this potential for confounding variables into account, another way to examine the veracity of the mechanism underlying the insurance framework is to ask whether executive turnover predicts any meaningful change in the four measures above. The insurance model would suggest that under normal circumstances,[5] swapping one executive for another should produce, if anything, positive but likely negligible (in the sense of being substantively small) changes in levels of judicial independence. This is because what is at issue is the competitiveness of the electoral arena and the likelihood of replacement, which is already "priced in" when executive turnover occurs. In other words, the probability of losing power and there being executive turnover to another party is the impetus for establishing or maintaining judicial independence, and its primary effects should have occurred well before actual executive turnover. Thus, the *act* of turnover is unlikely to be consistently associated with large increases (or decreases) in respect for the judiciary. This empirical expectation runs precisely counter to the skeptical take on the insurance framework. For such an account, the idea is that incoming leaders are in no way bound to respect the insurance policies previous leaders paid for in the form of independent judiciaries, and because of this these insurance policies never pay out; recognizing this fact, rational leaders therefore refrain from buying insurance and the explanatory framework of the insurance model fails to obtain.

In the rest of this section I present graphical results drawn from models of the respective outcome, restricting the presentation of tabular model results to the chapter appendix. I do this for two reasons: first, the visualization of the

[5] I specify under normal circumstances because there are conditions where electoral change *should* produce meaningful changes in the level of judicial independence. These circumstances are landslide elections that reshape the electoral arena, granting massive majorities to one party and allowing it to reshape the institutional environment, or the reverse.

implications of models conveys more clearly the relevant issue at hand, the effect of change in leadership (modeled in a variety of ways) on the independence of the judiciary. Second and more important, however, is the fact that what I seek to examine is the *lack* of any meaningful relationship. That is, the goal is to find the most robust evidence possible for the contention that there is a negligible (at best) relationship between executive replacement and these measures. When looking to examine the *lack* of a relationship, Rainey (2014) argues that social scientists should follow best practices in biostatistics (Berger & Hsu 1996) and explicitly test theorized negligible effects, as opposed to asserting that the lack of a statistically significant relationship is evidence (i.e. the tables presented in the chapter appendix). This is because a lack of statistical significance is neither necessary nor sufficient evidence for the claim that no meaningful relationship exists between two variables (Westlake 1979). Large sample sizes, for example, can produce statistically significant yet negligible effects, as the large number of observations allows for precisely estimated trivial effects; small sample sizes, on the other hand, can mean large errors around estimates, and thus lead researchers to reject large, meaningful results because their confidence intervals overlap zero (Gill 1999).

Recognizing this, instead of presenting simple tabular model results, I test the skepticism of a binding constraint on new leaders by presenting plots of 90% confidence intervals, simulating the parameters of the model by draws from the posterior distribution (Rainey 2014). This practice is functionally equivalent to the "two one-sided tests" (TOST) framework forwarded as a more appropriate way to test the argument that a variable has a negligible effect on an outcome (Berger & Hsu 1996). While showing that the data are consistent with there being "no effect" (i.e. showing that there exists no statistically significant relationship) is neither necessary nor sufficient evidence for a negligible relationship, the use of 90% confidence intervals coupled with substantively meaningful values allows a researcher to show that "the data are *inconsistent with meaningful effects*" (Rainey 2014, 1085, emphasis original). Key here is the determination of a minimum substantively meaningful value for such an effect, which can only be determined by scholars in a given area and context (Wellek 2010); Rainey (2014), for example, in his reanalysis of Clark & Golder's (2006) work on electoral systems chooses the average difference in the effective number of parties between the US and Britain.

For the purposes of analysis here, to robustly test the mechanism of the insurance framework the choice of the value for the independent variables of interest is obvious; because whether or not an executive was replaced by an individual of their own or a different party is binary, the decision is to estimate the expected change in the value of each of the four measures when an executive is replaced in each manner. The question of minimally meaningful values for the outcome measures is less obvious: choosing too large a minimum value means that the test is not robust, whereas choosing too small a value means that most any effect can be deemed meaningful. To ensure that the test of a negligible effect is a difficult one, I employ as the minimally meaningful effect one fourth of one standard deviation of the given measure of infringement on the judiciary. For high court independence, for example, this is approximately the difference in the V-Dem measure's estimation for South Korea before and after its 1993 legal reforms.

2.2.4 Executive Turnover in Democracies

Disaggregating the question of the degree to which new leaders are bound by the levels of judicial independence respected by their predecessors is more straightforward in the context of democracy, as it restricts analysis to the prosaic issue of electoral outcomes, rather than issues of regime change or autocratic replacement. It allows us to look at how the four factors related to infringements of the judiciary are associated with new leaders, including those who replace co-partisans and those who replace executives of another party. To do so, I estimate a series of linear regression models with country-fixed effects, and in doing so account for two potential confounders: the level of economic development and the duration of democracy.[6]

The level of economic development has been shown to be strongly associated with both levels of judicial independence, and as much as poor economic performance is strongly associated with incumbent losses in elections, development might also affect the likelihood of executive turnover. The duration of democracy is a potential confounder because one might expect long-standing democratic regimes to have both more established liberal orders respecting the rule of law, and thus fewer attacks on courts, while simultaneously having more established party systems and more regular alternation in power. To assess these two potential confounders, the log values of per capita GDP (measured in constant 2000 US dollars) and the years a state has been democratic, drawn from Boix, Miller, & Rosato (2013), are included in the models underlying the visualized results. These numeric variables are standardized (by two standard deviations) to make their estimated coefficients directly comparable to each other as well as the dichotomous variables of replacement by a different party and replacement by the same party.

Figure 2.3 follows the procedure described previously, showing the estimated values and their 90% confidence intervals for two sets of linear models (presented in the chapter appendix). In the first, models are fit to each measure of means of undue influence over the judiciary in the year of executive turnover. In the second, models are fit for each measure but also include changes in the subsequent

[6] I discuss the reasons for using the Boix, Miller, & Rosato (2013) measure of democracy and dictatorship in Chapter 3.

year, offering a more thorough test, as it is possible that the year of turnover fails to capture how new executives are unconstrained by existing executive–judicial relationships. There are two potentially overlapping reasons for this. First, it might simply be the fact that a significant amount of turnover that occurs happens at the end of the year, rather than at the beginning, and thus the year of executive turnover is inappropriate. Second, it might be the case that in many instances it takes time for a new executive to need to put the screws to the judiciary, as it takes time to enact new polices, find the courts an impediment, and engage in activities that address the perceived problem. To account for this, models that examine the effect during the year of executive turnover and in the subsequent year are also shown.[7]

Figure 2.3 therefore examines the skeptical hypothesis that the insurance framework is flawed because new executives are not bound by existing respect for the judiciary, and thus insurance does not pay out. And given the procedures employed it does so in a highly conservative manner, in effect stacking the deck against the insurance model. I suggested that if this skeptical take is correct, then a meaningful effect of executive turnover should be discernible, defined extremely conservatively as one quarter of one standard deviation change in each outcome measure. Were this the case, then the 90% confidence intervals would be overlapping or entirely outside the left dashed gray line; that is, having a meaningful negative effect on the outcome measure. The results shown in Figure 2.3 demonstrate that, even after accounting for potential confounding variables and including country fixed effects, there is little evidence supporting the skeptical hypothesis that executives are not bound by past executive behavior and fail to respect the judicial branch.

Instead, the plots in Figure 2.3 illustrate that the data strongly suggest that executive turnover has a negligible effect on attacks on the judiciary. In no instance do the data suggest a meaningful effect. This is true either in the form of replacement by a co-partisan or individual from a different party, as well as whether one looks only at the year of executive replacement or the year of replacement and the subsequent year. In other words, no matter how you slice it, there is no evidence to suggest that new executives in democratic regimes target the judiciary, but rather strong evidence to suggest that they, on balance, respect the institution. This is true whether the measure is of attacks on the judiciary, government compliance with unfavorable judicial decisions, or either the V-Dem or LJI measure of more general de facto judicial independence.

[7] Though not shown, results are almost identical if solely a one- or two-year lag is employed, or if any change between the previous two years and the current year is considered.

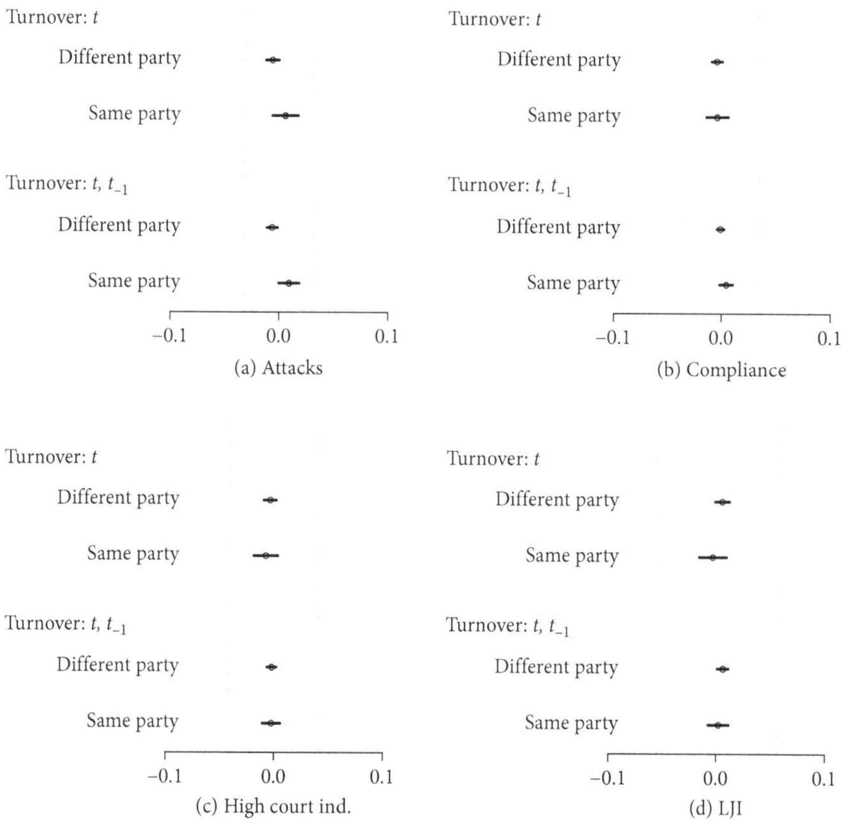

Figure 2.3 Estimated effects of executive turnover in democracies. Plots showing the estimated effects of executive turnover on attacks on the four measures of interference with the judiciary. These plots test the hypothesis that the insurance framework is incorrect that new executives are bound by past respect for the judiciary. 90% confidence intervals show that there is no meaningful effect on the outcome measures (meaningful defined as at least one quarter of one standard deviation).

2.2.5 Executive Turnover in Non-democracies

The above discussion of skepticism of the insurance framework's assumption that future leaders do not renege on the insurance policy was raised in the context of democratic insurance models. This is unsurprising, as until recently the insurance framework had not been explicitly forwarded in a non-democratic context (Epperly 2017), and in fact the reverse account is more popular in comparative case studies of electoral authoritarian regimes (Popova 2010). In non-democracies, however, some skeptics might think that the impetus for new leaders to influence the judiciary is even greater than in democracies. In their study of electoral authoritarian regimes in African states, for example, VonDoepp & Ellet (2011)[8] contend that the personal insecurity of leaders is so fraught in these contexts, and the need to influence courts to validate electoral wins so great, that there is a much greater need to pressure courts than in solidly democratic contexts.

On the other hand, the idea that this insurance mechanism is less efficacious in non-democratic contexts is puzzling, because roughly 90% of autocratic regimes that fail due to elections (as opposed to popular uprising, coup, insurgency, etc.) are replaced with democratic rather than autocratic regimes. This is decidedly *not* the case for non-electoral failure, where only a third of the subsequent regimes can be classified as democratic (Geddes, Wright, & Frantz 2014). Making the fairly tenable assumption (which will be shown correct later) that newly empowered democrats are more likely to treat former dictators more favorably than newly minted despots, it follows that it is far better to be replaced by choosing not to run in or losing an election than by other means. Although the likelihood of losing power electorally is certainly not exogenous to other relevant regime factors, it remains the case that the general distribution of how autocratic regimes fail and what they are replaced by raises a question for skeptics of the binding nature of judicial institutions. Unless new democrats are decidedly more likely to take aim at the judiciary, insurance would appear a potentially lucrative investment for autocrats facing increasingly competitive electoral contexts.

This impressionistic take, however, much like the pooled distributions presented in Figure 2.2, calls for more systematic analysis. This analysis will largely mirror that on democracies: linear models with country fixed effects, controlling for a few key potentially confounding variables, presented via a visual examination of whether the effects drawn from these models are in fact negligible. As autocratic regimes continue to exist until replaced by democracy or another autocratic regime (Geddes 1999), rather than examine whether an incumbent government was replaced by a co-partisan government or another party, however, here the key explanatory variable for testing the causal logic of the insurance model is regime failure.

For scholars interested in the specificities of autocratic breakdown, the phenomenon can occur in a variety of ways; here, however, as the focus is on the potential for the provision of insurance against electoral loss, the critical distinction is whether an autocratic regime is replaced via electoral or other means. Using the award-winning data on autocratic regime breakdown developed by Geddes, Wright, & Frantz (2014), I consider electoral failure to occur when either an incumbent loses an election, or when no incumbent runs in a competitive election

[8] Although the title characterizes the study as one focused on "New African democracies," the authors acknowledge that they are also looking at "semi-democratic" regimes; in fact, four of the five country cases are coded as autocracies by the Cheibub, Gandhi, & Vreeland (2010) and Boix, Miller, & Rosato (2013) dichotomous democracy/dictatorship measures, and as one-party or personalist autocracies by Geddes, Wright & Frantz (2014).

and the result is an opposition victory. Non-electoral autocratic regime failure is thus when a regime collapses due to other factors. Both the level of economic development and the time a regime has existed (both logged and standardized) are considered as potential confounders. The former for reasons previously discussed, and the latter because there is some reason to expect that the duration a regime has been in power might affect both its propensity to breakdown (Ulfelder 2005) as well as its relationship towards its judiciary (Moustafa 2007). Finally, I include a dichotomous variable flagging when a democratic transition occurs, as democracy is associated with more respect for the independence of the judiciary and is obviously closely related to (some) autocratic regime failure. As with the models underlying Figure 2.3, the tabular results for autocracies are presented in the chapter appendix.

Because statistical significance is, for reasons discussed, an incomplete way of assessing whether an effect is negligible, Figure 2.4 returns to the method used in biostatistics to assess non-effects that was first presented in Figure 2.3 (Rainey 2014), once again using one quarter of one standard deviation as the minimum meaningful effect.[9] Unlike in the analysis of democracies, Figure 2.4 shows that there is some evidence for meaningful effects for the measures, as the 90% confidence intervals overlap the dashed gray lines representing the minimal meaningful effect.

The fact that some effects are not negligible, however, does *not* provide support for skepticism of the insurance framework's underlying mechanism. Rather than having a meaningful negative effect on the four measures in Figure 2.4, in over half the models an autocracy suffering collapse via elections is associated with slightly *improved* outcomes for the judiciary, i.e. opposite what the skeptical take would expect. And in no case is electoral failure associated with a negligible negative effect. This is the case for the expectations from models of compliance, and high court independence the year of regime collapse; there is no evidence of meaningful effects of electoral collapse if one considers these measures and electoral collapse in the preceding year as well. The only instances in which there is a minimally meaningful *negative* effect on an outcome measure is for *non*-electoral regime collapse in the model fit to the V-Dem attacks on the judiciary measure. However, the insurance framework as presented here, and in all previously published examples, is about insurance against electoral loss, this minimal amount of evidence that non-electoral regime collapse is associated with slightly more attacks is of no concern. If anything, this only further supports the contention that when *elections* change autocratic regimes, the judiciary is not targeted, even controlling for when those electoral collapses occur alongside democratic transitions.

[9] Like in Figure 2.3, the values for years democratic and economic development are held constant at their mean values for the simulated model parameters and effects; the democratic transitions variable is set to zero for the purposes of simulation.

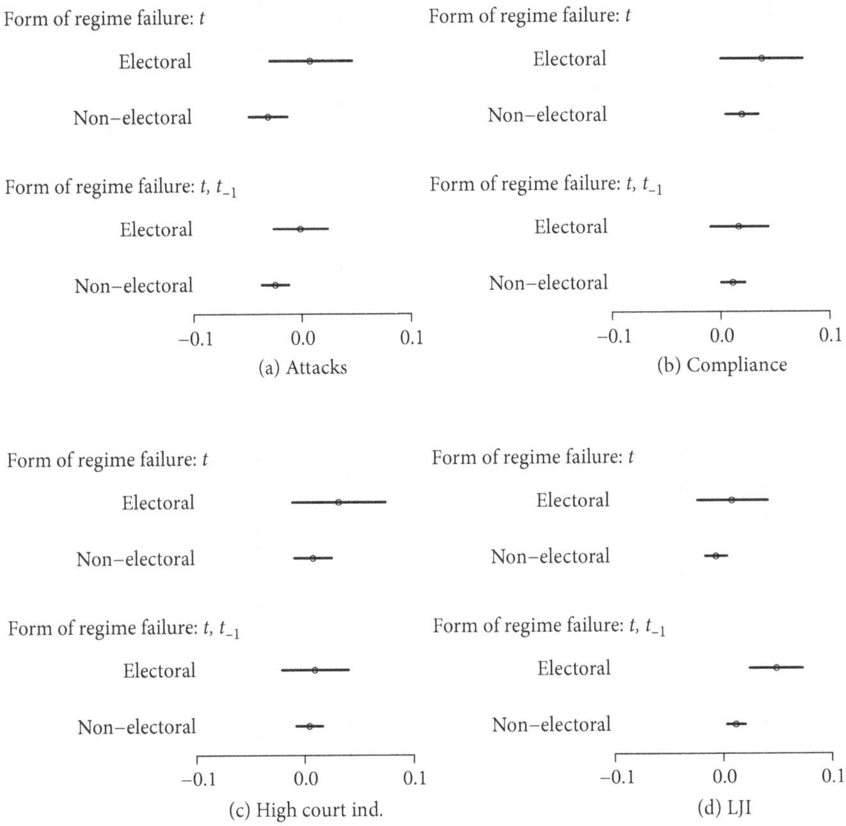

Figure 2.4 Estimated effects of executive turnover in autocracies. Four plots showing the estimated effects of executive turnover on the judiciary measures. These plots test the hypothesis that the insurance framework is incorrect that new executives are bound by past respect for the judiciary.

Extending the analysis to autocratic conditions finds no evidence to call into question the assumption of the insurance framework that future leaders are bound by past actions. Rather, much like in the democratic analyses presented previously, the weight of the evidence sides strongly with those advancing an insurance framework, not with those who question the mechanisms supporting its causal logic.

2.2.6 From Democracy to Autocracy

The final piece of the puzzle with regards to whether existing institutional arrangements bind future leaders and whether judiciaries are capable of providing insurance, and the link to whether they *do* provide insurance, is the occasion of democratic breakdown. While obviously no democratic leader hopes to be removed from office by undemocratic means, much like autocrats in competitive authoritarian regimes who have to face the non-zero probability of losing elections, the possibility is present at times, as the experiences of countless states around the world attest. This raises two important questions. First, are new autocrats significantly more likely to pressure the judiciary such that insurance would not be viable? And second, does this even matter?

Addressing the second question first, one must consider that, if it is the case that insurance is a viable strategy for democratic replacement, is there any reason to think that a democratic leader who considers the possibility of replacement by a dictator would prefer a *less* independent judiciary, and would this preference outweigh the far greater likelihood of electoral replacement? This returns us to a simple informal account of a leader's expected utility function. Assuming an independent court in no way whatsoever constrains the new autocrat or decreases the likelihood the former democratic executive suffers at his hands, does its existence increase the likelihood of bad outcomes for the former democrat? It is difficult to imagine how such a situation might arise. Even if there is, however, some small probability that such an independent court would be less preferable under autocratic replacement, the (dis)utility of such a court and the likelihood of autocratic replacement would have to outweigh the utility of an independent court after democratic replacement and the likelihood of democratic replacement. Given that democratic leaders are orders of magnitude more likely to be replaced by normal electoral means rather than dictatorships, it would take a massive difference in utility functions to compensate for the difference in the expectations over their realization. It simply does not matter even if autocracies that succeed democratic regimes are not constrained by the judicial institutions they inherit, because even were these institutions somehow worse for the former democrats, the likelihood of losing power to democratic breakdown is minuscule compared to through the electoral process.

This makes the first question, whether autocrats that replace democrats are uniquely unconstrained and more likely to not be bound by existing institutions, largely moot. But in the interests of the most thorough examination of the mechanisms of the insurance framework possible, I nonetheless offer an account. While it seems plausible that those who topple democracy (or assume power after its toppling) would fail to be constrained by the prior institutions, it is unclear why it is any *more* plausible than those who topple another autocratic regime, the institutions of which presumably have less legitimacy and support than a democratic regime's.

Given the Section 2.2.5 shows that autocrats who replace other autocrats are not more likely to put the screws to the courts, a brief account here should put to rest the concern that autocrats who replace democracies are unique. The models visualized in Figure 2.5 employ the Geddes, Wright, & Frantz (2014) autocratic regime data to provide such an account. Models are fit to each of the four measures, using the prior regime type to assess whether autocrats who replace democratic regimes are more likely to produce ill outcomes for courts than autocrats who replace autocratic regimes. This is captured by a covariate for prior democracy, as the default reference category is prior autocracy. Here we are dealing with small sample sizes: in the data used for the first three models (using V-Dem measures), out of 310 total observations there are only sixty-three examples of democratic regimes being replaced by autocratic regimes, and only 149 examples of autocratic regimes replacing other autocratic regimes (the remaining observations include incidencies of foreign occupation, collapse into warlordism, etc.). As the Linzer & Staton (2015) data have more limited temporal and cross-sectional coverage, for the model fit to the LJI measure the numbers are 51 and 130, respectively.

Once again, rather than report tabular results, Figure 2.5 presents the results of simulated model parameters and expected values, plotting them with 90% confidence intervals to assess whether there exists any minimally meaningful effect. The results presented in Figure 2.5 are largely consistent with those in Figures 2.3 and 2.4, with there being a negligible effect for the compliance measure, and slight positive for the attacks and LJI measures. Figure 2.5 does, however, offer the first—albeit very minimal—support for the skeptical account, as there is some marginal evidence that autocrats who replace democratic regimes (as compared to other autocratic regimes) are associated with lower scores on the V-Dem high court independence measure. It is important to note that this result is not consistent across either the V-Dem or LJI measures (both measuring high court independence) or among the various V-Dem measures. And it is, of course, the only instance in the visualization of twenty models testing the causal mechanism

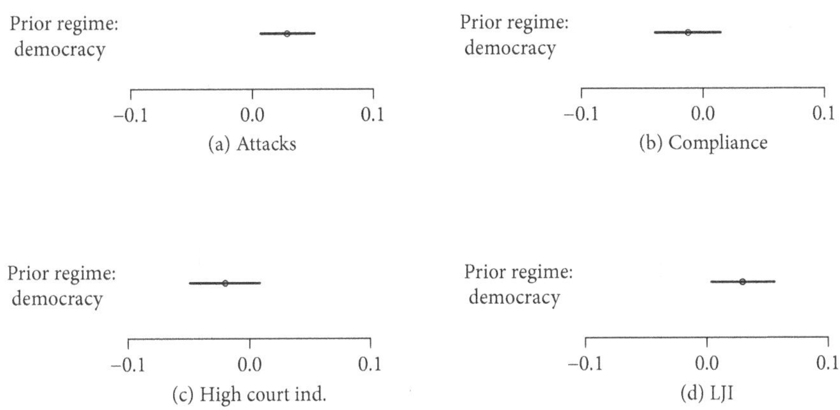

Figure 2.5 Estimated effects of prior regime type. Four plots showing the estimated effects of an autocratic regime replacing a democratic regime as opposed to another autocracy.

that provides even the slightest support for the skeptical account.[10] That is, in 95% of the analyses, results provide evidence that supports the insurance framework and undermines the skeptical challenge. As such, I am confident that once again a thorough and systematic examination reveals strong evidence for the mechanism underlying the insurance framework, and the most scant in the way of support for those who rather suspect incoming leaders run roughshod over existing judicial institutions.

To this point, this chapter has focused on persuading the reader that, despite potential reasons to be skeptical otherwise, new leaders do not appear to target courts and renege on existing levels of respect for judicial institutions. It might be somewhat unsurprising that democracies which replace autocracies do not go about dismantling judicial independence. More surprising, however, is the consistent and robust evidence that the past binds regardless of the prior regime, and regardless of whether it is being replaced by a democratic or non-democratic system. This evidence is itself an important contribution to the literature on comparative law and courts, showing as it does that a fundamental assumption of the insurance framework—one previously unexamined by either those advancing the framework or skeptical of it—is in fact strongly supported by systematic evidence. These uniform findings of no relationship between executive turnover and attacks on the judicial branch provide robust support for the mechanism undergirding the insurance framework, namely that judiciaries are able to offer insurance that is not simply voided by incoming executives. Whether or not they *do* provide such insurance is the matter to which I now turn.

2.3 The Provision of Insurance

Section 2.2 provides substantial evidence for a key mechanism of the insurance framework that has until now been assumed rather than shown: that new leaders are in fact bound by the past and are do not overturn the institutions of insurance established or maintained by previous leaders. What it does *not* do is provide evidence for the subsequent mechanism in the insurance framework by showing that independent judiciaries do in fact provide insurance to those previously in power. The disconnect between these two related mechanisms is clearest if one considers that a skeptical reader might argue the very evidence marshaled to demonstrate that the first mechanism undercuts the second. That is, an insurance skeptic might contend the fact that there is such persuasive evidence that new leaders do not target courts upon assuming power is indicative of independent

[10] And, as presented in the chapter appendix, despite there being some negligible effect, the estimate for the covariate for prior democracy has a p-value of >0.45.

judiciaries not providing insurance, as it is only because they do not provide such insurance that new leaders refrain from attacking their independence.

Absent evidence and thorough analysis, debating—let alone deciding for—one asserted relationship vs. another advances our understanding not at all. Thankfully, bringing evidence to bear on this question is entirely possible, and is the focus of the remainder of this chapter. To achieve this, I present analyses of the relationship between what happens to leaders after they leave office and the degree to which courts exercise independence at this point.[11] Although the insurance framework is predicated on the idea that courts are not only able to provide insurance but that they in fact do provide it, there has been little attempt to assess whether this assumed mechanism is consistent with its observable implications. Critical to the insurance framework is that courts decrease uncertainties associated with being out of power; independent judiciaries serve as insurance, decreasing the likelihood that a number of negative outcomes come to pass after a leader or party leaves office.

Ginsburg's (2003, 32) conception is that independent courts serve most fundamentally as a "risk-reduction device," offering protection to leaders and parties once they no longer hold the reins of power. Ginsburg's monograph is arguably the most exhaustive treatment of the insurance model to date, and he goes to great lengths to demonstrate the role that competition played in creating independent courts in Taiwan, Mongolia, and Korea and to explain the variation in the degree to which constitutional courts in these countries were able to assert themselves as independent actors after the establishment of democracy. When it comes to a systematic analysis of whether these courts were effective at providing insurance in the cases studied, however, Ginsburg's otherwise impressive work is less convincing, offering a handful of cases in which courts ruled against those in power as evidence of the efficacy of insurance. Excellent studies of other countries that employ an insurance framework observe a similar pattern, with scholars showing persuasively that competition was critical in prodding those in power to strengthen judicial independence while simultaneously paying little attention to whether these courts actually provided effective insurance (Finkel 2005, Ríos-Figueroa 2007).

2.3.1 Tests of Insurance

For a number of reasons, I contend that a highly critical test of whether a judiciary is able to offer insurance to an outgoing leader is whether said leader is able to save his (or her) skin. Although traditional conceptions of the insurance model focus

[11] Section 2.3 draws in part on Epperly (2013).

primarily on policy continuity, there is no reason why the logic of the framework stops there (Epperly 2013, Dixon & Ginsburg 2017); as I develop in Chapter 1, one's freedom from arbitrary punishment is also an important factor that those formerly in power must consider. In fact, I contend that a leader's post-tenure fate is the *fundamental* test of the insurance assumption: most former leaders would find policy continuity a small consolation if they are exiled, imprisoned, or killed, and it is hard to conceive of a judiciary that is willing to protect a former leader's policies but not the leader herself. In other words, if courts do in fact provide the risk-reduction mechanism assumed by the insurance framework, then independent courts should be able to provide insurance for the physical security of leaders after leaving office. This is doubly true when one considers that Section 2.2 demonstrates that levels of judicial independence show remarkable continuity in the years immediately after executive turnover or regime change. It follows that courts highly dependent on the executive—whose increased potential for politicized justice I discuss in the Chapter 1—will remain so, and thus be beholden to those newly in power. In Section 2.2 I demonstrated that this remains the case regardless of the nature of power transitions.

The first reason why a leader's post-tenure fate is a particularly effective test of the insurance framework's assumed causal logic is because it is commensurable and measurable within states over time, across states, and in both dictatorships and democracies in a way that protecting policy outcomes is not. There are two key reasons for this. First, in its most simple sense, data on policy continuity is extremely difficult to measure over time and space. The most comprehensive attempt to date to assess cross-nationally the degree to which high courts maintain or block government policy via decisions is the CompLaw database developed with National Science Foundation support by Carrubba, Gabel, Helmke, Martin, & Staton (2012). As ambitious and important as this project is, the fact that it assesses only a cross-section of forty-three states—most of which are consolidated democracies—makes it unable to adjudicate the matter at hand. Second, even were one to have comparative measures of policy continuity with decent temporal scope, it remains far from clear the degree to which these measures would be commensurable. In the context of advanced industrial democracies, with long-established partisan landscapes following some semblance of a left/right spectrum, assessing policy continuity across successive governments is likely unproblematic. This is not the case in most emerging democratic regimes, let alone autocracies. For example, the first twenty-five years after the collapse of communism in Central and Eastern Europe were typified not by the establishment of stable and effective parties with clear and consistent policy positions, but rather by inconsistency, a lack of clarity, and at times an indifference to policy as opposed to personal gain (Gryzmala-Busse 2007, Pop-Eleches 2010). Similarly, it is difficult to assess just how one might assess policy continuity as being indicative of the rule of the judiciary, as broken promises are endemic to democratic politics. This is perhaps exemplified most clearly by the phenomenon of leftist parties throughout Latin America campaigning against pro-market reforms and economic adjustment policies, and upon winning shifting almost overnight to the very policies they campaigned against (Stokes 2001). These factors make ascertaining what policy continuity might be the function of judicial insurance and what might simply be a result of parties indifferent to policy or enthusiastic converts to previous policies difficult.

The second reason the fate of leaders after exiting power is a valid and important test of the insurance function has less concern with what a focus on policy continuity cannot achieve and more with what post-tenure fates *can* achieve. What happens to leaders after leaving office is comparable across space and time, and as important for my purposes across regime type and regime change. While it might be unclear the degree to which a personalist dictator who comes to power via coup as opposed to a democratic leader who spent decades within a party structure cares about the continuity of policy after leaving office, it is far more obvious how both care about not being imprisoned, exiled, or killed after losing power.[12] To the degree that a significant aspect of ruling the state in both democracies and non-democracies alike is access to redirecting state assets and spending to friends and family via the privatization of public wealth (Levin & Satarov 2000, Gryzmala-Busse 2007, Dawisha 2014), establishing insurance against post-tenure prosecution—or worse—is an important hedge when electoral loss threatens.

In fact, the question of what happens to leaders after exiting office follows readily even from Stephenson's (2003) strategic model in which independent courts exist because they provide a third-party signal in a context of imperfect information: independent courts can credibly signal that if a former leader is punished, such punishment is not due to the politicization of justice but is rather "valid" punishment. With a dependent judiciary, however, no credible signal exists, and cooperation (i.e., only punishing former leaders who truly deserve it) breaks down. Therefore, independent judiciaries should allow for an equilibrium of cooperation in which politicized punishment is absent or rare because they provide a signal (e.g. upholding a conviction) that any punishment which occurs is valid.

Finally, any truly effective test of the insurance mechanism needs to determine whether judicial independence is associated with an outcome that those who might no longer be in power in the future would care about (and whether such an outcome might be minimized by an independent judiciary), but one that is not directly implicated by a strategic or attitudinal model of judicial decision-making. In other words, an outcome in which the existence of judicial independence might constrain other non-court actors from infringing on the rights of those who have

[12] Indeed, even among types of autocratic regimes, there should be variation in commitment to sustained policy after leaving office: compare for example the ideological commitments of (some) Leninist cadres in Moscow during the 1920s with the flexibility of those ruling the Kremlin today.

recently lost power. For this reason, as well as the reasons discussed above, what happens to leaders once they are no longer in power is an ideal test of the second assumed mechanism of the insurance framework.

2.3.2 An Example

Unfortunately, the role of an independent judiciary in deterring politicized prosecution is rarely directly observable, as independence makes the option of using the courts to target former political leaders unattractive, both because it is likely to be unsuccessful and widely criticized. As a result, when the prosecution and conviction of most former government leaders is successful in states with moderately independent judiciaries, it is for blatant and targeted human rights abuses and economic crimes for which there exists significant and significantly damning evidence (Lutz & Reiger 2009). The role that even moderate levels of judicial independence can play in making the successful prosecution of former leaders difficult is evidenced by the post-communist experience. While Nicolae Ceaușescu certainly did not avoid extra-legal punishment immediately after losing power, former leaders in states that established independent judiciaries and sought legal punishment fared well, with few being prosecuted let alone convicted. Even in the Czech Republic, where attempts to seek justice for communist-era crimes was most vigorous (Elster 2004), former state leaders have avoided conviction: although both Miloš Jakeš and Jozef Lenárt were prosecuted for treason for their role in the suppression of the Prague Spring, both were acquitted by Czech courts in 2002.

There are, on the other hand, countless examples of the politicized prosecution of former leaders in those states where judiciaries lack autonomy and power (Lutz & Reiger 2009). The recent case of Yulia Tymoshenko, the former prime minister of Ukraine, illustrates the danger of being a former leader in a situation where judicial independence is severely constrained.[13] In the 2010 presidential elections, Tymoshenko was the sitting prime minister, running for the presidency against two main opponents: her former Orange Revolution ally (and the incumbent president) Viktor Yushchenko, and the leader of the opposition Party of Regions, Viktor Yanukovych (the former prime minister, and the loser in the electoral disputes of the 2004 Orange Revolution). In reality, the contest was between Tymoshenko and Yanukovych, as Yushchenko's approval—along with Ukraine's GDP—had plummeted, and nearly 80% of voters listed his name in response

[13] It should be noted that although Ukraine's executive is difficult to code (Zadorozhnii 2010), in the Archigos data the leader is coded as the president and thus Tymoshenko is not a leader who would be included in the subsequent statistical analysis. It serves as an exemplary case, however, because of its recency and because it highlights two important issues worthy of future research: the role of courts in moderating conflict between leaders in semi-presidential systems, and the role of international legal institutions, as the European Court of Human Rights played a significant role in the resolution of the issue.

to the survey question "Who would you vote for under no circumstances?" (Interfax-Ukraine 2009). Being the two candidates with the most votes in the first round, the second round of the elections, held in early February, was a choice between Tymoshenko and Yanukovych. In results widely regarded as free and fair, Yanukovych won the elections with 49% of the vote to Tymoshenko's 45.5% (ODIHR 2010). Despite at first appealing the results of the election, Tymoshenko soon declined to take her legal challenge to the Supreme Court, and Yanukovych was the uncontested winner of the presidential election.

Two months later, a case that had been closed five years prior was reopened, and Tymoshenko found herself under investigation for trying to bribe judges. This was simply the first in a series of criminal cases against the former leader, to which were added investigations or prosecutions for a variety of offenses, including abuse of office when signing a gas deal with Russia, misappropriation of funds, non-delivery of goods by a firm she controlled in 1996, the reopening of a 2001 investigation of tax evasion, involvement in the 1996 murder of businessman and member of parliament Yevhen Shcherban, bribery of former Prime Minister Pavlo Lazarenko by a Cypriot company co-owned by Tymoshenko, and four further charges of tax evasion and embezzlement covering the period 1996–2000.

Both domestic and international observers, including the US, Russia, and the European Union, considered these actions to be politically motivated prosecutions by the Yanukovych administration.[14] Many suggest that the additional charges filed against her while in prison were to prevent her from running in the 2015 presidential election, which would have been possible if the European Court of Human Rights had ruled in her favor with regards to her conviction for abuse of office (Danilova 2013), a conviction the Council of Europe has called the "criminalization of normal political decision-making" (Spillius 2012). In 2014, before the European Court could decide the case, the Euromaidan "revolution" that ousted Yanukovych made the issue moot, as Tymoshenko was released from prison and the criminal code revised such that the charges brought against her for the gas deal with Russia were decriminalized, with the Ukrainian Supreme Court declaring her innocent (Interfax-Ukraine 2014).

These politically motivated prosecutions were successful for as long as they were in no small part because of the fact that in Ukraine the judiciary is subject to intense political pressure (Futey 2011). In the early 2000s the judiciary was severely lacking in independence (Popova 2012), and this situation deteriorated

[14] In 2012, European Commission President Jose Manuel Barroso reiterated this position, saying that the ratification of further agreements between Ukraine and the EU "will not be possible unless Ukraine urgently addresses this stark deterioration of democracy and the rule of law. In the immediate term, this applies to the above cases of selective justice and politically motivated prosecution. Solutions need to be found, enabling Ms. Tymoshenko, Mr. Lutsenko and others to regain their freedom and fully participate in political life" (Interfax-Ukraine 2012). Similarly, in early 2013 the then Secretary of State Hillary Clinton wrote to Tymoshenko to "reaffirm that the United States supports your immediate release," reiterating previous State Department releases on the matter (Reuters 2013).

significantly under the Yanukovych presidency: multiple Constitutional Court justices critical of Yanukovych resigned and were replaced by loyalists, changes to the Supreme Council of Justice gave the executive wide latitude in the appointment and dismissal of judges, and the discretion of courts was severely curtailed (Freedom House 2011). In 2011 a vote of no confidence was taken against the chairman of the Supreme Court (the highest appellate court), seen as independent of Yanukovych. Though it failed, his term expired later in the year and he chose not to run again, coincidentally immediately after a district court dropped criminal charges against his son-in-law (Freedom House 2012). Indeed, the very fact that it was only after the Euromaidan revolution and upheaval in Ukrainian politics that the Supreme Court ruled for Tymoshenko is further evidence of the dependent nature of the judiciary.

It is highly likely that were it not for the severe lack of judicial independence in Ukraine, Tymoshenko would not have been forced to appeal her conviction to international courts, and in fact had not been prosecuted or convicted at all, given the weak nature of the cases and the politicized nature of the prosecution and trial. That the prosecution was highly politicized remains the official position articulated by individual European governments, the European Union, the US, and Russia, and was further evidenced by the fact that it was not until her political opponents took power that she was implicated in a murder that took place fifteen years prior, an implication that was only made *after* she lodged a complaint with the European Court of Human Rights appealing her prosecution for abuse of office (European Court of Human Rights 2011). Additionally, the trial itself was marred by practices that an independent judiciary would immediately flag as serious violations. Among other blatant problems, the court refused to allow certain defense witnesses to be called, and allowed witnesses for the prosecution to testify when counsel for the defense was not present (Pifer 2012).

2.3.3 Analysis

If the second mechanism assumed by the insurance framework is correct—that is, that courts are in fact able to provide insurance—then independent judiciaries should be more highly associated with observable outcomes that such insurance can offer as compared to non-independent judiciaries. It is this mechanism that I aim to test here, and to do so by assessing whether or not independent judiciaries are associated with "better" (i.e. unpunished) outcomes for leaders once they leave office.

Post-tenure fate

In the past decade, international relations scholars have begun to scrutinize the effects of how leaders enter into and exit from power, and as an ancillary question what happens after leaving office. The most widely used data on these factors are the Archigos data produced by Goemans, Gleditsch, & Chiozza (2009). Although the Archigos data classify post-tenure fate in four categories (histograms of which are presented by regime type in Chapter 1) they need not be used in this manner, and I analyze these data dichotomously to better understand the relationship between judicial independence and post-tenure fate. Thus, I consider instances of all three forms of post-tenure punishment as one category. Given the lack of data within each punishment category compared to the "baseline" category of no punishment, there are methodological reasons for doing so.[15] Perhaps more compelling, however, is the theoretical reason: a leader worried about his or her post-tenure fate is likely most worried about any punishment, rather than the specific nature of the punishment imposed by those succeeding in power. Put simply: exile, imprisonment, and execution are unhappy outcomes to be avoided, and insurance if effective would likely be insurance against all forms of extreme punishment. If a leader is "only" exiled, it can probably be said that any insurance policy that he or she hoped an independent judiciary might provide was in fact an insurance policy that could not be collected.

Analyzing insurance

Table 2.4 presents a preliminary test of the insurance assumption. Here, the Linzer & Staton (2015) latent judicial independence (LJI) measure is used. Given that multiple measures of the same concept should not be included in analyses, I conduct Bayesian model averaging (not presented for reasons of space) to determine which of the two de facto judicial independence measures is preferable (Montgomery & Nyhan 2010). Results are decisive, with the V-Dem measure's estimated probability of not equaling zero itself being 0.0, and the cumulative posterior probability of the top two models—each including the LJI measure—being 99.5.[16]

Model 2 in Table 2.2 adds two potential confounding variables to the estimation: whether a state is a democracy and the level of economic development. The first of these is included because democracy is both associated with higher levels of independence, as well as a lower likelihood of a leader being punished after leaving office (model averaging is as insistent on its inclusion as it is the LJI measure). While one might consider it plausible that the relationship between independence and punishment is conditional on democracy, such is not supported by the data:

[15] This is also done to simplify interpretation. As demonstrated in Epperly (2013), the results are robust to analyses using post-tenure fate in ordinal and multinomial models. That is, treating the four possible categories as either ordered (being unpunished is better than being exiled, which is better than prison, which is better than death) or distinct and unordered categories produces comparable results.

[16] Regardless of the better model fit, if the V-Dem high court independence measure is used instead of the better-fitting LJI measure, the coefficient estimate of de facto judicial independence remains statistically significant and substantively important. Recall that although the LJI and V-Dem high court independence measures are highly correlated ($r = 0.7$), the underlying data used to create them are entirely separate.

Table 2.2 Tests of post-tenure fate and judicial independence. Two logistic regression models assessing the probability that a leader is unpunished after leaving office across varying levels of the latent judicial independence measure.

	Model 1	Model 2
Intercept	-1.01^{***}	-0.39
	(0.15)	(0.20)
Judicial independence	5.46^{***}	2.60^{***}
	(0.41)	(0.57)
Democracy		1.33^{***}
		(0.23)
log(GDP/capita)		0.37^{***}
		(0.09)
AIC	924.06	837.64
BIC	934.04	857.47
Num. obs.	1085	1052

$^{***}p < 0.001$, $^{**}p < 0.01$, $^{*}p < 0.05$

interactions between independence and democracy are neither significant in any model, nor do they improve model fit. Results are furthermore robust to fitting the data separately to democratic and non-democratic observations, suggesting that the relationship between independence and punishment is independent of regime type. Per capita GDP is included because it is plausibly related to independence for reasons previously discussed, and as wealthier states are more stable generally leaders of these states should be less likely to find themselves facing post-tenure punishment (though less decisive here, model averaging suggests that the probability of GDP being non-zero is greater than 0.4).

The results of Table 2.2 provide strong support for my claim that independent judiciaries do in fact provide insurance. Regardless of the inclusion of potential confounders, judicial independence remains highly significant and, as Figure 2.6 illustrates, substantively important. Because interpreting coefficients in nonlinear models is not straightforward, I plot the expected probability of a leader's unpunished post-tenure fate for Models 1 and 2 in Figure 2.6. In each plot, the value of judicial independence is allowed to vary from its observed minimum its observed maximum, while all other covariates are held constant at their mean values. Rather than use confidence intervals drawn solely from the standard errors of the estimates, to take into account the uncertainty in the modeling process itself I plot individual model fits drawn from simulation, along with the mean of these simulations.[17]

[17] Specifically, I take 1,000 draws from a multivariate normal distribution, with means set to coefficient estimates of the covariates in each model and the deviation around these means set to the

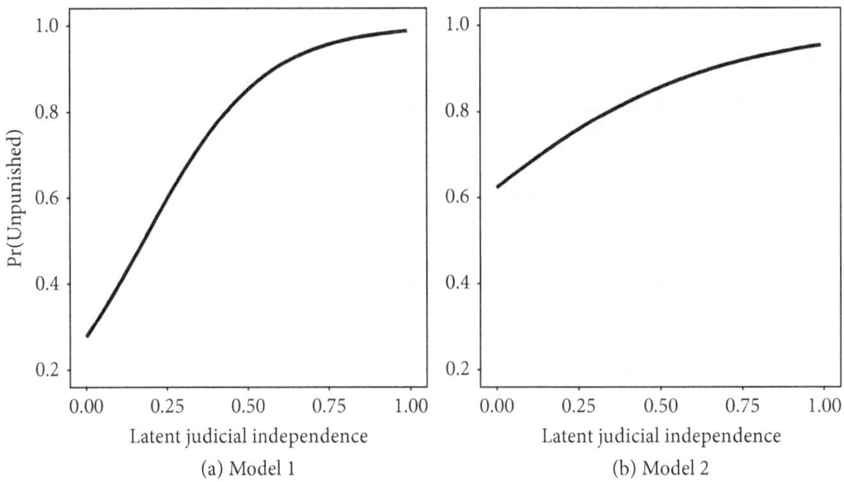

Figure 2.6 Leader fate and judicial independence. Two plots showing the expected probability (black line) of a leader not being punished at different levels of judicial independence when other covariates are held at their mean values. 95% confidence intervals are shown in gray.

Figure 2.6 visualizes the strong relationship between independence and post-tenure fate observed in the two models presented in Table 2.4: as judicial independence increases, the probability of not being punished after leaving office increases rapidly. When the LJI measure is approximately 0.6, for example, the probability of an unpunished fate reaches 0.9, and by the time judicial independence is at its maximum, in neither of the models is the probability of being unpunished after leaving office less than 0.99. In fact, using the LJI measure, which model averaging decisively recommends over the V-Dem measure, the probability of being unpunished reaches 0.9 before a state even reaches the third quartile value of latent judicial independence.

These results provide striking evidence in support of a strong relationship between independent judiciaries and personal insurance for leaders once they have left office. They are also extremely robust, as demonstrated in the secondary analyses and appendix of Epperly (2013). The relationship demonstrated is robust to using ordered and multinomial logistic regression of all four possible outcomes (unpunished, exiled, imprisoned, or killed), as well as using multilevel logistic and ordered logistic regression. The inclusion of other potential confounders does not change the results, which remain strong after including how a leader enters

corresponding variance–covariance matrix. Each of these 1,000 draws thus produces a distribution of simulated model parameters (estimates and standard errors). Using matrix multiplication of these simulated model parameters and specified quantities of interest (varying judicial independence here and holding all else constant) builds up a distribution of 1,000 observations for each level of independence.

power (via regular or irregular means), the number of years a country has been democratic, or the form of the executive.[18]

There are, of course, possible alternative explanations for these consistent and substantively important results. One such alternative could be characterized as a "bad leader/bad system" explanation. Here, in those systems in which leaders act in a lawless fashion more generally, there is unlikely to be judicial independence, and because of the lawless nature of rule they are more likely to be punished. While the models presented cannot fully adjudicate between these two explanations, the results provide more evidence for an explanation consistent with the insurance framework. This is because in polities where leaders act lawlessly—and are thus more likely to be punished—judicial independence is not the only thing that should suffer: we should also see significantly lower levels of economic development, no long-standing democracy, and especially more entry into power by irregular means, and as a result these should also be strongly associated with the dependent variable. Given that these other covariates that should also capture the lawfulness or quality of a political system (for lack of a better term) fail to show any relationship with the dependent variable, support for this alternative explanation is weak.

2.3.4 Further Implications

Although the above findings provide strong support for the relationship between more independent judiciaries and leaders insured against punishment after leaving office, and are thus highly consistent with the insurance framework, they do not explicitly consider whether it is party competition that is driving these better outcomes, as they pool all leaders and treat them as equivalent regardless of *how* they leave office as well as *who* they are replaced by. To show that these results are consistent with an insurance logic and not some alternative explanation for the relationship, I examine two further empirical implications of the argument: who replaces leaders and how they leave office.

[18] A potential limitation of the Archigos dataset for my purposes is that it assigns the same fate to leaders who are executed after losing power and those who are assassinated. The logic presented here suggests that independent courts can serve as an insurance mechanism because they make politicized prosecution less likely. If such prosecutions at times lead to executions, the utility of courts according to this argument is clear. The utility of an independent court in preventing an assassination, however, is far from clear. As the data conflate execution and assassination, it is possible that this conflation affects the inferences of the models. Conducting the analysis while excluding those who were killed from the punished post-tenure fate category produces no meaningful differences, however: coefficients of covariates are highly similar, and in no instance does a covariate become or cease being statistically significant.

Co-partisan replacement

A further empirical implication of the insurance framework is that there should be a difference between how judicial independence is associated with post-tenure fate when those replacing a former leader are from the same party. If the observed relationship is actually being driven by the causal logic developed in the insurance framework, it should be observed that independence is more important when a leader is replaced by an opposition figure. The reason behind this is simply that when a leader is replaced by members of her own party, the need for insurance against post-tenure punishment should be much lower and, often, nonexistent. Here, a new leader of his or her own party would include new prime ministers or presidents hailing from the same party and, for non-elected leaders, those hailing from the same ruling circle, be it a family in a monarchy or a fellow junta member in a military dictatorship (presuming the leader left office regularly and was not deposed in a coup). While on occasion we might expect a leader who engaged in particularly egregious actions while in office to be punished if replaced by his own people, on balance any incentives that those in power have to punish former leaders should be less when the leader is of the same party, for both loyalty reasons and because associating the party with individuals punished for crimes in office is bad publicity. This is clearly supported by the percentages of leaders who faced post-tenure punishment during 1960–2004: only 14% of leaders replaced by their own party were punished after leaving office, while 47% of those replaced by their opponents faced post-tenure punishment.

To determine whether independent judiciaries are more strongly associated with an unpunished post-tenure fate after the opposition assumes power, Table 2.3 reanalyzes the models presented in Table 2.2 across two subsets of data. The first subset includes only those instances in which the leader in question was replaced by a member of her own party (denoted as Models 1a and 2a); and the second, only when the replacement was an opposition figure (Models 1b and 2b). Results are highly consistent with the hypothesis that the mechanism explaining the relationship between judicial independence and what happens to leaders after they leave office is the one derived from the insurance framework: comparing Model 1a to 1b illustrates a coefficient for opposition replacement more than three times greater than non-opposition, and comparing Models 2a and 2b shows it more than double. In fact, once the confounders are included, non-opposition replacement is no longer statistically significant. Furthermore, the magnitude of the effect in Models 1b and 2b is greater than in Models 1 and 2 in Table 2.2, with the coefficient for judicial independence substantially larger when only analyzing the opposition subset.

In other words, although those replaced by their own party are on balance *less* likely to be punished after leaving office, the role of judicial independence in insuring this is not nearly as obvious or robust as when one is replaced by an

Table 2.3 Tests of post-tenure fate and judicial independence by opposition replacement. Four logistic regression models assessing the probability that a leader is not punished after leaving office, depending on who replaces the leader. Models 1a and 2a consider non-opposition replacement, while Models 1b and 2b consider opposition replacement.

	Model 1a co-partisan	Model 1b opposition	Model 2a co-partisan	Model 2b opposition
Intercept	1.86***	1.01***	1.66***	0.16
	(0.18)	(0.12)	(0.27)	(0.17)
Judicial independence	2.18**	7.14***	1.59	4.08***
	(0.68)	(0.57)	(1.06)	(0.75)
Democracy			0.50	1.82***
			(0.51)	(0.27)
log(GDP/capita)			−0.03	0.16
			(0.20)	(0.13)
AIC	226.14	601.57	218.95	530.70
BIC	233.61	610.72	233.73	548.90
Num. obs.	309	719	297	699

$^{***}p < 0.001$, $^{**}p < 0.01$, $^{*}p < 0.05$

opponent. These results are highly consistent with and provide further support for the mechanism developed by the insurance framework, that independent courts serve to minimize the success of arbitrary punishment as well as deter attempts to politicize justice.

The manner of replacement

The second empirical implication of the mechanism for the insurance framework is not the relationship between post-tenure fate and who replaces a leader, but rather the relationship between post-tenure fate and how that replacement occurs. Specifically, differences between autocratic and democratic leaders can be leveraged to assess whether competition is driving the observed relationship between independence and outcomes.

Insurance policies do not hold for all leaders, but especially not for all autocrats. It is precisely those leaving office via normal means such as electoral defeat or regular replacement that benefit from independent judiciaries; those removed via coup or extra-legal force should more likely face non-institutionalized, extra-judicial punishment. In other words, when threats to power come from legal and institutionalized electoral competition, a stronger legal and institutionalized minoritarian institution such as an independent judiciary should offer insurance. In instances where threats to power are extra-legal, extra-legal punishment should be far more likely and judicial independence should have no consistent relationship with whether a former leader is punished after leaving office.

This implication can be tested because the Archigos data code not only what happens to leaders after they leave office but the manner in which they exited, most crucially whether exit was by regular or irregular means.[19] In the Archigos data, regular exit means voluntary retirement, removal due to term limits, or defeat in an election; irregular exit violates established rules and is "overwhelmingly the result of the threat or use of force as exemplified in coups, revolts and assassinations" (Goemans, Gleditsch, & Chiozza 2006, 4). The implication here is straightforward: if the mechanism advocated by the insurance approach is correct, it is those autocrats who leave office due to regular means who should benefit from the insurance provided by courts, while those exiting irregularly should see no consistent benefit from an insurance policy designed to guard against the electoral transition of power. This is because if leaders exit via an institutionalized transfer process, an empowered court is more likely to remain a player in politics. Recall that Figure 2.4 suggested that electoral turnover in autocracies is associated with a minimally meaningful improvement. On the other hand, if a regime is toppled by coup or revolution, the insurance provision should be far less robust: groups competing electorally in autocracies are operating under the (typically unfair or unfairly applied) rules of the game, whereas coup plotters and revolutionaries are by definition subverting those rules and rejecting the game (obviously, in the case of assassination any insurance function becomes wholly irrelevant). Recall also that non-electoral turnover in Figure 2.4 is associated with a minimally meaningful negative effect for three of the judicial measures, and is associated with a positive effect in none.

Put another way: autocrats who leave office via elections should look similar to democrats, who overwhelmingly leave office through regularized means, and there should be a consistent relationship between independence and post-tenure fate. Conversely, the highly attenuated importance of a judiciary in circumstances of extra-legal regime change means that no systematic relationship between independence and post-tenure fate should be observed. Note, however, that it is entirely possible that leaders exiting via irregular means feared leaving via regular means and thus increased judicial independence; eventually losing power to a coup does not mean that an autocrat never faced electoral competition, after all. This possibility should further weigh *against* the empirical implication as it would strengthen the connection between independence and irregular exit, making it appear more like regular exit. This raises another barrier to confirmation and leads to further confidence that the empirical implication supports the mechanism of the insurance framework.

[19] These data also account for whether a leader died of natural causes while in office or was deposed by another state. As these two methods of exiting office are unrelated to the process being studied here, these leaders are omitted from the analysis.

Table 2.4 Judicial independence and regular vs. irregular exit. Four logistic regression models of the probability of being unpunished after leaving office. Models test the empirical implication of whether autocrats leaving office via regular means benefit from independent judiciaries when compared to those who leave office via irregular means.

	Model 1 Dem. & Autoc. Reg. & Irreg. exit	Model 2 Democrats Regular	Model 3 Autocrats Regular	Model 4 Autocrats Irregular
Intercept	0.68***	2.78***	2.60***	−1.38***
	(0.15)	(0.23)	(0.42)	(0.33)
Judicial independence	2.61***	2.61†	2.83†	−0.20
	(0.55)	(1.36)	(1.70)	(1.23)
log(GDP/capita)	0.31**	0.37	−0.09	0.10
	(0.11)	(0.34)	(0.26)	(0.19)
Democracy	1.50***			
	(0.23)			
AIC	819.13	176.76	123.09	236.81
BIC	838.86	189.89	132.60	247.15
Num. obs.	1024	589	176	232

$^{***}p < 0.001$, $^{**}p < 0.01$, $^{*}p < 0.05$, $^{\dagger}p < 0.1$

Table 2.4 presents results of four logistic regression models of leaders' fates after leaving office. Each examines the relationship between judicial independence and the probability of being unpunished through a different set of observations. Model 1 is a reference point, pooling autocrats and democrats and those exiting office via regular and irregular means (it is highly similar to Model 1 in Table 2.2, fit to a slightly lower number of observations due to removing those leaders who are deposed by foreign states). Models 2 and 3 look at regular exit for democrats and autocrats, and Model 4 autocrats who exit irregularly. The results of these models illustrate that the empirical prediction of the autocratic insurance argument holds: autocrats exiting office via regular means look shockingly similar to democrats, whereas autocrats exiting via irregular means do not. In both Models 2 and 3 in Table 2.4 there is a consistent and positive relationship between higher levels of independence and being unpunished after exiting, with the coefficient for independence almost identical across the democracy/dictatorship divide.

While this effect is significant at only the attenuated $p < 0.1$ level (likely due to the small number of observations), it should be noted that the point here is not to ascertain the strongest of relationships, but rather to see whether the relationship looks similar for democrats and autocrats exiting office via regular means. These models demonstrate that this is the case as clearly as they demonstrate that the effect of judicial independence for autocrats exiting office via irregular means (Model 4) looks vastly different than it does for autocrats exiting via regular means, where the effect of independence is indistinguishable between democracies and autocracies. These findings further support the interpretation of the relationship between judicial independence and what happens to leaders after leaving office as being strongly consistent with the insurance framework's logic. Clearly, the weight of the evidence demonstrates that not only do courts provide insurance, but that such insurance is highly consistent with the causal logics articulated by the insurance framework.

2.4 Conclusion

Despite more than two decades of attention to the role that competitive electoral environments play in the establishment and maintenance of independent judiciaries, to date two key mechanisms that allow for this relationship have remained unexamined.

First, for the contention that courts are able to provide insurance to those formerly in power to hold, it must be the case that incoming leaders refrain from simply undermining the judiciary. If new leaders regularly attack the integrity of the court, undermine its independence, or refuse to comply when it rules against the government, then any insurance policies put in place would never actually pay out. In other words, if the case of Argentina in the second half of the twentieth century is the norm, then skeptics are right to think there is little binding constraint on those assuming office, and little in the way of insurance. Even if this condition holds, a second condition must also hold for the insurance framework to offer an effective explanation, namely that courts do in fact offer insurance. Carefully examining both aspects of the theorized causal mechanism is critical because the two could be in tension: perhaps courts only remain free from attack by new executives precisely because they do *not* provide insurance.

In this chapter I present the first ever attempt to address the first condition for the insurance framework, offering a response to the many skeptics who have rightly questioned whether this key mechanism, previously only assumed, holds (Helmke & Rosenbluth 2009). I systematically examine whether political actors are more likely to undermine the judiciary after executive turnover: assessing four different relevant measures, I show that there is no difference between the distribution of these measures before and after a change in power. That is, there is no evidence supporting the empirical implication of the skeptical account that these should be distributed quite differently, as those newly empowered can and do run roughshod over courts. I then show that in democracies, a different party taking power is no more strongly associated with bad outcomes for courts than a co-partisan, or even no executive turnover. Similarly, in autocracies, regime breakdown—be it by electoral or non-electoral means—does not produce attacks on the judiciary. Finally, I tie the autocratic and democratic stories together and show that autocratic vs. democratic collapse also fails to predict worse outcomes for courts. In laying out all three, I demonstrate that not only are these factors not statistically significant, but furthermore show that they are irrelevant by assessing the negligibility of their effects (Rainey 2014). The evidence marshaled in the first half of this chapter demonstrates that the Argentine story that opened this chapter is the exception, not the rule, and it is now incumbent on skeptics of the descriptive accuracy of the insurance framework's assumption that future leaders are in fact bound by past decisions regarding the judiciary—who like supporters have to date not brought to bear evidence supporting their position—to offer systematic analysis in defense of their position. To the extent that they do not, such skepticism is unwarranted going forward.

If leaders are—as the insurance framework has to date assumed and this analysis now shows—empowering courts because courts can actually provide some insurance function, then independent courts should be associated with positive outcomes for leaders after leaving office. I demonstrate here that this is clearly the case: the provision of insurance is robust. Rather than merely show that there exists a strong correlation between the presence of a more independent judiciary and positive post-tenure fates for leaders, I show strong evidence by way of two further empirical implications that this is in fact a function of the causal logic articulated by the insurance framework. By looking at the relationship between being punished after leaving office and first who replaces leaders and second how they exit, I am able to offer three clear and differentiated empirical implications highly consistent with the insurance model and unexplained by any other explanatory framework.

Combined, the two broad empirical foci of this chapter offer a persuasive defense of the descriptive accuracy of the assumptions and mechanisms undergirding the insurance framework's structure. In doing so, I construct a thorough foundation for assessing the predictive accuracy of the insurance model. Given that we now know that courts provide insurance, it is to the important question of whether more competitive electoral environments predict better insurance policies that I now turn.

2.5 Appendix

In Sections 2.2.4–2.2.6 I present visualizations of whether the lack of statistical significance in the models referenced (but not shown) is in fact "negligible" in the sense of being statistically *and* substantively unimportant. I do so with the equivalent of the TOST (two one-sided tests) framework (Berger & Hsu 1996, Rainey 2014), plotting 90% confidence intervals of the predicted effects of the key covariate across the four outcome measures,[20] to see whether these cross a substantively meaningful threshold. To be as conservative as possible in my tests,

[20] The first three of these are drawn from the V-Dem data, and consist of attacks on the judiciary, compliance with judicial decisions, and high court independence. The fourth is the Linzer & Staton latent judicial independence (LJI) measure.

the threshold I choose is a scant one-quarter of one standard deviation of the relevant outcome variable; given the covariates of interest are dichotomous, if their predicted effects fail to consistently reach even this threshold, I can safely conclude that they are not only statistically insignificant but also substantively irrelevant. For flow, and because Figures 2.3 and 2.4 contain more stringent tests, I omit the regression tables from the main chapter text. Here I report all relevant regression output, to further demonstrate the impressive array of evidence supporting the first mechanism of the insurance model.

Executive turnover in democracies

Tables 2.5 and 2.6 report results for the models used to produce Figure 2.3. Table 2.5 reports the results of those models fit to the four outcome measures, assessing the effect of executive turnover (of the same or different party) in democratic regimes. Table 2.6 expands the analysis, including when turnover occurred in the previous year as well.

Executive turnover in non-democracies

Tables 2.7 and 2.8 report results for the models used to produce Figure 2.4. Table 2.7 reports the results of those models fit to the four outcome measures, assessing the effect of autocratic breakdown (either electoral or non-electoral

Table 2.5 Influence on the judiciary and executive turnover in democracies. Linear models with country fixed effects (not reported) for the four different measures of infringement of the judicial branch and the effects of executive turnover. These are the models used to produce the estimated effects presented in Figure 2.3 for Turnover: *t*.

	Attacks	Compliance	High court ind.	LJI
Intercept	0.10***	0.30***	0.32***	−0.81***
	(0.03)	(0.02)	(0.02)	(0.04)
Different party	−0.01	−0.00	−0.00	0.01
	(0.00)	(0.00)	(0.00)	(0.00)
Same party	0.01	−0.00	−0.01	−0.00
	(0.01)	(0.01)	(0.01)	(0.01)
Duration democratic	−0.02***	−0.02***	0.03***	0.03***
	(0.00)	(0.00)	(0.00)	(0.01)
log(GDP/capita)	0.06***	0.08***	0.06***	0.28***
	(0.00)	(0.00)	(0.00)	(0.01)
AIC	−9734.50	−11612.33	−10091.40	−6504.13
BIC	−9030.77	−10908.61	−9387.67	−5863.18
Num. obs.	3743	3743	3743	2507

$^{***}p < 0.001$, $^{**}p < 0.01$, $^{*}p < 0.05$

Table 2.6 Influence on the judiciary and prior executive turnover in democracies. Linear models with country fixed effects (not reported) for the four different measures of infringement of the judicial branch and the effects of executive turnover in the preceeding or current year. These are the models used to produce the estimated effects presented in Figure 2.3 for Turnover: t, t_{-1}.

	Attacks	Compliance	High court ind.	LJI
Intercept	0.08**	0.29***	0.32***	−0.86***
	(0.03)	(0.02)	(0.02)	(0.05)
Different party	−0.01*	−0.00	−0.00	0.01
	(0.00)	(0.00)	(0.00)	(0.00)
Same party	0.01	0.00	−0.00	0.00
	(0.01)	(0.00)	(0.00)	(0.01)
Duration democratic	−0.03***	−0.03***	0.03***	0.02*
	(0.00)	(0.00)	(0.00)	(0.01)
log(GDP/capita)	0.07***	0.08***	0.06***	0.29***
	(0.00)	(0.00)	(0.00)	(0.01)
AIC	−9529.69	−11592.20	−9956.82	−6369.09
BIC	−8841.31	−10903.82	−9268.43	−5750.06
Num. obs.	3647	3647	3647	2405

$^{***}p < 0.001$, $^{**}p < 0.01$, $^{*}p < 0.05$

Table 2.7 Influence on the judiciary and autocratic breakdown. Linear models with country fixed effects (not reported) for the four different measures of infringement of the judicial branch and autocratic regime collapse. These are the models used to produce the estimated effects presented in Figure 2.4 for Turnover: t.

	Attacks	Compliance	High court ind.	LJI
Intercept	0.52***	0.44***	0.48***	−0.35***
	(0.02)	(0.02)	(0.02)	(0.03)
Electoral failure	0.01	0.04**	0.03*	0.01
	(0.01)	(0.01)	(0.02)	(0.01)
Non-electoral failure	−0.03***	0.02**	0.01	−0.01
	(0.01)	(0.01)	(0.01)	(0.01)
Democratic transition	0.01	0.03**	0.07***	0.12***
	(0.01)	(0.01)	(0.01)	(0.01)
Regime duration	0.21***	−0.11*	−0.15**	0.34***
	(0.05)	(0.04)	(0.05)	(0.05)
log(GDP/capita)	−0.02**	−0.01*	−0.02**	0.13***
	(0.01)	(0.01)	(0.01)	(0.01)
AIC	−9442.23	−9935.93	−9125.90	−8808.18
BIC	−8718.74	−9212.45	−8402.41	−8111.63
Num. obs.	3778	3778	3778	3328

$^{***}p < 0.001$, $^{**}p < 0.01$, $^{*}p < 0.05$

Table 2.8 Influence on the judiciary and prior autocratic breakdown. Linear models with country fixed effects (not reported) for the four different measures of infringement of the judicial branch and autocratic regime collapse in the preceding or current year. These are the models used to produce the estimated effects presented in Figure 2.4 for Turnover: t, t_{-1}.

	Attacks	Compliance	HC ind.	LJI
Intercept	0.51^{***}	0.45^{***}	0.48^{***}	-0.34^{***}
	(0.02)	(0.02)	(0.03)	(0.03)
Electoral failure	−0.00	0.02	0.01	0.05^{***}
	(0.01)	(0.01)	(0.01)	(0.01)
Non-electoral failure	-0.02^{***}	0.01^{*}	0.00	0.01^{*}
	(0.01)	(0.00)	(0.01)	(0.01)
Democratic transition	0.02	0.05^{***}	0.08^{***}	0.09^{***}
	(0.01)	(0.01)	(0.01)	(0.01)
Regime duration	0.15^{**}	−0.02	−0.06	0.47^{***}
	(0.05)	(0.05)	(0.06)	(0.05)
log(GDP/capita)	-0.02^{**}	-0.02^{**}	-0.02^{***}	0.12^{***}
	(0.01)	(0.01)	(0.01)	(0.01)
AIC	−9330.97	−9822.20	−8961.02	−8587.58
BIC	−8616.49	−9107.72	−8246.55	−7900.86
Num. obs.	3688	3688	3688	3220

$^{***}p < 0.001$, $^{**}p < 0.01$, $^{*}p < 0.05$

Table 2.9 Influence on the judiciary and regime breakdown. Linear models with country fixed effects (not reported) for the four different measures of infringement of the judicial branch and democratic vs. autocratic collapse. These are the models used to produce the estimated effects presented in Figure 2.5 for the effect of prior democratic regime.

	Attacks	Compliance	High court ind.	LJI
Intercept	0.55^{***}	0.44^{**}	0.14	-0.40^{**}
	(0.13)	(0.15)	(0.16)	(0.15)
Prior democracy	−0.00	−0.01	−0.02	0.01
	(0.02)	(0.02)	(0.03)	(0.03)
Prior other	0.02	−0.00	0.01	−0.03
	(0.02)	(0.02)	(0.02)	(0.02)
Duration democratic	0.03	−0.01	0.00	0.02
	(0.02)	(0.02)	(0.02)	(0.02)
Duration autocratic	−0.01	0.00	0.01	−0.00
	(0.01)	(0.02)	(0.02)	(0.02)
log(GDP/capita)	−0.04	−0.01	0.05	0.15^{***}
	(0.04)	(0.04)	(0.04)	(0.04)
AIC	−528.73	−474.37	−422.36	−454.68
BIC	−162.54	−108.19	−56.17	−121.06
Num. obs.	310	310	310	257

$^{***}p < 0.001$, $^{**}p < 0.01$, $^{*}p < 0.05$

failure), whereas Table 2.8 reports results including when breakdown occurred in the previous year as well.

From democracy to autocracy

Table 2.9 reports the results of models used to produce Figure 2.5. It assesses the effects of prior regime type to determine whether regime breakdown where new autocratic regimes replace democracies differs from those instances where new autocratic regimes replace previous autocratic regimes (the reference category).

3

Examining Insurance across Regime Type

Chapter 2 establishes that two critical—and previously unexamined—mechanisms of the insurance framework hold. First, that new leaders do not run roughshod over the judiciary, regardless of the form of leadership change. Second, that regardless of turnover in power or regime change, courts do in fact provide insurance to former leaders after they leave office, most saliently in the form of personal protection. This general pattern holds across regime type, and Chapter 2 further shows that who replaces the leader and the manner of their exit from office are both highly consistent with the empirical implications suggested by the insurance framework.

With this foundation in place, it is time to turn our attention to the edifice of the explanation itself. This chapter aims to show that electoral competition is associated with more independent judiciaries, and that the relationship is, as theorized in Chapter 1, highly conditional on regime type. It does so in three parts. The first part returns to matters of concept and measurement, this time focusing on how best to think about competition. Here I discuss how existing research has at times left large gulfs between the underlying concept of competition and how it induces a need for insurance, arguing that a better operationalization includes both the distribution of partisan preferences in all legislative houses, rather than simply the lowest, as well as the fragmentation of the opposition.

In Section 3.2 I present a thorough analysis of the relationship between the competitiveness of the electoral environment and de facto judicial independence by way of a cross-national, observational approach. After presenting my preferred specification I address competing explanations drawn from the law and courts literature, including explanations that focus on alternative factors as well as those focusing on hegemonic decline or judicial defection. The focus here is on the clarity of presentation and the substantive implications of the models, and more thorough details concerning model fit, robustness, and further alternative specifications are presented in detail in the chapter appendix. Of course, given the nature of complicated institutional and political arguments, concerns of endogeneity and omitted variable bias loom. Thus, in Section 3.3 I argue for the appropriateness of two instruments for political competition, and using an instrumental variable approach further analyze the relationship, taking the first steps in the literature towards a causal interpretation of the relationship between competition and independence

The Political Foundations of Judicial Independence in Dictatorship and Democracy. Brad Epperly, Oxford University Press (2019). © Brad Epperly
DOI: 10.1093/oso/9780198845027.001.0001

This chapter offers multiple important contributions to our understanding of judicial independence generally and the insurance framework specifically. First, it takes a careful approach to thinking about how to best measure competition given the causal logics of the insurance model. Second, it builds on the theoretical insights of the previous chapters and demonstrates strong and consistent support for the idea of autocratic insurance. The third contribution it makes is bringing causal inference techniques to bear on this important question. These three contributions combine to offer a consistent and persuasive case that electoral competition is strongly associated with more judicial independence in non-democracies, offering preliminary evidence suggesting that this relationship is causal. The final contribution is what the evidence of the chapter does not support, namely that there is a meaningful relationship between competition and insurance in democracies. This raises the final question of the book, which will be addressed in Chapter 4.

3.1 Competition, Independence, and Democracy

Attempting to accurately assess the validity of the insurance model requires an effective method of measuring the degree of threat posed by electoral competition. The specific manner of how different scholars go about operationalizing this threat varies, and rarely is the discussion of the connection between concepts and measures explicit, with clear reasoning provided as to why a given approach is being used. While careful attention to how we conceptualize and measure key concepts like regime type is critical in general (Wilson 2014), as I argue elsewhere it is of vital importance in assessing the relationship between political competition and judicial independence (Epperly 2018). In brief: because how we conceptualize democracy is so often inextricably tied up with either the competitiveness of the electoral arena (Boix, Miller, & Rosato 2013) or the independence of the judiciary (Marshall, Jaggers, & Gurr 2015), without careful attention to concept-measurement issues we risk making a proper assessment of the competition independence relationship impossible. To better address this, in this section I present a brief overview of how a handful of major contributions approach this, before discussing the concept and measure of competition (as democracy was addressed in Chapter 1) employed in the rest of Chapter.[1]

[1] What follows is far from exhaustive, focused on some of the most influential works, and many contributions to the literature go unaddressed; in general, the concepts and measures these employ are similar if not identical to works discussed.

3.1.1 Concept-measurement in Existing Work

In some instances, the role of competition is examined by way of broad comparisons between a handful of countries, with scholars employing ordinal frameworks, even if implicit and unspecified. Given comparisons of general levels of competition and general levels of judicial independence, these scholars consider that operationalizing competition—along with independence—in broad ordinal ways is able to effectively capture the underlying relationship. For Ramseyer (1994), for example, the United States has more competition than Japan, as well as more independence; this is indicated quite sensibly by the LDP's decades-long stranglehold on high office. For Ginsburg (2003), the levels of competition are structured comparatively across his three cases, indirectly assessed as the number of relevant parties engaged in constitutional negotiations during regime transition. These are then mapped out onto a discussion of the constitutional rules under which the post-transition judiciaries operate, as well as the behavioral responses of the political branches to judicial decision-making. For both, the conceptual importance of competition is well developed, while the measurement in a highly specified manner is neither well developed nor necessary, given the parameters of their studies.

In her important critique of the applicability of the insurance framework to electoral authoritarian regimes, Popova (2010) tackles political competition in two different ways. Conceptually, she inverts the incentive structures of insurance framework while still focusing on how the fear of losing elections induces specific behavior from those in power; Popova argues that in non-democratic/competitive authoritarian contexts the fear of losing power induces leaders to attack judicial independence because dependent courts can be effective tools to be used against the opposition. When it comes to measurement, she first considers via impressionistic accounts that Ukraine was far more electorally competitive than Russia. Popova (2010, 1210) notes that "as Ukrainian politics became increasingly competitive during the 2000s, Russian politics became less competitive." While this is hardly a contentious reading of the arc of the second decade of post-communism in the two states, the degree to which it is accurate in the first couple of years of the decade—her analyses cover parliamentary elections in 2002 and 2003 in Ukraine and Russia, respectively—is far less certain. Putin's project of dismantling electoral competition can hardly be said to have been settled, after all, before the first time his United Russia party even contested seats in the Duma. While the *result* of the 2003 parliamentary elections was a highly successful showing for the new United Russia party, in the previous elections the "party of power" (Unity) won less than a quarter of the total votes, coming in second place to the Communist Party and securing only a handful more seats than the third-place party.[2]

[2] Furthermore, this cannot even explicitly be a story of presidential elections rather than legislative: in his first presidential election of 2000, Putin received the support of only a bare majority of voters (53%).

Given her sub-national analysis, however, a key measure of competition for (Popova 2010) is at the level of the legislative district. Here, however, there is a confusing and problematic divergence between concept and measure. Conceptually, the phenomenon of interest for Popova is how competitive electoral contests at the district level affect the likelihood that judges rule for or against candidates aligned with the national governments in Kyiv and Moscow in electoral registration disputes that would determine "who can contest elections and who cannot" (Popova 2010, 1211). The measure of competition, however, is the electoral *result* at the district level.[3] While it could be argued in some instances that it is not a problem for a measure of an explanatory variable to be measured temporally subsequent to the phenomenon it explains, in this instance it most certainly is.[4] This becomes clear if one focuses on the fact that successful electoral disputes—the outcome—should seriously affect the result of elections; one's vote share is naturally endogenous to whether or not one bars one's opponent from the ballot.

As the approach I employ here is comparative and quantitative, it calls for a more thorough discussion of how the handful of works of this nature handle competition. To date, the only cross-national look at the relationship between competition and de facto judicial independence in democratic regimes is a cross-section of nearly 100 states in the 2000s (Aydın 2013).[5] Arguing that competition inhibits independence in emerging democracies for reasons similar to Popova's "strategic pressure" argument, Aydın employs the difference between the share of seats of the government party or coalition and the largest opposition party, averaged over the 2000–2008 time period. The connection between concept and measure is far clearer in this instance: the size of the largest opposition party, relative to the size of the government, should indicate the degree to which a credible electoral threat is presented.[6] An issue might arise from the specific

[3] As Popova (2010, 1211) notes, "I measure district competitiveness through a dummy variable, where I assigned 1s to all SMDs where the difference between the winner and the runner-up was less than 10%."

[4] This is not to minimize the important contribution of Popova's work: the careful attention to how electoral disputes (as well as media disputes in her 2012 monograph) can provide information regarding judicial independence is itself a substantial contribution. Unfortunately, however, given the ex post measure of competition it can tell us far less about how competition might affect such independence.

[5] Though Stephenson's (2003) formal model assumes a democratic regime, his empirical examination of its assumptions analyzes both democratic and autocratic regimes. The degree to which the piece assesses democracies remains an open question, however; Aydın's idiosyncratic measure of democracy considers Putin's Russia and Mubarak's Egypt democratic. For an extended discussion of her conceptualization of democracy, and a replication using standard classifications, see Epperly (2018).

[6] The appropriateness of the use of all government parties as opposed to the largest government party remains an open question. While in many cases a party might govern with only a handful of votes provided by small minority parties, in other instances the largest party of government might control a closely comparable number of seats as compared to the largest opposition party. That this measure does not take into account the degree to which government is divided thus might, under some circumstances, underestimate the level of electoral threat that an opposition party poses. Put concretely: a governing party with 30% of the seats and support from small parties to push it above 50% where an opposition party controls 25% of seats should be in a very different position than a governing party with 51% of seats that faces an opposition with 25%.

implementation of this measurement, however, due specifically to its aggregation of competition over nearly a decade. While Aydın (2013, 123) argues that this averaging of competition is appropriate due to the slowly changing nature of electoral competition, it remains unclear the degree to which electoral competition is slowly changing. While electoral volatility is generally low in advanced industrial democracies, it is remarkably high elsewhere, including Latin America and the post-communist states of Eastern Europe and the former Soviet Union (Roberts & Wibbels 1999, Birch 2003, Epperly 2011), a fact not missed by those studying how competition affects other state outcomes (Frye 2010). As Aydın (2013, 119) herself notes in a discussion of Moldova, there can be significant changes from election to election: her score for competition in 2001 is 0.52, whereas in 2005 after the next election it is less than half that, at 0.22. Thus, if one thinks competition might matter—positively *or* negatively—for judicial independence, masking significant swings in competition by averaging across time periods means that making such an inference is far more difficult.[7]

Randazzo, Gibler, & Reid (2016) offer an analysis that at first glance appears to be closely related to the argument I offer here, as it looks at both democratic and non-democratic regimes. Rather than arguing, however, that competition increases judicial independence in non-democracies, they hypothesize—following the logic articulated by Popova (2012) and Aydın (2013)—that it inhibits independence. Furthermore, they contend that competition is not only conditional on regime type, but so too are ethnic heterogeneity and the size of the winning coalition. The latter concept draws on the popular "selectorate" idea in international relations research, which Randazzo, Gibler, & Reid (2016, 583) suggest captures "the potential for inter-group trust across society as a whole." This trust, according to the authors, should be associated with higher levels of judicial independence, though they omit any discussion of how or why this is the case.[8] The issue of gulf between concepts and measures arises once again, for both their measures of competition and the size of the winning coalition, and this combination makes it difficult to draw inferences from their empirical results.

To measure political competition, the authors rely on Vahanen's (2000) index of democracy, which attempts to capture the two contestation and participation components of Dahl's (1971) idea of polyarchy. This measure subtracts from 100 the largest party's vote share, and then multiplies it by the percentage of the population (total, not electorate or voting-age population) that voted. Thus, "higher values are associated with greater levels of political competition within

[7] It also follows from the cross-sectional nature of the analysis that any statistical patterns observed are between countries rather than within, despite the conceptual matter at hand generally considered inter-temporal rather than merely cross-sectional.

[8] Although the authors do note that larger selectorates should be associated with more widely distributed provisions of private goods by leaders, it is unclear how this relates to inter-group trust, or how they would increase the amount of private goods, rather than just distribute fewer private goods more widely.

the state that should increase pressure for judicial independence" (Randazzo, Gibler, & Reid 2016, 587). Unfortunately, as the authors do not attempt to link the relevance of voter turnout to the pressure competition places on leaders or the desire for insurance, any connection between concept and measure here remains obscured.[9] At purely a measurement level, however, the focus on voter turnout produces methodological results that run precisely counter to assessing the effects of competition. Take, for example, an electoral situation where the largest party took 51% of the vote: if turnout was 55%—US voting age population turnout in 2016—then the Vanhanen index score would produce a competition measure of 28 (were it to use voting age and not total population). At the same margin of victory, if turnout was 77%—the turnout in the 2017 Dutch elections—the Vanhanen score would be more than a third greater, at 39.[10] If one compares the score for the 2015 Swiss elections to the 2014 Belgian, an identical margin of victory would produce a score for Belgium of more than double that of Switzerland (44.5 vs. 19.7). Without a clear conceptual reason for thinking turnout is *exactly as important* for the insurance impulse as the distribution of votes or seats by party, using the product of the two numbers introduces massive amounts of noise into the key explanatory variable. This noise is further amplified by the fact that total population and voting age population vary dramatically by country for reasons of both demographics and immigration: almost 42% of the Kenyan population is under the age of 15, for example, while in Japan the proportion is less than 13%.[11]

[9] While one might think that lower turnout at one election could mean less popular interest in politics or political change, one could just as easily interpret it to mean that at the subsequent election there is more ability for the opposition to mobilize previous non-voters and thus produce higher levels of electoral volatility and a higher likelihood of turnover.

[10] In fact, as a result of the nature of measurement, the highest level of competition recorded by the Vanhanen index in the analysis of Randazzo, Gibler & Reid (2016) is 49. I thank the authors for sharing replication data for the article.

[11] The difficulty of drawing inferences from these results is amplified by the authors' use of the size of the winning coalition (*w/s*) measure common to selectorate work in international relations. As Clarke & Stone (2008), Kennedy (2009), and Gallagher & Hanson (2015) illustrate, the *w/s* measure fails to capture the underlying concept of size of the winning coalition, and is rather a measure of the degree of competitiveness of legislative elections. This presents two further problems. First, that the *w/s* measure in fact measures competitiveness means the piece thus improperly uses multiple measures of the same concept, which as Montgomery & Nyhan (2010) note further makes inference problematic (this is also evidenced not only by studies of the selectorate measures but also by the fact that the two measures, unrelated in the authors conceptual schema, are correlated at greater than 0.8). Second, that there is significant contamination across these measures: not only does *w/s* rely entirely on a component of Polity that it is then interacted with, but the measure of judicial independence Randazzo, Gibler & Reid (2016) employ on the left hand side of the equation itself draws on the Polity executive constraints component, which appears four times (due to three separate interactions) on the right hand side of the equation.

3.1.2 Conceptualizing and Measuring Competition

It is important to keep in mind that according to the insurance logic articulated in Chapter 3, electoral competition is a key component not because there is something important about a specific share of seats controlled by a given opposition party, but rather because of the signal it sends to those in power about the credibility of the electoral threat to maintaining power.

To best capture the credible threat of electoral replacement, I employ a measure that neatly captures the degree to which opposition parties offer such a threat. Originally developed by Henisz (2000, 2002) to measure the viability of policy change at any given point in time, the manner in which such viability is measured fulfills both goals laid out above: it captures the degree to which the party of the executive dominates the political environment and conveys not only the number of seats controlled by the opposition but also the degree to which the opposition is unified (Epperly 2017). Henisz's 0–1 measure captures the number of executive and legislative veto points,[12] the extent of party alignment (of those parties in the legislature) with the executive, and the fragmentation of parties in the legislature. This last point is critical, because more fragmentation of the opposition means less of a credible threat of replacement: four opposition parties each controlling 12% of the seats offer a far less credible threat of replacement to a governing party than one unified opposition party with control of 48% of seats.[13] Contemporary Hungary—to be discussed at length in Chapter 4—offers a case in point: despite significant opposition to Fidesz after more than half a decade in power, the contentious fragmentation of opposition parties means there is no credible threat of replacement. Polls from October 2017—slightly more than half a year before the next parliamentary elections—showed that opposition to the Orbán government is fractured, with the two largest parties being far-right and left-wing (Adam 2017b), and further that opposition voters were highly divided on the issue of whether these parties should work in concert, with one third thinking each party should run independently, which, given the Hungarian electoral system, would ensure

[12] Henisz also develops a constraint on the executive measure that includes whether there exists an independent judiciary able to serve as a veto point on policymaking. For obvious reasons, this is not the measure I employ.

[13] I should note that the fact that the Henisz measure effectively captures the underlying logic for why more competitive systems should induce different preferences for those in power, this strength could also be viewed as a weakness. This is because there is reason to expect that there remain distinctions—although for a perspective that treats them as effectively identical see Ríos-Figueroa (2007)—between aspects relevant for the insurance logic such as competition per se and fragmentation. This is perhaps best illustrated by a comparison of the US and Israel: even if those in power in each state viewed their likelihood of losing office as identical, the extreme fragmentation of the Israeli electoral system might be a relevant factor (Yadav & Mukherjee 2014). Although I address this empirically by assessing the role of electoral systems, the Henisz measure does conflate the two conceptually. While I consider this a strength given the logic articulated here, it remains the case that anyone interested specifically in the distinction between competition and fragmentation (rather than how each contributes to the demand for insurance) will need to consider alternative measures.

Fidesz victories in most districts (Balogh 2017), which is precisely what occurred in the 2018 parliamentary elections.

The Henisz measure is higher when the executive is highly constrained, i.e. when large, homogeneous opposition groups exist in the legislature. On the other hand, a legislature completely aligned with the executive has a constraint measure of 0. This means that in those instances where a single party aligned with the executive has all seats in the legislature (i.e. a one-party regime), the level of constraints will be lowest. Thankfully, it is also the context in which political competition is lowest. Similarly, if the opposition controls a given percentage of the legislature, its ability to provide an effective constraint on the executive is also affected by its degree of fractionalization. This also effectively operationalizes the logic of the political competition model outlined previously, as a number of small opposition groups controlling any given share of seats should provide less of a credible threat than a single opposition group controlling the same share, and governments of one party are not as threatened as weak coalitions (Tate & Vallinder 1995, Smithey & Ishiyama 2002, Ginsburg & Versteeg 2013).

It is worth stressing that one reason why the political constraints measure better captures the underlying logic of the insurance model than other commonly used measures is specifically because it does not just look at solely the lower legislative house (obviously irrelevant in the Hungarian example above), as do all other measures used. These measures that look at only the distribution of seats in the lower house relative to one another or the presidential vote share ignore that in most political systems (and unlike in Hungary) there exists a second legislative chamber able to if not veto at least check executive policy preferences, regardless of whether those policies are infringing on the rights of political minorities or undermining the policies of their predecessors. The constraints measure I employ, on the other hand, refrains from this problematic assumption and instead includes the distribution of political preferences in the upper house. This measure is thus, among commonly used indicators of competition, uniquely able to capture the logic of the insurance model, which is specifically about how competition constrains those in office in the future from pursuing policies that are to the detriment of those currently in office.

3.1.3 Democracy

As I discuss in Chapter 1, the conceptualization of regime type I employ is dichotomous, focused on the categorical distinction between democracy and dictatorship. To operationalize this dichotomy of democracy and non-democracy I employ the regime-type measure developed by Boix, Miller, & Rosato (2013). Following in the footsteps of the recent popularization of dichotomous measures (Alvarez et al. 1996, Cheibub, Gandhi, & Vreeland 2010), these authors create a clearly specified set of factors that a given state must meet (in a given year) to be classified as a democracy according to their minimalist conception (Schumpeter 1950, Dahl 1971, Przeworski, Alvarez, Cheibub, & Limongi 2000). Boix, Miller, & Rosato lay out two criteria of contestation and one of participation. The latter requires a majority of adult men to vote, whereas the former requires an executive directly or indirectly elected by popular elections that is responsible to either the voters or the legislature as well as a legislature chosen in free and fair elections.[14]

The key manner in which the authors differ from Przeworski et al. (2000) is that turnover of the executive is viewed as neither a necessary nor sufficient condition for democracy. Not necessary because of the situation exemplified by Sweden between 1936 and 1976, when turnover in office failed to occur because the socialists succeeded in winning every election, which they rightly contend "would qualify as democratic even before knowing the electoral outcome of 1976" (Boix, Miller, & Rosato 2013, 9). And not sufficient because of the not uncommon phenomenon of executive turnover to the opposition occurring in a non-democratic regime that then fails to produce democracy. Thus, while they consider executive turnover as strongly indicating free and fair elections, it is nonetheless not determinative, and they augment the estimation of free and fair elections with historical data and election reports. Practically, while significant overlap thus exists between these two most commonly used dichotomous indicators of democracy and dictatorship, differences arise from coding certain instances of regime type and *when* regime change occurs; rather than coding autocracy or democracy backwards from the election that originally precipitated the regime type, they ascertain at what point transition occurs. For example, Boix, Miller, & Rosato do not code Russia as undemocratic in its entire post-communist experience because of Putin's dismantling of democracy (as thus no turnover to the opposition occurred), and code Venezuela as undemocratic not from 1999 when Chavez was elected as do Przeworski et al., but rather from 2005 when an opposition party boycott led parliament to give Chavez decree powers.

3.2 Analyzing Competition and Independence

Figure 3.1 shows the distribution of competition and de facto independence across regime type (like the histogram in Figure 1.1, it excludes those autocratic country-years where competition is zero to better convey the distribution in autocratic regimes where a competitive electoral environment is present).[15] It

[14] Although for research focused on the mid to late-twentieth century the participation criterion is rarely relevant, Boix, Miller, & Rosato (2013) code democracy back to 1800 to allow for historical work covering time periods where participation varies considerably.

[15] As noted in Chapter 1, autocratic country-years with competition comprise a large minority, slightly more than 20% of the observations in the 1960–2006 data. Furthermore, the phenomenon is of increasing salience over time, with that number doubling to 40% in the post-Cold War era.

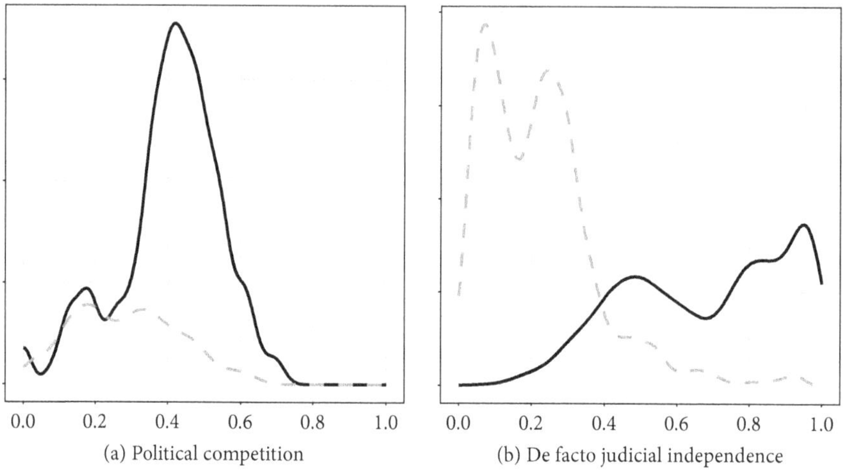

Figure 3.1 Political competition and de facto independence across regime type. Density plots showing the distribution of political competition and de facto judicial independence in democratic (black solid lines) and non-democratic (dashed gray) regimes from 1960 to 2006 (each measure ranges from 0 to 1). Plot (a) shows all country-years for democracies and the non-zero levels of competition in autocracies to better visualize the variation in the more than 20% of autocratic country-years where this is the case; plot (b) shows judicial independence in all country-years across regime type.

demonstrates visually what was conveyed earlier in Chapter 3: while competition and independence are on average higher in democratic contexts, there nonetheless exists substantial variation both within and across regime type for both. The goal of this section is to convince the reader that not only do these two factors vary in such a manner, but that variation in competition is strongly associated with variation in independence; the goal of Section 3.3 is to provide evidence that this relationship is causal.

In empirically assessing the manner in which competition is related to independence, conditional on democracy and autocracy, there are a handful of factors that, being related to both competition and independence, might potentially confound the relationship between them. The first of these is the level of economic development. States at low levels of development may lack the resources, human capital, and infrastructure required for effective courts, let alone courts operating independently of political power. States at high levels of development, on the other hand, are not only potentially more likely to have the resources to empower courts, but also to have—even in autocratic regimes—economic actors independent of the state who may demand some degree of independence for the protection of their property (Clague et al. 1999). Simultaneously, the level of political competition has been shown to be related to economic performance in both democracies and autocracies (Gryzmala-Busse 2007, Frye 2010), as competition restrains rent-seeking and state predation of economic resources and over economic actors. To account for this potential confounding I include a measure of economic development, specifically the log of the per capita gross domestic product (GDP) in international dollars at 2000 prices (Haber & Menaldo 2011).

The second potential confounder is the occurrence of democratic breakdowns and transitions. The analysis presented in Chapter 2 demonstrates that democratic transitions are associated with (slight) improvements in multiple measures capturing the status of the judiciary. Transitions to democracy are also associated with political competition for the obvious reason that democratization typically ushers in more democratic politics at both the elite and popular level (Urban 1997); similarly, transitions to autocracy often (though not always) significantly restrain the amount of electoral competition. Given that such transitions are associated with both competition and de facto independence, I include a trichotomous measure, drawn from the Boix, Miller, & Rosato (2013) data, that notes when either a democratic breakdown or transition to democracy occurs (the default reference category being neither event occurring).

A number of other factors are theorized by qualitative scholars to affect the level of judicial independence, especially in autocratic regimes (Moustafa 2007), and these and other covariates are included in existing quantitative analyses (Aydın 2013, Randazzo, Gibler, & Reid 2016, Epperly 2017, Epperly & Sievert 2018). These include the level of foreign direct investment, the need for regime legitimacy, and inter- and intra-state conflict. It remains untheorized, however, how these might specifically affect both competition and independence. That is, rather than being possible confounders, these are best conceived of as alternative explanations; from a causal inference perspective, their inclusion has the potential to bias results, and thus I omit them in the subsequent analyses. From a purely predictive perspective, however, one might be interested in their relationship with the outcome. For this reason, the chapter appendix includes a number of these factors to assess their association with de facto judicial independence.

The relationship between competition and independence is presented in Table 3.1. As discussed, the threat of replacement produced by electoral competition is operationalized via the Henisz (2002) measure, de facto judicial independence is operationalized via the widely used Linzer & Staton (2015) latent judicial independence measure, and democracy is coded according to the minimalist dichotomy produced by Boix, Miller, & Rosato (2013). The data cover just over and just under 6,000 country-year observations from 155 and 152 countries, respectively, spanning the 1961–2007 time period.[16] Both models report

[16] Although the Boix, Miller, & Rosato (2013) democracy measure codes over 200 countries from 1800 to 2007, the measures of political competition and latent judicial independence are more typical, and available from 1960. Analysis begins in 1961, as covariates are lagged one year to prevent simultaneity bias.

Table 3.1 Judicial independence, political competition, and regime type. Standardized coefficient estimates of two linear models with country fixed effects (not reported) of the relationship between political competition, conditional on regime type, and de facto judicial independence, with robust standard errors clustered by country.

	Model 1	Model 2
Intercept	0.11***	−0.51***
	(0.02)	(0.02)
Political competition	0.14***	0.12***
	(0.01)	(0.01)
Democracy	0.18***	0.19***
	(0.01)	(0.01)
Political competition*Democracy	−0.05***	−0.05***
	(0.01)	(0.01)
Democratic breakdown		−0.15***
		(0.01)
Democratic transition		0.12***
		(0.01)
log(GDP/capita)		0.22***
		(0.01)
AIC	−12791.87	−13741.94
BIC	−11724.28	−12677.06
Num. obs.	6090	5987

***$p < 0.001$, **$p < 0.01$, *$p < 0.05$

standardized coefficients (by two standard deviations) to make comparisons among the continuous covariates and between these and the dichotomous clearer, and include country fixed effects (not reported), with robust standard errors clustered by country. Model 1 includes the electoral competition and democracy measures, along with the interaction between the two; Model 2 adds the potential confounders of democratic breakdown/transition and the level of economic development.

The results of Models 1 and 2 provide strong support for the contention that competition is highly associated with judicial independence, and that this is true across regime type. In Model 1, competition shows a positive association with de facto independence, but this effect is tempered in democracies. That is, while independence is greater in both democracies and autocracies when competition is greater, this effect is more pronounced in non-democratic regimes, as theorized in the Chapter 1. The inclusion of the potential confounding variables in Model 2 has almost no effect on competition, democracy, or the interaction of the two: there are only very slight changes in the estimates of the two covariates and no change for the interaction, with all three remaining statistically significant at the $p < 0.001$

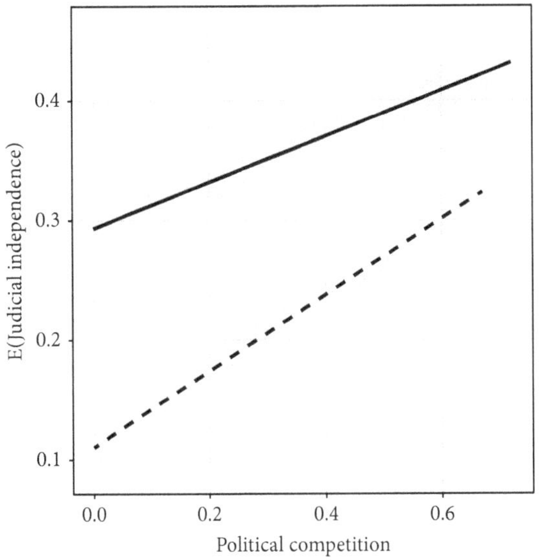

Figure 3.2 Independence as competition varies by regime type. The expected value of latent judicial independence from Model 1 when competition is allowed to vary from its observed minimum to maximum by regime type. The solid black line reports the expected value for democracies, while the dashed black line reports non-democracies, with 95% confidence intervals shaded around each.

level even with standard errors robust and clustered by country. As one would expect, democratic breakdown is associated with worse judicial independence, while transitions to democracy are associated with more independent judiciaries, as is economic development.[17]

Figure 3.2 illustrates visually the inferences to be drawn from Model 1 in Table 3.1. Model parameters are simulated using point estimates and the robust variance–covariance matrix to include model uncertainty, and expected values (the lines) and their 95% confidence intervals (the shaded regions around the lines) are created by 10,000 simulations, allowing competition to vary in both democracies and non-democracies. Figure 3.2 thus shows the implications of all three parameters from Model 1.

[17] The results also offer some insight into Popova's (2010, 2012) "strategic pressure" findings that suggest Ukraine, despite having greater levels of competition than Russia, had less judicial independence: economic development has a strong, positive effect on judicial independence, and by all measures the level of economic development in Russia is multiple times that of Ukraine. Thus, even if Ukraine showed more competitive politics, it is possible that the economic factor outweighed this.

First, there is a positive effect of democracy, which is illustrated by the greater expected value for judicial independence in democracies (the solid black line) than non-democracies (the dashed black line), regardless of the level of political competition. Second, there is a positive effect of competition in both democracies and autocracies, as evidenced by the upward trajectories of the expected values for both. Third, this effect, however, is far stronger in autocratic regimes than in democratic (i.e. the negative coefficient estimate for the interaction term); while the point estimate in democracies increases almost 50% (0.29 to 0.43) from the minimum to the maximum observed value of competition, the estimate in non-democracies increases (0.11 to 0.32) shows an almost 200% increase (and this despite having a lower observed maximum value in autocracies). Figure 3.2 thus shows clearly the key implication of the models in Table 3.1: while judicial independence is higher in democracies than in autocracies, the effect of competition is greater in non-democratic regimes.[18]

3.2.1 Autocratic Twilight

As I discuss in Chapter 3, some explanations of judicial independence in autocratic regimes in the literature focus on the instances of regime breakdown, and one might think that these are driving the results here. In other words, results may be either a function of judges engaging in strategic defection against incumbents who have begun to lose power (Helmke 2002) or a result of decisions by incumbents in the process of losing power (Hirschl 2000, Finkel 2005). These alternative explanations suggest that only when transition has begun will competition be expected to incentivize those in power to establish judicial independence as a political insurance policy, and that the results presented above are driven by such instances. The difference between these arguments and my own is that I argue that competition, when present, should incentivize actors even under conditions of "stable" authoritarianism (regimes that successfully remain in power for long periods of time, regardless of levels of electoral competition), and not only after seeing that the writing is already on the wall and they reached the end of their rule. Thus, my argument in some sense subsumes these arguments forwarded for contexts of regime transition and change: competition is the driving force, and while it may be driving decisions made by judges (Helmke) and leaders (Finkel, though see Magaloni 2008), its effects should not be restricted to moments of transition.

[18] If Model 2 is represented visually this pattern replicates itself, with 22% and 72% increases in democracy and non-democracy, respectively, as competition varies from its observed minimum to maximum. The difference in the overall expected values is greater, however, as holding economic development constant at its mean by regime type means that its positive effect is more pronounced in democracies, as they are wealthier.

While the concern over the final years of autocratic regimes driving the results is plausible, the strong relationship demonstrated in Table 3.1 and Figure 3.2 is not driven by autocratic twilight. As I show here, removing various numbers of years prior to regime transition (either two, four, or seven years) in no way attenuates the relationship between competition and independence in autocratic regimes, providing strong evidence that insurance is not merely a function of an autocracy's twilight years, but rather that, when competition is present, autocrats desire insurance in case of electoral loss, regardless of whether any electoral loss ends up occurring in the future. This comports with both the theoretical model I offer in Chapter 1—where the uncertainty surrounding the future is specifically why I employ an expected utility framework—and the work of scholars of democratization who note that autocratic regimes often institute competitive (to varying degrees) elections well before any democratization occurs (Lindberg 2009), as well as Roessler & Howard (2009), who find that in many autocracies elections are not harbingers of future openness.

It should be noted that this is not necessarily a story of regime *weakness*, in which either weak regimes create independent courts or lack of control over the judiciary is part of what it means for a regime to be weak. This is because of the fact that in democracy or non-democracy, elections are not the equivalent of regime weakness; as Levitsky & Way (2002, 2010) and other contemporary typologists of autocracy like Lindberg (2009) elucidate, elections are often the norm in autocracy and not signals of weakness. Furthermore, even contexts of not insignificant opposition should not be viewed as a sign of regime weakness per se; as Roessler & Howard (2009) discuss, moderate amounts of electoral competition in fact define one of the most studied forms of authoritarian regime and do not presage democratization. Rather, it is a question of contexts in which regime breakdown is occurring, and such breakdown need not be a result of electoral competition.[19]

If competition is, as previous work suggests, only salient when autocratic regimes are breaking down, then excluding the twilight years of autocratic tenure from analyses should significantly change the results: competition would no longer be strongly associated with independence as the independence measure would pick up significantly different patterns. If, on the other hand, competition affects independence even in times of autocratic stability, then the empirical results of models excluding the years before a regime transition should look similar to those presented in Table 3.1.

[19] A caveat relates to the fact that identifying regime breakdown ex ante is difficult, which is why here it is "identified" ex post by removing years before regime transitions. It is still possible that unsuccessful transitions in which executive control unravels (but not completely) can also lead to more independent courts. While the robustness of the results in Table 3.2 suggests such should not reverse the inferences presented here, the effects of unsuccessful regime transitions in autocratic states deserve further examination.

Table 3.2 Judicial independence, political competition, and regime type with years before transitions omitted. Coefficient estimates of linear models with country fixed effects (not reported) of the relationship between political competition, conditional on regime type, and de facto judicial independence, with robust standard errors clustered by country. For each model, the subscript is the number of years prior to an autocratic transition to democracy that are omitted from the analysis.

	Model 2_2	Model 2_4	Model 2_7
Intercept	-0.50^{***}	-0.51^{***}	-0.51^{***}
	(0.03)	(0.03)	(0.03)
Political competition	0.12^{***}	0.12^{***}	0.12^{***}
	(0.01)	(0.01)	(0.01)
Democracy	0.21^{***}	0.22^{***}	0.22^{***}
	(0.01)	(0.01)	(0.01)
Political competition*Democracy	-0.05^{***}	-0.04^{***}	-0.04^{***}
	(0.01)	(0.01)	(0.01)
Democratic breakdown	-0.08^{**}	-0.08^{**}	-0.08^{**}
	(0.03)	(0.03)	(0.03)
Democratic transition	0.08^{***}	0.08^{**}	0.08^{**}
	(0.03)	(0.03)	(0.03)
log(GDP/capita)	0.22^{***}	0.22^{***}	0.22^{***}
	(0.01)	(0.01)	(0.01)
AIC	−12563.76	−11882.31	−11882.31
BIC	−11530.23	−10862.54	−10862.54
Num. obs.	5122	4695	4695

$^{***}p < 0.001$, $^{**}p < 0.01$, $^{*}p < 0.05$

Table 3.2 presents the results of three models replicating Model 2 from Table 3.1 while removing years preceding a democratic transition from the analysis (Model 1 replications are omitted for brevity). Model 2_2 removes two years immediately preceding a regime transition. A two-year exception is the baseline as it was number of years prior to regime change employed by Helmke (2002) in her influential analysis of judicial defection in Argentina. She argues that this is the earliest possible time before transition that justices could plausibly foresee change. However, since transitions may be more protracted beyond Argentina, I include models removing observations four and seven years prior to a regime transition, offering a more robust test of my argument. These are subscripted 4 and 7, respectively.

Results of models presented in Table 3.2 are clear: electoral competition is associated with increased levels of independence even when years preceding regime transitions are excluded. This empirical implication of my argument clearly diverges from previous work examining courts in transitioning autocracies, and provides significant evidence that results presented in this chapter are not driven by either judges strategically defecting against autocrats losing power or merely the result of autocrats strengthening judicial independence as they leave office.

3.2.2 Alternative Explanations

As noted, there are a number of alternative explanations that have been forwarded both in case studies of judicial independence and in the handful of quantitative cross-national analyses of the phenomenon. Although some of these are forwarded in the context of either democracy *or* autocracy, in almost all cases the logic articulated for why they should matter is not restricted to one or the other, but rather ought to obtain under both types of regime. These alternatives can generally be split into three categories: the focus on common law by those focusing on "legal origins," especially Glaeser & Shleifer (2002) and La Porta et al. (2004); the explanations of autocratic judicial empowerment that Moustafa (2007) forwards; and the covariates included in cross-national analyses of de facto independence (Aydın 2013, Randazzo, Gibler, & Reid 2016, Epperly 2017).[20]

Table 3.3 presents regression results from a model designed to illustrate how these alternative explanations stack up against the role of competition, as well as demonstrating that these are not confounding variables, the omission of which biases results (however, note that their inclusion might introduce backdoor relationships between competition and independence, one of the reasons why they were excluded from the previous analyses). Due to the inclusion of time-invariant covariates, especially common law but including for many states the form of the executive and the incidence of conflict, Table 3.3 presents the results of hierarchical (multilevel) linear models with random intercepts by country.[21] Models 1 and 2 here replicate Models 1 and 2 in Table 3.1, fit to less than half the number of observations, due to more limited data availability for a number of the alternative explanation covariates included in Model 3. Models 1 and 2 here are included for comparison purposes, both with Model 3 as well as with the models in Table 3.2 (in fact, the highly similar estimates despite highly restricted data provide further support for the robustness of the main models).

Despite the significant criticism that the focus on legal origins has received (see, for example, the 2009(6) issue of the *BYU Law Review* dedicated to this question), the common-law heritage covariate here finds some support for being associated with higher levels of de facto judicial independence. Moustafa (2007) argues that autocrats desire independent judiciaries to monitor state agents, bolster legitimacy, and make credible commitments to property rights to encourage foreign

[20] Related to this third category is the work of Yadav & Mukherjee (2014), who consider how electoral institutions intersect with the likelihood of losing power in developing democracies. Given they restrict their logic to democratic regimes, analyses accounting for electoral system are not reported. Results, however, suggest that electoral systems are not predictive in analyses across all regimes, the full set of democracies, or just autocracies.

[21] As the first two models in Table 3.3 illustrate, even with significantly restricted data the estimates for competition and democracy, as well as their interaction, are highly similar to the fixed effects models presented in Table 3.2 (preferred by Hausman tests); if one fits random effects models to the full data used in Table 3.2, the coefficient estimates and errors are identical as the fixed effects until the third decimal place.

Table 3.3 Alternative explanations. Three hierarchical linear models to test alternative explanations. Due to data limitations on alternative covariates, these models are fit to far fewer observations. Models 1 and 2 are references to Models 1 and 2 in Table 3.1, using these restricted data. Model 3 adds measures of phenomena argued to be important, but unrelated to competition, by other scholars.

	Model 1	Model 2	Model 3
Intercept	0.36***	−0.25***	−0.12*
	(0.02)	(0.05)	(0.06)
Political competition	0.11***	0.10***	0.09***
	(0.01)	(0.01)	(0.01)
Democracy	0.14***	0.15***	0.13***
	(0.01)	(0.01)	(0.01)
Political competition*Democracy	−0.04***	−0.03***	−0.03**
	(0.01)	(0.01)	(0.01)
Democratic breakdown		−0.14***	−0.15***
		(0.02)	(0.02)
Democratic transition		0.08***	0.09***
		(0.01)	(0.01)
log(GDP/capita)		0.16***	0.11***
		(0.01)	(0.01)
Common law			0.07*
			(0.03)
FDI inflows			0.00
			(0.00)
Government share of GDP			−0.01*
			(0.00)
Autocratic tenure			−0.02***
			(0.00)
Parliamentary executive			0.07***
			(0.01)
Presidential executive			0.01
			(0.01)
Years democratic			0.11***
			(0.02)
Conflict			−0.00
			(0.00)
AIC	−5756.74	−6006.66	−6159.56
BIC	−5721.62	−5953.99	−6060.08
Num. obs.	2571	2571	2571
Num. groups	93	93	93

$^{***}p < 0.001$, $^{**}p < 0.01$, $^{*}p < 0.05$

investment. While advanced strictly in the context of non-democratic rule, the first and third clearly apply to democracies as well, given that democrats also need to effectively monitor state agents and can also create economic environments hostile to foreign investment. I include measures of FDI inflows (drawn from the World

Bank), the government share of GDP from the Penn World Tables, and the years a given autocrat has been in office from the Database of Political Institutions (Beck, Clarke, Groff, Keefer, & Walsh 2001). As previously, all covariates are lagged one year, and continuous covariates are standardized to ease interpretation. This second set of additional covariates fails to provide consistent support for Moustafa's arguments: the government share of GDP, for example, is associated with (very slightly) less, not more, judicial independence, and FDI inflows have a non-significant zero coefficient. Longer autocratic tenure is associated with less independence, which provides some support for Moustafa's (2007, 2008) argument, but how much is unclear. Although he argues that new autocrats might empower courts as a means of distancing themselves from previous leaders, he also suggests that longer-serving autocrats might do so when other policies have failed.[22]

The nature of the executive, the number of years a state has been democratic, and the incidence of conflict have been suggested by those conducting cross-national examinations of judicial independence to be worthy of inclusion, despite neither being a focus of any analysis nor receiving well-developed theoretical expectations (Aydın 2013, Randazzo, Gibler, & Reid 2016, Epperly 2017). As such, they are included here for the sake of completeness and to further demonstrate that they are not confounders whose exclusion biases results. Table 3.3 demonstrates the continued predicative accuracy of the competition, democracy, and their interaction despite the inclusion of nearly a dozen covariates, and analysis conducted on less than half the data as in Table 3.1.

The primary goal of this chapter is to illustrate that the relationship between competition and judicial independence is conditional on regime type, and that this relationship is substantively important. Table 3.1 and Figure 3.2 provide the first evidence of this, and Tables 3.2 and 3.3 demonstrate that these results are robust to alternative explanations common in the literature. Additionally, these results are robust to alternative specifications, tests of fit, and robustness checks. These further analyses—being of limited interest to many readers—can be found in the appendix to this chapter. Here, however, I will provide a summary of the information provided there. First, cross-validation procedures demonstrate that the model specification presented in Table 3.1 is highly effective at capturing the data-generating process, with out-of-sample fit being remarkably similar to model fit in-sample. Second, the results are robust to the use of a second measure of de facto judicial independence, constructed with entirely different underlying data. Finally, concerns of missing data and multiple imputation are discussed.

[22] This is highlighted by the case of Anwar Sadat: rather than enshrining a (somewhat) autonomous high court immediately upon assuming power after Gamal Nasser's death, he waited nearly a decade to do so.

3.3 Competition, Independence, and Causal Inference

While the analyses presented are strong, consistent, and as the appendix demonstrates have high out-of-sample predictive accuracy and remain robust to a host of alternative specifications, they remain observational analyses lacking an identification strategy. For two reasons, this is far from damning. First, there is to my knowledge no existing research on judicial independence that attempts to determine whether there exists a causal relationship between the determinant of interest—be it political competition or something else—and the independence of the judiciary. This is not an indictment of these works, but rather a recognition that scholars of comparative courts recognize the difficulty of using causal inference strategies in the analysis of judicial institutions across space and time (Carrubba, Gabel, Helmke, Staton, & Martin 2015): field experiments are extremely difficult, natural experiments few and far between, and instruments rarely plausible.

Second, despite a justifiable desire for making causal claims, and reason to privilege those done effectively, there are good reasons to not denigrate observational research, be it careful case studies[23] or correlational in nature. First, as many note, the quest for clean identification can lead to highly specific but also irrelevant findings (Rogeberg & Melberg 2011); "mere" description is an important goal in itself (King, Keohane, & Verba 1994); and mature scientific disciplines include iterative processes of theory generation, description, and causal inference (Elman & Burton 2016, Lieberman 2016). Placed in a broader context, description is not "mere," but in fact necessary. As Gelman (2011) notes, "Descriptive statistics is not just for losers. There is value in revealing patterns in observational data, correlations or predictions that were not known before." Indeed, a casual perusal of the theoretical relationships tested by experimental political science in recent years demonstrates just as much, with countless works explicitly building off—and often simply confirming—regularities observed time and again by observational and case study research.

More specifically, applied to the matter at hand: there is value in knowing there exists a strong, consistent relationship between the amount of electoral competition and the amount of de facto judicial independence, and that this holds across regime type. Even absent any theoretical account to make sense of it, or causal identification strategy to assess such an account, there is value in being aware of such an observed regularity. This is the case for two reasons. First, because this observed regularity, if we lacked a reason for expecting it, should give us as scholars pause and provoke us to search for reasons why we might observe this relationship, be those reasons causal or spurious. Second, this descriptive

[23] For an important recent argument that deep qualitative and historical knowledge is a necessary condition for natural experiments, and thus equally valid for generating generalizable knowledge, see Kocher & Monteiro (2016).

observation runs directly counter to published work in comparative law and courts. Popova's (2010, 2012) well-crafted, regarded, and cited work uses a paired comparison of Russia and Ukraine to suggest that there are theoretically grounded and generalizable reasons for expecting the exact opposite of the relationship observed here. The work of VonDoepp (2009), VonDoepp & Ellet (2011), and Aydın (2013) forward similar theoretical arguments with the same empirical expectations,[24] and Ginsburg & Moustafa (2008) contend that there is no reason to expect the electoral logic to apply outside of democratic regimes.

For these reasons, there is good reason to think that the analyses I have presented so far offer a significant contribution to our understanding of comparative law and courts: after examining the assumptions and mechanisms underlying the insurance framework, I offer an analysis that is consistent and robust to alternative explanations and model specifications. If the goal, however, is to provide the most thorough and convincing account of the insurance framework to date, then an attempt to properly identify the causal relationship that the insurance model suggests has much to offer. Given the challenges to structuring a field experiment of something as complex and elite-driven as the way electoral uncertainty conditions political leaders to empower courts, and the difficulty of finding natural experiments as well as their potential inability to offer any causal account more plausible than a well-crafted case study (Kocher & Monteiro 2016), I turn to an instrumental variables approach in the hopes of convincing the reader that some evidence exists to suggest that the correlations presented above are perhaps causal.

3.3.1 Instrumental Variables Analysis

One goal and use of instrumental variables analysis is to address the fact that often the relationship between our key explanatory variable and the outcome we seek to explain might be affected by reverse causation, omitted variable bias, or measurement error. A canonical example is the relationship between years of education and income: while we may have good reason to believe that education is associated with higher earnings, we know that education is not randomly assigned. As such, simply estimating the relationship will produced biased estimates of the effect of education. One potential solution to this is the use of an instrument, which should produce change in the explanatory variable without having any direct effect on the outcome of interest. Fundamental to any instrumental variables analysis is a plausible instrument that, among other things, meets the exclusion restriction. In the popular education and income example, one such instrument proposed

[24] Inasmuch as these works are focused on "emerging democracies" that look highly akin to (and are often coded as) electoral authoritarian regimes.

is a person's distance from a college while in high school.[25] In the context here, however, this means that what is required is a variable that is correlated with electoral competition but which is only related to the level of de facto judicial independence through its relationship with competition.

3.3.2 Justifying the instruments

The focus of my instrumentation strategy is the fact that better economic performance and more government spending, while keeping taxes low, are, unsurprisingly, quite popular with the citizens of both democracies and dictatorships. As such, these factors increase popular support for incumbents, and decrease the threat of electoral loss. If it is the case that neither short-term economic performance (as opposed to the long-term level of economic development) nor the sources or level of non-tax revenue have direct effects on the level of judicial independence, then measures operationalizing some aspect of these two factors are good candidates for instruments, because the only way they should relate to judicial independence is through their effects on the level of political stability of incumbents. Below I introduce two potential instruments, exploring how they should relate to a decreased risk of losing power for incumbents and how they should not relate to judicial independence in any other way.

That spending helps political leaders—autocratic or democratic—is uncontroversial. State spending allows leaders to reward supporters as well as make side payments to those who might otherwise threaten the regime. This can be done in a problematic way, in the sense of granting state resources to regime loyalists or directing state revenues to their bank accounts (Dawisha 2014), or in the sense of the firms of loyalists receiving a disproportionate degree of state support (Gryzmala-Busse 2007), as has been the case in Hungary since 2010 (Than & Dunai 2012, Byrne 2016). It need not be nefarious, however: public goods provision is popular, and can be used to reward regime supporters and shore up support with groups who might otherwise be less loyal; this is the case in both dictatorship and democracy, as the influential work of Acemoglu & Robinson (2006) on the role of redistribution in maintaining regime stability demonstrates. As a whole, research shows that state spending in general increases support for incumbents (Levitt & Snyder Jr. 1997, Akhmedov & Zhuravskaya 2004).

This spending, however, typically requires taxation of the population, which is *unpopular* with the citizens of both democratic and autocratic systems, and decreases regime support and the likelihood of re-election (Sobel 1998, Paler 2013). In arguably the most systematic treatment of the issue to date, Morrison

[25] The logic being that this should have some effect on the propensity to attend college while simultaneously not having an effect on one's later wages; whether or not this instrument is truly exogenous is not the issue here, as one could think of a number of plausible reasons distance from a college might have an effect on wages (e.g. an improved local economy).

(2014) shows that increased taxation is strongly related to higher levels of regime instability and decreased support for incumbents, be they democratic or autocratic. Critically, Morrison also shows that *non-tax* revenue allows regimes to spend, which is popular, without having to tax, which is not. What regimes need to do this is a ready source of non-tax revenue, and the more of it the better. The most common of such sources is natural resource rents, particularly oil revenue. Morrison's important synthesis provides a clear reason that his earlier work (Morrison 2009) and the work of scholars such as Smith (2004) and Andersen & Aslaksen (2013) all find that oil wealth is strongly associated with increased regime stability.

An ideal instrument would therefore be the amount of non-tax spending as a portion of state revenue. Unfortunately, such a direct measure is not readily available. As Morrison (2014) lays out, the most reliable source of data—the International Monetary Fund's *Government Finance Statistics*—changed its method for calculating these measures, which both limits their temporal coverage as well as calls into question the previous coding.[26] Because of this, I rely on an adequate proxy for a state's access to non-tax sources of revenue, total oil reserves, which has significant—almost complete—temporal and cross-sectional coverage for the 1960–2007 era I analyze (Haber & Menaldo 2011).[27] There is little reason to believe that oil resources should directly affect the level of judicial independence in a country. Not only has such a claim, to my knowledge, never been made in the literature, but furthermore it lacks any intuitive reasoning behind it. While there have been many arguments concerning how natural resource wealth inhibits *democracy*, these have focused on how it provides autocrats with the ability to buy off potential regime opposition and decreases the demand for change among the population.[28] While these abilities are certainly bad for political competition, this is hardly a problem, since they are the entire point of thinking that oil resources might be a justifiable instrument in the first place. As such, I use the oil resources as an instrument for political competition in the subsequent two-stage least squares estimation.

The contention that economic performance affects support for incumbents is even less contested than the idea that the availability of larger amounts of non-tax revenues should increase support and stabilize governments, and is

[26] These more complicated measures on government finances also contain significant missingness, concentrated in poorer and non-democratic regimes, further limiting their utility for my purposes.

[27] As I noted at the beginning of this section, finding good instruments is a difficult task. The differential coverage of Haber & Menaldo's oil *reserves* measure and their measure of fiscal reliance on natural resources is indicative of the lack of coverage of fiscal measures. While the former has coverage for 91% of the observations used in the models in Table 3.1, the latter is available for less than 10% of these observations.

[28] Similarly, in their comprehensive treatments of oil-producing states, Luong & Weinthal (2010) and Mazaheri (2016) demonstrate that inasmuch as oil wealth is a "curse," it is because of the strategies pursued by leaders with regards to state-owned firms, small businesses, and innovation rather than any systematic policies towards legal institutions such as the courts.

a long-standing finding in both politics and economics.[29] Although much of the early literature focused on elections in the United States, and presidential elections in particular, the insight that economic performance affects support for incumbents—democrats and autocrats alike—has found significant purchase in comparative studies. Work on Latin America, post-communist Europe, and elsewhere all finds that economic performance affects the incumbent vote share (Remmer 1991, Pacek & Radcliff 1995, Tavits 2005), as well as increasing electoral volatility in general (Roberts & Wibbels 1999, Birch 2003). This holds true in competitive authoritarian regimes (Magaloni 2006), and Reuter & Gandhi (2011) find that hegemonic parties face serious threats of defection and electoral loss when economic conditions are particularly bad.

Long-run economic development has been shown to be related to judicial independence, with scholars arguing that an independent judiciary's protection of property rights is an important pillar of long-term economic success (Voigt & Gutmann 2013). Short-term economic performance, however, should have little direct effect on the level of judicial independence in a country. This is particularly true for inflation, which along with unemployment is especially shown in comparative research to decrease vote shares for incumbents because it is a far more easily visible signal than growth rates (Palmer & Whitten 1999, Chappell Jr. & Veiga 2000, Leigh & Wolfers 2006). In addition, it also produces other behaviors that are electorally disadvantageous for both autocrats and democrats, such as protest (Lehman-Wilzig & Ungar 1985, Hendrix, Haggard, & Magaloni 2009). Unlike unemployment, however, inflation rates are commonly available and comparable across countries. Looking at the data used in the models presented in Table 3.1, for example, unemployment rates are missing in over 60% of observations. The rate of missingness for inflation, on the other hand, is a third that of unemployment. For this reason, I use the rate of inflation as an instrument for political competition in the subsequent two-stage least squares models.

3.3.3 Analysis

Table 3.4 reports the (second-stage) results of two two-stage least squares models of judicial independence, instrumenting competition with measures assessing the inflation rate and the oil reserves of a state. As the endogenous variable (here competition) is interacted with an exogenous variable (regime type), the interaction is thus also endogenous and must be instrumented. In the first-stage regression I account for this by interacting the instruments with the measure for regime type, allowing for unbiased estimates of the interaction term as well as the constituent competition term (Balli & Sørensen 2013). Unlike in previous models, coefficients are not standardized due to the 2SLS procedure; per previously,

[29] For reviews of this literature, see Monroe (1984), Lewis-Beck (1990), and Lewis-Beck & Stegmaier (2000).

Table 3.4 Instrumental variables analysis. Two models using two-stage least squares to assess the affect of competition on de facto judicial independence. Second-stage results are reported along with test statistics.

	Model 1	Model 2
Intercept	−0.03	−0.71***
	(0.04)	(0.06)
Competition (instrumented)	0.77***	0.61***
	(0.14)	(0.13)
Democracy	0.53***	0.37***
	(0.12)	(0.09)
Competition*Democracy (instrumented)	−0.94***	−0.64***
	(0.21)	(0.18)
Democratic breakdown		0.20***
		(0.02)
Democratic transition		−0.16***
		(0.02)
log(GDP/capita)		0.04
		(0.04)
Adjusted R^2	0.72	0.83
Num. obs.	4953	4953
F-test (competition)	10.92***	10.62***
F-test (interaction)	6.10***	6.46***
Wu-Hausman test	24.83***	19.68***
Sargan test	2.5	1.38

$^{***}p < 0.001$, $^{**}p < 0.01$, $^{*}p < 0.05$

however, coefficients are robust and clustered on country, and country fixed effects are included but not reported. Unfortunately, despite the fact that I chose two specific measures to instrument for competition because their data availability was far greater than other comparable measures capturing the relationship, the result of including inflation and oil reserves in the first-stage regression is losing roughly one fifth of the observations due to missing data.[30] Despite this, results are broadly similar to those reported in Table 3.1: once again, both democracy and political competition are associated with higher levels of de facto judicial independence, but the effect of competition is highly attenuated in democratic regimes; the estimates for the confounders remain highly similar to the standard OLS approach used, as well.

Although assessments of the exclusion restriction remain at the level of theory, the models in Table 3.4 pass a number of other tests of the appropriateness of the

[30] The structure of the missingness of the data is primarily entire countries for long spans of time rather than occasional years; see the chapter appendix for a discussion.

instrumental variables approach used here. Two f-tests are reported in Table 3.4, to assess first if the instrument for the independent effect of political competition is weak, and second whether the interaction of the instrument and democracy is weak, as weak instruments and poor first-stage prediction can result in large variance and bias (Bound, Jaeger, & Baker 1993, 1995). In both instances, the f-test rejects the null hypothesis that the instrument is weak. The Wu-Hausman tests the null hypothesis whether OLS is equally consistent with the two-stage least squares estimation. Here, again, the rejection of the null provides support for the appropriateness of the instrumental variables approach.

One of the benefits of using two instruments for competition rather than a single instrument is that doing so allows me to conduct a Sargan test for testing over-identifying restrictions in the model. This assesses the null of whether these instruments are uncorrelated with the model results; that is, whether they are in fact exogenous. The insignificance of the test here (the p-values are 0.34 and 0.50 for Models 1 and 2, respectively) means that we cannot reject the null that the instruments are actually exogenous (unlike the other tests, a non-significant result here is preferable). This is, however, at best supportive evidence and not dispositive, as these are just failures to reject the null. The actual exogeneity of the instrument remains untestable and guided by theoretical concerns.

The results of Table 3.4 show that both inflation and oil resources are strong instruments that produce unbiased estimates of the effect of political competition on judicial independence across the autocratic/democratic regime divide. Naturally, while only theory and what we know about the world can guide the selection of instruments that are appropriate and meet the exclusion restriction, the use of two instruments allows for a Sargan test, which confirms the null hypothesis that the instruments are exogenous cannot be rejected, providing statistical support for the exogeneity of the instruments. Whether or not the reader is convinced of the true exogeneity of the instruments depends on their read of the literature and whether or not inflation and oil reserves should affect judicial independence via a pathway besides competition. There exists significant evidence for the connection between inflation and decreased support for incumbents, as well as for the connection between non-tax sources of revenue and the ability of incumbents to spend without taxing. I find no evidence in the literature to support a relationship between either of these and judicial independence, however, and contend that these are as reasonable as any instrument for the relationship between significant institutional and political phenomena is likely to be.

Table 3.4 has two important implications. First, the instrumental variables analysis makes clear that strong evidence exists not only for the correlation between competition and independence in non-democratic regimes, but furthermore preliminary evidence that this relationship is causal. The second implication concerns the relationship in democratic regimes. Here, the evidence is not persuasive, with the instrumental variables models suggesting that no substantively meaningful relationship exists, as the interaction term washes out the estimated effect of competition (as the effect of the competition estimate effectively shows competition's effect in non-democratic regimes, whereas the sum of competition and the interaction shows the effect in democracies).

Combined with the weaker results for the effect of competition in Table 3.1, this finding calls into question the relationship between competition and de facto judicial independence in democracies, or in other words, a not insignificant portion of the literature on democratic insurance. This finding produces the third question that calls for an answer. Namely, why do we see such a distinct difference between the findings of this chapter, which offer the most sophisticated and comprehensive cross-national take on insurance to date, and the existing cross-sectional quantitative research and the myriad case studies of the phenomenon? Chapter 4 offers a preliminary theoretical and empirical answer.

3.4 Conclusion

The results of the modeling strategy pursued in Tables 3.1 and 3.4 provide solid and consistent support for the theoretical proposition I articulate in Chapter 1: competition—when present—should be far more salient a factor for judicial independence in non-democratic rather than democratic regimes, because an autocrat's expected utility calculation is dominated by the far larger downside risks of losing power. This is shown not only through standard OLS models with country fixed effects, but also through instrumental variables analysis via two-stage least squares. In this chapter I offer four important and novel contributions to the study of de facto judicial independence.

The first important contribution has nothing to do with the statistical models or their findings, but rather the well-developed connection between concept and measure advocated in Section 3.1. Much, though certainly not all, of the existing quantitative work on insurance has given less attention to this matter than it deserves.[31] As a result, at times the ways in which competition is operationalized capture the underlying logic of the insurance model less effectively than they otherwise could. Recall that vote or seat shares or any other way of operationalizing competition is actually an attempt to proxy the risk assessment of those in power regarding the likelihood that they will lose power and that their policies, property, or persons will be at risk under those who follow. As such, operationalizing the concept in a manner exhibiting the greatest fidelity to the logic is ideal. I argue that a measure capturing the distribution of parties within both legislative houses is better than one capturing only the distribution in the lower house, as too is one

[31] This is in no way to indict any of this work: the constraints imposed by the article format are no doubt the primary culprit.

that captures the fragmentation within the opposition. After all, an opposition that consists of six parties each barely passing a 5% threshold in the lower house and possessing even fewer seats in the upper offers a far less credible threat than a single unified opposition party that controls 30% of the seats in each.

The second important contribution is the findings concerning the strong and consistent relationship between competition and de facto independence. Not only is this relationship robust to a host of alternative specifications (see the appendix), but it also comports perfectly with the theoretical analysis offered in Chapter 1. Combining the results of the book to this point, it is evident that the first question has been definitively answered: there are theoretical reasons why autocrats would seek the insurance via courts, it is clear that courts can and do offer insurance, and the empirical relationship between competition and independence is well demonstrated. The insurance model surely has analytical purchase outside the democratic world.

The third contribution this chapter makes is by offering the first steps towards a causal interpretation of a theory of judicial independence. This is a contribution not because I think progress is impossible without identification strategies; I concur with leading methodologists that there are important contributions to be made by descriptive analyses of all stripes, both for their own sake and for their necessity in theory generation. Regardless, the analysis here is neither experimental nor conclusive, and while it makes some contribution by way of offering a plausible identification strategy for understanding the insurance model, it makes a far greater contribution by suggesting—though it is hardly unique in doing so—to scholars of comparative law and courts that we should and can employ these methods in our research on the often intractable institutional questions that fascinate us.

The final contribution is the lack of agreement between the results presented here, especially in the instrumental variables analysis, and existing research forwarding the insurance framework in democratic regimes. The degree to which this is a *contribution* is likely dependent on how successfully I resolve the lack of agreement and provide an answer to the question it generates. That is the subject of Chapter 4.

3.5 Appendix

As one of my goals is to present the most comprehensive quantitative examination of the insurance framework—and do so across regime type—to date, a number of alternative model specifications and tests of fit are presented here to further convince the reader of the robustness of the autocratic insurance argument on offer.

3.5.1 Model Fit and Robustness

Cross-validation

Cross-validation is a technique that examines model fit based on one of the gold-standard means of model testing: out-of-sample predictive accuracy. Rather than collect new data (often extremely diffcult in some fields, particularly the study of comparative political, including judicial, institutions) and test models on these data, cross-validation partitions the data into separate datasets. The number of sets varies. One popular form of cross-validation is k-fold, where the data are partitioned into k datasets, with one sample retained for testing and $k - 1$ for training, i.e. creating the model whose parameters are used to predict the values in the test set. Here I conduct $k = 2$ cross-validation, partitioning the data into two sets, one for training and the other for testing. I first estimate a model in the same manner as traditional quantitative analysis. The estimates from this model are then used on the second test set of data. As the data in this test set are themselves not used to derive the model estimates, the model is thus being tested out-of-sample. A researcher can then use the differences between the model fit in the training and test sets to determine the degree to which the model is capturing the underlying data-generating process (Ward, Siverson, & Cao 2007). If the model fit out-of-sample is comparable to the model fit in-sample, evidence exists that the model fits the underlying empirical process of interest that has generated the data, as opposed to just being a collection of statistically significant effects that fail to accurately capture this process.

Figure 3.3 shows the in-sample and out-of-sample fit for Models 1 and 2 from Table 3.1, plotting the actual observed value of latent judicial independence against the predicted value for each observation; predictions are derived in-sample from the models in plots (a) and (c), whereas in plots (b) and (d) they are derived out-of-sample from the parameters of the models that they were not part of creating. The solid diagonal line in each is where $x = y$, in other words when the model fits perfectly. The dashed lines are each twice the root mean squared error (RMSE), effectively showing 95% confidence intervals around the line of best fit. As can be seen, almost all of the 3,000 observations in each plot fall within these two lines.

The RMSE of the in-sample model shown in plot (a) of Figure 3.3 is 0.082, whereas the RMSE of the out-of-sample fit (it is not a model, but rather predicted values using the model estimated on in the 'training' data) shown in plot (b) is 0.085. In other words, the RMSE when used on out-of-sample data is only 4% higher than in-sample; the RMSE in plots (c) and (d) are 0.074 and 0.078, meaning the out-of-sample fit is only 5% worse than in-sample. Out-of-sample fit is an important and exacting standard in assessing model fit, and such high out-of-sample fit provides strong evidence that the models effectively capture the underlying data-generating process.

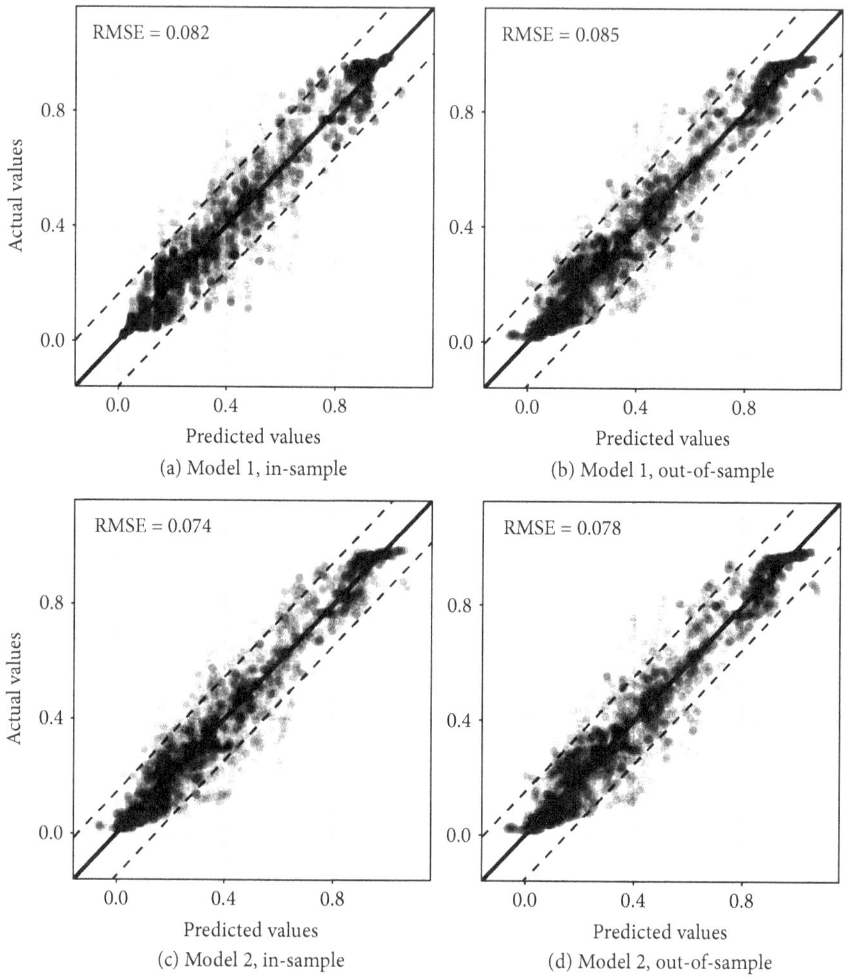

Figure 3.3 Cross-validation and predictive accuracy. In-sample and out-of-sample fit for Models 1 and 2 from Table 3.1. The data for each model was randomly partitioned (halved) into training and test datasets, and estimates from models fit to the training data (plots a and c) are applied to the data in the test sets (plots b and d) to produce out-of-sample predictions. The RMSE (root mean squared error) of the in and out sample fits is reported, and as can be seen increases only slightly.

Alternative measure of de facto independence

To illustrate that the results are robust to alternative measurement, Table 3.5 revisits the model specification in Table 3.1 (once again, standardized coefficients are reported, country fixed effects are included but not reported, and errors are robust and clustered by country), but rather than fit the models to the Linzer & Staton (2015) latent judicial independence measure it uses the Varieties of

Table 3.5 V-Dem measure of de facto independence. Coefficient estimates of two linear models with country fixed effects (not reported) of the relationship between political competition, conditional on regime type, and the V-Dem measure of de facto judicial independence, with robust standard errors clustered by country.

	Model 1	Model 2
Intercept	0.37***	0.22***
	(0.02)	(0.02)
Political competition	0.08***	0.07***
	(0.01)	(0.01)
Democracy	0.14***	0.14***
	(0.01)	(0.01)
Political competition*Democracy	−0.04***	−0.04***
	(0.01)	(0.01)
Democratic breakdown		−0.08***
		(0.02)
Democratic transition		0.09***
		(0.01)
log(GDP/capita)		0.05***
		(0.01)
AIC	−12858.20	−12725.94
BIC	−11790.61	−11661.06
Num. obs.	6090	5987

$^{***}p < 0.001$, $^{**}p < 0.01$, $^{*}p < 0.05$

Democracy (V-Dem) measure of high court independence (Coppedge, Gerring, Lindberg, Skaaning, Teorell, Andersson, Marquardt, Mechkova, Miri, Pemstein, et al. 2016*a*).[32] It demonstrates that using another measure of the outcome of interest produces highly similar results, despite using an entirely different procedure for producing the data (fitting an IRT model on contracted country expert codings as opposed to existing measures of de facto independence).

Examining the results of Table 3.5, competition is once again positively associated with independence (as is democracy), but this association is attenuated in democratic regimes, i.e. it is more salient in autocracies. This is true regardless of the inclusion of the potential confounders, and once again the effect is substantively important. This substantive importance is conveyed visually in Figure 3.4, where once again, although the expected value of independence is higher at every level of competition in democracies (due to the independent effect of democracy), the effect of competition is greater in non-democracies, conveyed here by the steeper slope of the dashed line. Again, the effect is substantively meaningful, with

[32] As in Chapter 2, I normalize the V-Dem measure to a 0–1 range, to make the visualizations comparable to the preferred LJI measure.

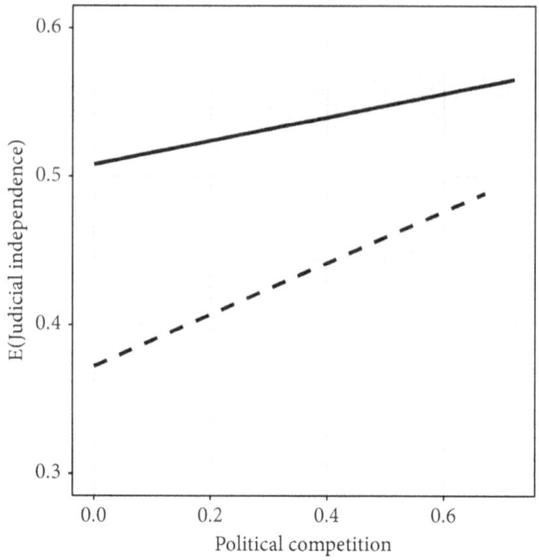

Figure 3.4 Using the V-Dem measure. The expected value of latent judicial independence from Model 1 when using the V-Dem measure of high court independence. Competition is allowed to vary from its observed minimum to maximum by regime type. The solid black line reports the expected value for democracies, while the dashed black line reports non-democracies, with 95% confidence intervals shaded around each.

the change in non-democracies being more than half the interquartile range for the Varieties of Democracy high court independence measure. The consistency of these results, considering the unrelated nature of data construction of the two measures, provides further support for the conclusion that competition is salient across regime type, and in fact of quite high salience in non-democracies, where it has to date been explicitly argued otherwise.

3.5.2 Missing Data

The issue of missing data remains an important concern for empirical work, especially that of a time-series cross-sectional nature, as there is little reason to expect that such data are missing at random. Unfortunately, the nature of the data used in the analyses in Tables 3.1 and 3.3 strongly suggest that the data are missing in a systematic manner: those instances where missing data arise are for specific states across most covariates, and typically for multiple years. A closer

Table 3.6 Multiple imputation. Results of four models fit to 15 imputed datasets. Models 1 and 2 are fit to restricted missing data, excluding all years without regime-type covariates; Models 3 and 4 are fit to all missing observations, including those without regime-type data.

	Restricted missing		All missing	
	Model 1	Model 2	Model 3	Model 4
Intercept	0.11	−0.40	0.10	−0.23
	(0.01)	(0.03)	(0.01)	(0.02)
Political competition	0.32	0.28	0.35	0.32
	(0.01)	(0.01)	(0.02)	(0.01)
Democracy	0.19	0.19	0.01	0.15
	(0.01)	(0.01)	(0.0)	(0.01)
Political competition*Democracy	−0.14	−0.13	−0.13	−0.13
	(0.02)	(0.02)	(0.02)	(0.02)
Democratic breakdown		−0.15		−0.11
		(0.01)		(0.01)
Democratic transition		0.11		0.08
		(0.01)		(0.01)
log(GDP/capita)		0.08		0.05
		(0.00)		(0.00)

Asterisks are omitted due to the use of the imputation model and the standardization across datasets.

inspection, however, suggests that a significant portion of the missingness is for states normally not included in such analyses (or many cross-national datasets): Barbados, Cape Verde, Maldives, Seychelles, Vanuatu, and the like. As such, any problems that arise from this missingness are endemic to similar work; cold comfort, perhaps, but recognizing the reality of both data limitations here and elsewhere is better than not, and as much as we expect the omission of these states to not systematically bias results in a substantively important manner likely an acceptable reality.

Given these facts, the problem with conducting imputation on these data is that basic regime characteristics like democracy vs. non-democracy are missing along with the other covariates, and often for an entire state's history. If one is to exclude, however, those states not included in the Boix, Miller, & Rosato (2013) data that are contained in Linzer & Staton (2015), the amount of missingness is trivial: less than 2% of observations for competition and for economic development. Without excluding these observations when considering missingness, the amount of missingness jumps considerably: 10% for regime type and economic development, and 3% for political competition.

Although multiple imputation is thus an incomplete fix to this problem, it nonetheless can provide some information as to the robustness of these results to the missing data. As such, Table 3.6 presents models fit to two types of imputed datasets (note that Table 3.6 omits asterisks to denote statistical significance).

Models 1 and 2 are fit to "restricted" missing data, excluding those observations that are missing regime-type data. Models 3 and 4 are fit to all missing observations (in each instance, reported coefficients and errors are averaged over the fit to fifteen imputed datasets). As coefficients are unstandardized, direct comparisons with the results of Table 3.1 are not obvious, but were the coefficients for competition, democracy, and their interaction Model 1 in Table 3.1 unstandardized they would be 0.32, 0.18, and –0.13—almost identical to the coefficients in Model 1 in Table 3.6, and highly similar to those for Model 3 (save the democracy covariate, which is heavily imputed and likely often "incorrectly"). Thus, despite facing significant difficulties in imputation and interpretation, the results of Table 3.6 provide some support for the assumption—which is all it can be—that the countries systematically excluded from the data do not significantly bias results.

4
Integrating De Jure Independence

In 2010, Victor Orbán led his center-right Fidesz party back to power in Hungary, winning enough seats to secure the country's first post-communist government in which a single party controlled a two-thirds constitutional majority. In the next few years, Fidesz recrafted the institutional order of the Hungarian state, changing laws affecting—among many other things—the electoral system, ordinary judiciary, and constitutional court. Much of this was done statutorily via "cardinal laws" requiring a two-thirds supermajority, as well as via amending and later replacing the constitution (also requiring a two-thirds supermajority). The result was widespread, justified criticism of democratic backsliding and creeping authoritarianism, even making it on multiple occasions to the opinion pages of the *New York Times*. Criticism of the dismantling of independent institutions by Fidesz was compounded by Orbán's professed admiration of "illiberal democracy" as practiced by states such as China and Russia. And yet there is widespread recognition by supporters and critics alike that while these developments have weakened the liberal and democratic character of Hungary, they have also been (with a handful of exceptions) fundamentally *legal*. This is especially the case with the weakening of the Hungarian Constitutional Court: rather than using informal means of pressure or illegal actions, the government has assiduously used de jure changes via statute and constitutional amendment to undermine the country's only other significant veto player.

The aim of this chapter is to provide an explanation for the post-2010 developments in Hungary, using the country's unfortunate experience to elucidate how the relationship between changes in electoral competition and judicial independence differs in democratic as opposed to autocratic contexts. In doing so, it also provides an answer to the final question motivating the book, which is a result of tension between existing research on judicial independence and the results presented in Chapter 3. Specifically, the counterintuitive conclusion that the insurance model, the dominant explanation for variation in judicial independence in democracies (VonDoepp & Ellet 2011, Vanberg 2015), is of rather limited explanatory power in cross-national analyses of the very phenomenon it became famous for explaining. Recall that in the fixed effects models presented, variation in the level of competition within a democracy was related to variation in the level of de facto independence, but that this association was of far less substantive importance than variation within non-democracies, a result even weaker in the subsequent

The Political Foundations of Judicial Independence in Dictatorship and Democracy. Brad Epperly,
Oxford University Press (2019). © Brad Epperly
DOI: 10.1093/oso/9780198845027.001.0001

tables assessing alternative explanations. More importantly, the results of the instrumental variables analysis suggest that while variation in competition causes changes in independence in non-democratic regimes, it has no substantive effect at all in democracies. Thus, the goal of this chapter is to offer a preliminary answer to this apparent contradiction: why the disconnect between the strongly robust and consistent empirical results presented in Chapter 3 and the large case study literature that has developed over the past two decades?

The answer to this question can be stated in brief: while it is the case that competition matters in both democratic and non-democratic regimes, *how* it matters differs. As Chapter 3 demonstrates, in non-democratic contexts competition matters because its increased presence causes increases in the level of judicial independence. On the other hand, in democratic contexts, as this chapter will show, changes in the competitiveness of the electoral arena are far more likely to produce changes in the level of de jure independence. Once this key distinction is realized, not only is the empirical anomaly of the Chapter 3 easily understood, but a unified insurance framework for explaining judicial independence also becomes possible. That is, competition is a key determinant of independence for both democratic and non-democratic regimes alike, and is vital for both de jure and de facto independence.

Section 4.1 makes the case for this differential impact. To do so I first synthesize existing work in the literature on comparative law and courts, suggesting that once we integrate work focused on the threat of public backlash into the insurance framework we are equipped with the tools to better understand how competition plays a differential role in dictatorships and democracies. I further develop the logics of this account in Section 4.2 via a case study of the constitutional and judicial environment in Hungary since 2010, when Fidesz won just under 53% of the vote in elections to the country's unicameral parliament and obtained 68% of the parliamentary seats. The record of this rather recent "historical" case study—which has received attention from scholars within Hungary and beyond—is augmented by expert interviews, both on and off the record, with Hungarian legal scholars, government officials, Constitutional Court judges, and relevant international actors. These interviews were conducted both in the spring of 2013, when the Fourth Amendment to the Fundamental Law (the new Hungarian constitution) was being considered by the Venice Commission and the Hungarian Constitutional Court, and the following year immediately after elections in which Fidesz was able to secure another 2/3 parliamentary majority, this time with less than 50% of the popular vote. The degree to which the explanation extends beyond the specific case used to develop it, however, remains in question. Therefore, Section 4.2 ends by taking the argument derived from the recent and unfortunate Hungarian experience and briefly examining it in a cross-national manner, once again relying on quantitative methods and data, some of it new but most of it familiar from previous chapters. The results are again highly consistent and robust, providing significant support for the claim that competition's association with independence in democratic contexts is overwhelmingly with the formal, de jure rules protecting the judiciary while in non-democracies it remains restricted to de facto, behavioral independence.

4.1 Competition and De Jure Independence

To better understand why de jure changes should be more likely in democracies requires moving away from what Vanberg (2015) calls endogenous explanations of judicial independence like the insurance framework, and integrating an exogenous explanation predicated on the possibility of public punishment of political actors who undermine the independence of the judiciary.[1] This exogenous perspective needs to be *integrated*, rather than *turned to*, because it in fact is highly contingent on the specific endogenous explanation offered by the insurance model, and is relevant only under conditions of diminishing competition. Thus, although the distinction between these two explanations is less clear than Vanberg suggests (as I will discuss), it remains a useful heuristic in framing the mechanisms underlying these two varying—but not competing—explanations. Before addressing why this is and how integrating these approaches offers a more thorough explanation, however, a brief presentation of the public support explanation is called for.

4.1.1 The Constraining Role of Public Backlash

The insurance framework's logic is "endogenous" because of the nature of the mechanism inducing political actors to embrace judicial independence; that is, the recognition by these actors that the values of an independent court is endogenous to the competition for political power between competing parties. "Exogenous" explanations for judicial independence, on the other hand, rely instead on the role played by a public that supports a court, as they are likely to punish political actors they view as attacking such a court (Epstein, Knight, & Shvetsova 2001*b*, Vanberg 2005, Staton 2010).[2] Fundamental to this perspective is the fact that the judicial branch can serve as a focal point for coordination among different public and

[1] Note that the focus here in on *changing* levels of of de jure independence, not on the question of the balance of power during constitution-drafting that scholars such as Ginsburg (2003) focus on. For a discussion of the importance of distinguishing the two, see Vanberg (2015).

[2] The degree to which either of these is in fact endogenous or exogenous is of course merely a function of where one draws the line; while I see no clear reason to privilege one form of self-restraint (induced by expectations of being out of power in the future or electoral backlash) over another with the term endogenous, I will conform with this existing usage for the sake of clarity.

private actors. This is the case in the first-order sense of the independence of a high court itself being a focal point around which coordination against transgressions is more likely to occur (Weingast 1997). It is also the case in a second-order sense of a high court being able to articulate to the population through its determination of the legitimacy of state action whether or not transgressions have occurred, and thus "serve as an unambiguous signal around which citizens can coordinate their evaluation of sovereign actions" (Vanberg 2011, 314). For this perspective on judicial independence, critical to public support is the role the court plays as a focal point and as an information clearing house,[3] in both instances clarifying to the population when the state is pursuing problematic policies.

The exogenous, public backlash explanation for independent courts is predicated on the idea that, as Gibson, Caldeira, & Baird (1998, 343) point out, "with limited institutional resources, courts are therefore uncommonly dependent upon the goodwill of their constituents for both support and compliance." Thus, such public support is able to induce compliance not only by the constituent public but also by political actors, who themselves fear the prospect of being punished by the public (both the court's and *their* constituents), presumably in the next electoral cycle (Vanberg 2000).

Perhaps the most influential account of this backlash is offered by Vanberg (2001), who constructs a formal model to ascertain the conditions under which democratic political actors will respect judicial independence and compliance with unfriendly court rulings will rule the day. Critical for this equilibrium outcome to exist is popular support for the court and transparency such that legislative responses to judicial decisions are observable by the public as well as the complexity of the issue, as highly legalistic or technocratic matters should lessen the public's understanding and thus its ability to monitor and sanction. To the degree that these two conditions hold, the model suggests that we should observe powerful courts whose independence is respected. To test this, Vanberg (2001, 2005) examines an empirical implication of his model (that transparency increases the likelihood of judicial annulment of government policies), looking at decisions of the German Federal Constitutional Court. He finds that increased transparency, i.e. public attention and the non-complexity of the issue, is strongly associated with an increased likelihood of the Court asserting itself. Moving beyond just the German case, Vanberg explicitly turns to the experience of Hungary during the 1990s, concluding that as long as courts are popular and transparency exists, judicial independence should be respected by political actors.

[3] For a thorough discussion of the information clearing house role of courts in federal and international systems, see Carrubba (2009) and Carrubba & Gabel (2014).

4.1.2 When Backlash Might Constrain

As is commonly pointed out, not only is this mechanism exogenous, but its source is rarely explained, with it remaining largely unexamined why courts that check popularly elected leaders and their policies obtain support (Stephenson 2003, Vanberg 2015).[4] This is, of course, not necessarily a problem. Countless phenomena in the social sciences are able to serve as perfectly adequate explanations without their own explanation being endogenous to the theory at hand; where political competition comes from is itself treated as exogenous in insurance explanations, for example.[5] What is far less commonly recognized, and of greater import, is the fact that the exogenous, public backlash explanation for judicial independence in fact assumes the conditions required for the endogenous, insurance-based explanation. Beyond the two conditions that Vanberg (2001, 347) contends are critical—public support and ability to monitor legislative responses to judicial decisions—there exists a third condition, without which the presence of the first two are likely insufficient to maintain an equilibrium of independence. This is the presence of a party able to credibly threaten the government with electoral loss. While those forwarding the public role in the maintenance of an independent judiciary explicitly assume that the public supports the court, the assumption that there exists a viable opposition for the public to vote for as a means to punish the government for infringing on judicial independence is not recognized. It might very well be the case that this, like popular support,[6] is *often* a fair assumption, but it is certainly not *always* so. This is made clear when one considers the fact that the first argument for the important role of political competition was Ramseyer's (1994) comparison of the United States and Japan, where it was precisely the lack of a viable opposition that allowed the latter's government to consistently undermine the formal independence of the judiciary. When a government faces a situation in which there exists no opposition party able to offer a credible threat to the electoral prospects of the government, there is no ability for the threat of public backlash to induce those in power to continue to respect the judiciary, regardless of the level of public support or transparency; when there is a credible threat of replacement, the role of the public becomes superfluous. When and how might public support be decisive, then? Looking at whether competition is stable or changing provides some clues.

[4] See, however, Staton (2010) for the most thorough treatment to date.

[5] Despite some claims to the effect, it is unlikely the case that judicial independence is critical in securing a competitive electoral arena, for reasons discussed and evidence presented in Epperly (2017), as well as the empirical results presented in Chapter 3.

[6] Krehbiel (2016) offers a formal model of unpopular courts and their support, examining its implications in an analysis of the European Court of Justice. The degree to which this generalizes to domestic courts, usually quite popular, remains an open question.

In times of stable levels of political competition, any threat posed by public backlash is unnecessary for strategic actors in power to respect the decisions of the judiciary and maintain existing levels of political competition, as the "endogenous" inducement of expectations concerning the future will already be salient. This is true regardless of whether the stable levels of competition are low or high. If the level of electoral competition has been and remains low, as noted previously there is and has been no credible risk to infringing on judicial independence, and the expectation should be a (continued) low level of judicial independence, regardless of the two factors Vanberg (2001) contends are critical; while it is the case that the incentives of public backlash should work opposite those of the insurance account, the fact that there is and has been no viable opposition by which the public can punish incumbents means that the insurance account should "win out", and incumbents should prefer fewer constraints (also assumed preferable in public backlash accounts) over more independent courts.[7] If the level of electoral competition has been and remains high, however, there is no need for public backlash to play any role: following the insurance logic, expectations of being out of power should induce incumbents to maintain existing levels of judicial independence without consideration of popular support for the court or the level of transparency.

If conditions are such that the competitiveness of the electoral system is increasing, there is similarly no need for the threat of punishment by the public to play any role in determining changing levels of judicial independence. While attacking a popular court would likely then be politically disadvantageous, it is also true that there are clear and obvious reasons for those in power to expect that the future might see them no longer in office, and thus a strong incentive would exist to maintain or deepen existing levels of judicial independence to safeguard against this possibility. Thus, in these situations the threat of public punishment should, if it has any effect, simply provide another incentive for positive outcomes from the perspective of the judiciary.

When the competitiveness of the electoral arena is stable or increasing, the threat of public punishment has effects that at best work in tandem with insurance pressures and at worst are superfluous due to their redundancy. In conditions of declining competition—the very conditions of interest for much of the work in the insurance vein—the threat of public backlash might, however, work at cross purposes with the insurance logic, and thus potentially temper declines in judicial independence. Recall that according to the insurance framework, declining levels of political competition should signal to those in power that their

[7] An empirical implication would be that in polities without at least some threat of replacement, the level of popular support for the judiciary is unrelated to any level of independence or its propensity to annul government policies. Given the lack of empirical examination of this assumption in existing work, however, I omit any such investigation here.

future electoral fortunes are more secure, with the result being a less pressing need for insurance and thus less reason to accept the constraints associated with more independent judiciaries. The reason why the exogenous, public backlash explanation becomes relevant in such a situation is precisely because—assuming no changes in public support or issues surrounding transparency of information provision—its incentive structure should now work against that of the insurance framework. Such is also the case, as noted previously, in stable levels of low competitiveness. The key difference here, however, is that competition is not stable, but fluctuating, suggesting to those in power that reversals are potentially possible (though attenuated by recent political developments), and that actions that might seriously threaten the recent electoral dominance of those in power should be avoided when possible. Thus, the result of a decreasingly competitive electoral arena should be a situation under which the logics of these two explanations are in tension: electoral dominance and the expectation of future successes lessening the need for insurance, with the previously competitive nature of politics simultaneously mitigating against undermining a respected institution and thus threatening popular support.

4.1.3 Regime Type, Competition, and De Jure Independence

Some pages ago I assured the reader that all of this had something to do with de jure judicial independence and democracy, and why changes in competition should affect primarily the de jure provisions ensuring judicial independence in democratic regimes, as opposed to de facto in non-democracies. It is the reasons for this—tied up in the potential constraints of public backlash—to which I now turn. In this section I focus on a number of key differences between democratic and autocratic regimes that should make the role of public backlash more salient in democratic regimes, as well as a number of reasons that undermining de facto independence should be more politically salient than changing the formal rules, and thus attacks on de jure independence are more prevalent in democracies. I first lay out two key distinctions between democratic and autocratic regimes before addressing why these should make autocratic regimes prone to target both de jure and de facto, and then addressing why democracies should prefer to target primarily de jure independence.

Two (of many) important differences

The first important distinction between democratic and autocratic regimes important for understanding the differential potential of public backlash to induce behavior is the role played by an independent media, which in democratic regimes has a far greater ability to popularize unconstitutional attacks on the de facto independence of the judiciary. The degree to which there exists significant differences in media independence across regime type can be illustrated by drawing on the the Global Media Freedom Dataset, which codes a categorical value denoting the degree of media freedom for every country-year from 1948 to 2012 (Whitten-Woodring & Van Belle 2017). The Global Media Freedom Dataset rates the media in each country-year as either free, imperfectly free, or not free.[8]

Table 4.1 shows the frequency of each of the three categories of media freedom by regime type. The differences between the two groups are striking: only 1% of non-democratic regimes are rated as having a free media, while 86% are considered to have a not-free media, such that it is government controlled or it is not possible to safely criticize the government. Only a scant 13% reach the level of imperfectly free, which Whitten-Woodring & Van Belle (2017) code as those where there are social, legal, or economic costs in criticizing the government, but such criticism does still on occasion occur. This contrasts sharply with democracies, where more than half the country-years have free media, i.e. those where criticism is a common part of politics. Only 15% of democratic country-years lack free media.

This is not, of course, to say that there is no variation *within* each constellation of democratic or autocratic states. The degree of media freedom varies within democracies, both consolidated and unconsolidated, as Table 4.1 illustrates. And there also exists variation across the scope of autocratic regimes, from "full blown" authoritarianism to the competitive or electoral authoritarianism receiving so much attention in the last twenty years. Highlighting the variation across autocracies, however, underscores the fundamental difference between these regimes and those that are democratic. As Levitsky & Way (2002, 57) note, the nature of the media in solidly authoritarian regimes is often such that it is "entirely state-owned, heavily censored, or systematically repressed." This can be as extreme as Leninist

Table 4.1 Media freedom across regime type. The frequency of each of three categories of media freedom across dictatorship and democracy, drawn from the Global Media Freedom Dataset (Whitten-Woodring & Van Belle 2017).

	Autocracy	Democracy
Free	0.01	0.55
Imperfectly free	0.13	0.31
Not free	0.86	0.15

[8] While Whitten-Woodring & Van Belle (2017, 2) also code those instances where there is no effective national media, they note that "Only the Congo (1960–1968) and Nepal (1948–1959) fall into the No Media category." I omit these from the presentation here, as they consist of less than one half of 1% of observations.

regimes, thankfully now few and far between, where by law no media is independent, and rather all media is directly controlled by state or party organs, from the most widely circulated newspapers to journals with the most niche of readerships. Less formal but no less effective is the de facto elimination of independent media that characterizes many autocratic regimes today. The situation of the media is, in general, far less dire in autocratic regimes where opposition parties are legal, participate in politics, and political competition exists to some degree. In such contexts, rather than the de jure or de facto elimination of independent media, strategies include the preferential allocation of state advertising contracts (and the financial viability and possibility for increased circulation that comes with them), the targeted use of tax laws to harass critical media (and signal to other media outlets what happens when lines are crossed), and restrictive and nebulous laws against crimes such as "extremism" that can be used to selectively prosecute those critical of the government.

The key distinction between the nature of media freedom and its watchdog role in general across the democracy/dictatorship divide is indicated by the fact that one of the strongest criticisms laid at the feet of Victor Orbán by domestic opposition figures and foreign actors since Fidesz took power in Hungary in 2010 involves the significant pressure placed on the media by government actions and policies (Scheppele 2012*b*). It is illustrative that Orbán has been open about his admiration for and goal to build an "illiberal democracy" of the sort found in Putin's Russia (Orbán 2014). What is noteworthy about the response to this is particularly the rejection of these practices towards the media (among other things), associated as they are with autocratic rather than democratic rule. Also noteworthy is the fact that, despite Orbán's definitive shift towards more illiberal strategies of rule, Fidesz has overwhelmingly refrained from unconstitutional attacks on the de facto powers of independent institutions, but has instead changed the formal rules, as will be explored in depth in Section 4.2.

A second distinction between dictatorship and democracy that should play out in the form of governmental action towards the judiciary when competition is in flux is the differential respect for constitutionalism, or more accurately differential constraints on respecting constitutionalism. This is *not* to say that autocratic constitutions are different, but rather that their relevance, role, and the respect for the ways they constrain actors are different. This can best be summed up in Okoth-Ogendo's (1993, 66) terminology describing the condition of constitutions without constitutionalism, the paradoxical and highly political situation of both a commitment on the part of "political elites to the idea of the constitution and an equally emphatic rejection of the classical or at any rate liberal democratic notion of constitutionalism." That is, conditions under which constitutions exist, and elites are committed to the idea of constitutions but unconstrained in practice by their content. This condition can obtain regardless of whether autocratic constitutions are operating manuals, window dressing, or both (Ginsburg & Simpser

2013): the focal point role of constitutions articulated by Barros (2002) does not require that the focal point be treated as inviolate by those whose activity is being coordinated. Operating manuals get ignored with regularity, after all.

Assessing the empirical accuracy of the idea that autocrats are far more enamored with the content of constitutions than obeying their dictates is not difficult. If autocratic constitutions contain but fail to constrain, then we should expect to see significant similarities between the constitutions of democratic and autocratic regimes. This is precisely what Ginsburg, Melton, & Elkins (2013, 21) find in their analysis of the content of authoritarian constitutions. The differences found are remarkably small, and "the most important finding may be the overall levels of similarity of formal texts across regime types... Constitutions have converged in form, if not in function." Although focusing on constitutions more generally, their findings hold when looking specifically at the de jure constitutional provisions protecting the independence of the judiciary. This is demonstrated in Figure 4.1, which visualizes the de jure constitutional rules securing an independent judiciary in the post-communist region, with darker shades of gray signifying higher scores on a factor analysis of various de jure provisions. What jumps out looking at Figure 4.1 is the fact that the solidly autocratic former Soviet Republics of Eurasia appear far darker than most of the Central and Eastern European democratic states that (mostly) consolidated democracy and joined the European Union. In fact, the only Central Asian state to perform below the global average is Turkmenistan, known for being by far the most autocratic regime in the region. But even here it outperforms Latvia, which effectively disappears from the map, seemingly creating a new body of water between the two other Baltic states.

If autocratic and democratic constitutions are similar, the intuition would be that by definition the functions of constitutions have not converged, given the

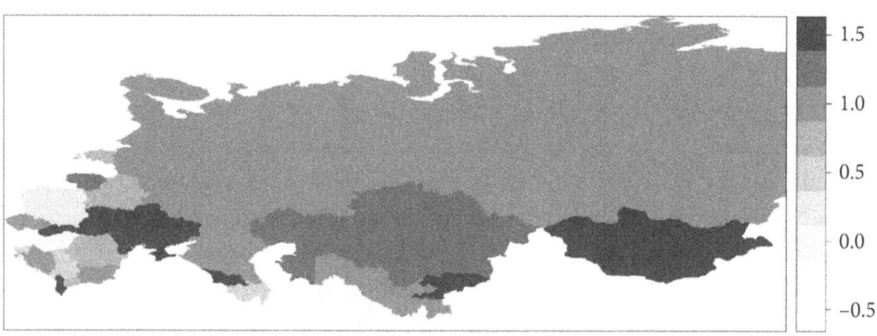

Figure 4.1 De jure independence in the post-communist world. Constitutional provisions for judicial independence in the post-communist region. Values are those of a factor analysis of seven constitutional provisions, with a global mean of zero (higher scores mean more de jure protections for the judiciary). See Tate & Keith (2007) for further discussion of the measure.

fundamental differences between autocracy and democracy. But we need not rely on intuition, as there is clear evidence that the window dressing aspect of autocratic constitutions sets them apart in a qualitative manner. While all regimes observe at times divergence between the goals and realities of their constitutional orders, autocratic regimes are particularly noteworthy in this regard, dominating the category of "sham constitutions" in Law & Versteeg's (2013) classification of constitutions by their correspondence to rights promised and rights respected.

Autocratic preferences to target de facto independence

This key difference between autocratic and democratic constitutional orders should have clear implications for our understanding of the insurance model. Put simply, autocrats do not face the same potential for domestic political punishment or international sanction for violating parchment barriers: as the corpus of research on comparative authoritarianism stresses, there exist expectations among their citizens and outside observers that formal rules respecting independent institutions and rights are mere parchment barriers, and that rhetoric regarding them is cheap talk.[9] These autocrats can fail to face the same level of repercussions for routinely and often blatantly violating the rules both because of the general cynicism induced by the idea that everyone is corrupt and democracy is no better (Paul & Matthews 2016); here the violation of norms is just common practice. Violations might also, however, be strategic, to explicitly decrease the likelihood of domestic political sanctions. As Simpser (2013) lays out, the undisguised violation of formal rules can be an effective tool to demoralize would-be opponents and signal the strength of the regime. The implication of the findings of the previous chapters would be that while such demoralization might work very well when opposition forces are fractured, weak, and competition is low, it might very well backfire when the opposition is none of these things; this is partly the story of the Color Revolutions. These factors are amplified by the lack or extreme fragility of independent media in autocratic regimes, which make the publication of attacks on the de facto independence of the judiciary (from exerting pressure to ignoring inconvenient decisions) far less likely.

In other words, if autocrats desire to influence the behavior or composition of the judiciary, they can certainly but need not go through the process of changing the formal rules of the game. As Mudde & Jenne (2012, 148) note, "Authoritarian leaders typically undermine democratic institutions by not respecting the law. Rather than changing the rules, they bend or break them," and do so because they

[9] This is not to say that autocrats do not sometimes end up surprised when these pieces of paper turn into focal points; this is in fact the reason that these regimes contain the seeds of their own destruction, with instability, democratization, or a slide into full-blown authoritarianism the medium-term options (Levitsky & Way 2010). Although perhaps more common in competitive authoritarian contexts, seeming parchment barriers can unexpectedly come to bind even in the most uncompetitive of autocracies, as the experience of the Helsinki Accords in Eastern Europe suggests (Thomas 1999).

can get away with it. They need not (but of course can, and also do) change formal rules, first, because if existing rules do not constrain autocrats from taking action to influence who is on the court, how it operates, or whether its decisions have force, they need not go through the effort of changing formal rules. And second, since such a disconnect between the content and form of constitutions exists, there is little reason to expect newly adopted formal policies would better track to behavioral changes given the failure of existing rules to do so. Furthermore, if the goal, in the end, is to affect outcomes, then the goal is to affect the behavioral independence of the court, not the formal rules under which it operates. If an autocrat faces the development of a credible electoral threat, he or she does not have to change the formal rules, given they are likely already such that they enshrine a level of judicial independence far greater than what is realized. This is even more the case when one considers that there are in fact costs to changing constitutions, given their content is something autocrats care about (Getty 1991, Okoth-Ogendo 1993), and the process requires the allocation of time and resources that could be better spent elsewhere; given the context being discussed is one in which the electoral environment is becoming increasingly competitive, these resources and effort could instead be spent on dealing with the emergence of credible challengers. If, on the other hand, the threat of electoral competition were decreasing, autocrats need not revise constitutions to achieve changes in the power and autonomy of courts, and can instead infringe on behavioral independence.

This discussion of the relative capabilities and benefits for autocrats of using de jure or de facto leverage over the judiciary underscores the argument made in the previous chapters, further stressing the point that only when they have reason to will autocrats respect judicial independence. A focus on de jure vs. de facto makes clear that what this means is that when induced to do so, autocrats should be more likely to follow the formal rules, enabling the judiciary to develop in a way that it is more capable at providing insurance if the threat of electoral competition turns out to have been credible enough to remove the autocrat from office. The first half of this argument is examined in previous chapters by reference to fixed effects "within" models assessing change in levels of judicial independence over time. Later in this chapter I assess it with reference to changes in the competitiveness of the electoral environment and changes in both de facto and judicial independence, with the expectation that changing competitiveness should be associated with changes in both de facto and de jure independence in autocratic regimes.

Democratic preferences to target de jure independence

The different roles of constitutionalism and the media in democratic regimes, on the other hand, should have significant effects on the ability of the government to engage in what are at heart unconstitutional attacks on the judiciary, i.e. the ability to systematically undermine the judiciary's de facto independence.

Recall that in the formal model developed by Vanberg (2001, 347) a necessary condition for voters to impose costs on government actors for violating de facto independence of the judiciary is for those voters to "be able to monitor legislative responses to judicial rulings effectively and reliably." As Vanberg is interested explicitly in the logics of legislative–judicial relations in democracies (specifically, in his empirical tests of his model, Germany), the existence of a media capable of providing the transparency required is both assumed and constant. The same is true for Staton (2010, 25), who argues that constitutional courts can "go public" and use the media to help them secure compliance with decisions, but notes that the public's role in constraining governmental noncompliance requires that

> [P]eople must be sufficiently informed about the cases that courts resolve in order to identify and deter potential noncompliance. It only makes sense to invoke the public as an enforcement mechanism for judicial decisions, indirectly or directly, if people are aware of what they are enforcing...If they are not, then noncompliance will go undetected.[10]

In democratic regimes the transparency required for these models to work is far more prevalent than in autocratic regimes, and for this reason the potential for the public to gain the information required to monitor government actions towards the judiciary is far greater. This relationship is supported by existing research on the role of an independent media on the knowledge and attitudes of citizens, which finds both that where citizens are more politically informed governments are more response to the public and that a more independent media means a more informed public (Adsera, Boix, & Payne 2003, Leeson 2008, Snyder Jr, & Strömberg 2010).

The public has a greater ability to know about the manners in which the government may undermine judicial independence in democratic regimes, and as discussed the threat of public backlash can constrain democratic leaders from attacks on the judiciary's de facto independence (Gibson, Caldeira, & Baird 1998, Stephenson 2004, Vanberg 2005), but that this requires some degree of political competition. In cases where competition is falling, we should expect attacks to take the form most conducive to maintaining electoral dominance (or, in the reverse situation of it rising, most conducive to long-term insurance). The question that follows is what form of independence should be most politically safe to attack given the conditions of constitutionalism and media independence which characterize democratic regimes.

I contend that in democratic contexts it is the de jure protections that safeguard courts that should bear the disproportionate share of a government's attention as a means to undermine judicial independence explicitly because in doing so they are

[10] Similarly, in Weingast's (1997) model of the political foundations of the rule of law, for the court to signal the sovereign has transgressed and create a focal point around which the public might coalesce requires at least a decently unimpeded flow of information.

"playing by the rules" as opposed to engaging in extra-legal attacks, and that such playing by the rules should be less dangerous given the increased role of constitutionalism and an independent media in democratic regimes. Whereas in contexts of increasing competition, the possibility of setting rules that might obtain into the future should encourage attempts to reset the formal rules when possible; in other words, actors should engage in hegemonic preservation (Hirschl 2004). Attacking de facto independence, that is using extra-legal means to influence behavior, should produce two risks for those in power that legal means do not. First, attempts to subvert the judiciary behaviorally in conditions of decreasing competition are far riskier as judges appointed under conditions of de facto independence assert their constitutionally protected prerogatives and use existing means of publicizing such attempts (Staton 2010). Second, that these attempts, likely to be resisted, can create a focal point around which a recently depleted opposition can attempt to re-establish itself as a viable force (Weingast 1997). The result should be that attempts to subvert judicial independence become "formalized," with the formal autonomy and competencies (often constitutionally-derived) of the courts targeted. Instead of undue pressure being placed informally on the judiciary, there instead should be attempts to legally constrain the court. This argument would predict that in consolidated democracies changes in the degree of political competition should primarily result in these de jure changes, including examples such as changing judicial appointment or retention procedures and restricting access to or the scope of judicial review, or in the "classic" examples of court-packing and changed retirement requirements.

A simple thought experiment might further illustrate my argument about the constraining nature of formal rules in democratic polities and the greater likelihood to change these rules rather than use extra-legal means of subverting de facto independence. Imagine the response by political actors, the press, and the public if a party with control of the executive and the legislature decided that it would appoint high-ranking officials without following any of the procedures laid down by the constitutional and statutory rules governing the process. That is, if a party were to, for example, place judges able to rule on the constitutionality of executive and legislative actions onto high-ranking courts for life and in doing so openly reject the existing rules constraining their ability to do so. As an alternative, imagine if the party instead decided to first change the rules by which the process was formally supposed to happen, using a simple majority to remove supermajority requirements on such appointments, with the end result being precisely the same.

To the degree that one thinks these two actions would produce differential responses—the latter perhaps only hand-wringing by some journalists and elite observers and shrugs by the general public—is the degree to which one thinks changing de jure protections for institutions (in this example minoritarianism) is far less likely to produce any public backlash, and thus far more likely to occur in democratic regimes. Of course, this is not merely a hypothetical. To the degree that a reader's reference point in this thought experiment was Senate Majority Leader Mitch McConnell changing the rules for appointing Supreme Court justices in 2017 or then Senate Majority Leader Harry Reid changing the rules for appointing the other 1,183 executive branch posts requiring Senate confirmation in 2013 is more likely an indication of one's partisanship. And while this specific change was not *constitutional*, such changes very often are, as Section 4.2 on Hungary will discuss at length. And regardless of whether a rule change is constitutional or not, the decision to change the way in which judges are selected—and which actors are involved in the selection is most assuredly important—has important implications for the degree of judicial independence, as debates in comparative law and politics and the study of US state courts have long recognized (Rosenn 1987, Epstein, Knight, & Shvetsova 2001*a*, Hall 2001, Feld & Voigt 2003, Rios-Figueroa 2006).[11]

This thought experiment can be extended to survey research to ascertain whether the intuition from the thought experiment laid out above is correct, which I have done. To do this, I prompted self-identified Republicans (to minimize any partisan negativity in responses) with the following vignette:

> The Supreme Court and lower federal courts often rule against Republican and Democratic Presidents. Since taking office, President Trump and Republicans in Congress have experienced a string of defeats in court, losing key battles over their policies. They say these policies are part of the mandate to govern they received when they won the White House and both Houses of Congress in the last election.

After reading this, respondents rated the plausibility of a number of Republican responses to this situation. Five of these are de jure changes affecting the independence of court (including selection, removal, and size), cribbed directly from actual actions taken by the Hungarian and Polish governments in recent years, while a further three are de facto attacks on the powers and composition of the court. The majority of (self-identified Republican) respondents answered that changes to four of the five de jure powers were plausible,[12] whereas only one third of respondents rated each de facto attack on the court (removal of judges for partisan bias, statement of court decisions being non-binding and

[11] In their important analysis of whether de jure judicial independence matters, Melton & Ginsburg (2014) consider the number of institutional actors involved in selection of constitutional (or highest appellate) court judges. What this thought experiment, and the Hungarian experience, illustrates, however, is that even within a single institutional actor the number of partisan actors is critical for maintaining judicial independence. It is far more important to require consent by legislative minorities in the selection of judges than having the involvement of a second actor with the same partisan preferences as the legislative majority, as Fidesz well recognized.

[12] The only one rated as implausible by a majority of respondents involved requiring the national debt to be below 50% of GDP for the court to be able to rule on the constitutionality of tax and budget laws.

refusal to comply with all adverse rulings, prior statement of refusal to implement upcoming ruling if adverse) as being plausible. While these results do not show that behavior would change, they provide preliminary evidence that even in a consolidated democracy co-partisans of the government view attacks on the de jure independence of the judicial branch as plausible, whereas attacks on their de facto independence are viewed as unlikely.

These survey results, along with both the thought experiment and the actual public response to the de jure changes of the independence of federal courts (via weakening selection procedures) under the Obama administration and the Supreme Court under Trump administration, as well as the evidence of what we know about media freedom and constitutionalism in democracies, all provide a solid basis for thinking that democratic leaders are, when faced with low or falling levels of political competition, far more likely to attack the de jure rather than the de facto independence of the judiciary, as this is far less likely to provoke public backlash that might threaten their political dominance.

A final reason for thinking this is the case is that changing the formal rules can not only be less politically disadvantageous from a public support standpoint, but also more politically advantageous from a medium-term perspective with regards to dead-hand control of state institutions staffed with preferred agents. This was precisely one goal of Reid's removal of the filibuster for federal judges: staffing a significant minority of the federal judgeships, appointed for life, with preferred agents. It can be even more effective if one changes the rules in such a way as to make future removal of a myriad of one's agents extremely difficult. This extreme version of this dead-hand control over state institutions that formal rule changes can bring about is observed in the Hungarian experience, to which I now turn.

4.2 Competition and De Jure Independence in Hungary

In April 2010, the right-wing Fidesz party won a landslide victory in Hungary, doing what no party had done in the the country's five previous post-communist elections and winning an outright majority of votes; in the previous two elections they had lost out to the then incumbent MSZP (the Hungarian Socialist Party) by a single percentage point, and remained the primary opposition party against the governing coalition of the MSZP and the Alliance of Free Democrats. In 2010, however, due to the details of Hungary's mixed electoral system, Fidesz's 52.7% share of votes translated into 68% of the seats in the country's unicameral parliament.[13] The result of a 10.5% increase in the popular vote share was an increase of 26% of the seats in and 2/3 majority control of the Hungarian parliament.

[13] One key aspect of this disproportionality is the overrepresentation of rural voters, which the new electoral system in place for the 2014 elections only worsened (Bozóki 2015).

The story of the collapse of competition in the Hungarian electoral arena and its subsequent effects on judicial independence is striking, but the degree to which it is an outlier is up for debate. In the 2015 Polish elections, the then incumbent Civic Platform party lost almost half of its popular support, and like in Hungary the party to take third place in the elections was entirely new to politics. Outside of Eastern Europe, most striking are probably the recent French elections, in which the presidential contest saw a second round consisting of no candidates from the established parties of the left or right, and the legislative contest saw an alliance consisting of a party entirely new to politics and another that won only two seats in 2012 winning 350 in 2017. I raise the French example not to wade into debates over the collapse of mainstream or the rise of "anti-system" parties, but rather to stress that the degree to which high levels electoral volatility—long common in democracies outside Western Europe and North America—are far from rare. The jury is still out on the degree to which the second half of the story, the experience of the Hungarian judiciary and Constitutional Court after 2010, is in fact an outlier. It is undoubtedly an exemplary case, and an important one given recent developments elsewhere, and for this reason better understanding the dynamics of constitutional change is vital.[14] For these reasons, I leverage the Hungarian example to understand the logic of the account developed in Section 4.1 in a case where the constraints on actors are few; to the degree that there are, of course, greater constraints on actors we should perhaps see fewer attempts to influence the judicial branch, but these should be visible nonetheless.

In the rest of this section I will discuss first the conditions that led to Fidesz's constitutional majority, as well as the political and constitutional environment leading up to the 2010 elections.[15] I then turn to the ways in which Fidesz shifted the de jure protections for and powers of the Hungarian judiciary and Constitutional Court after its victory, as well as the ways in which the new constitution adopted by Fidesz continued and furthered these changes. Finally, I discuss the (lack of) public response to Fidesz's "constitutional revolution," as well as the ways in which this was fundamentally a story of de jure, not de facto, attacks on the courts. What I do not do, however, is focus on the myriad other actions taken by Fidesz that have produced widespread criticism in governmental, academic, and civil society sectors around Europe and the world. This is not because Fidesz's policies concerning religious groups, the electoral system, or the media are unimportant, but simply because they are issues for another day.[16]

[14] Developments in Poland in 2015, for example, postdate the 2013–14 field work upon which the insights of this chapter are based.

[15] For the sake of brevity and clarity, I restrict my analysis to the years immediately after the 2010 victory, and do not address the important "Fourth Amendment" to the Fidesz constitution or the 2014 election that produced another (this time fleeting) constitutional majority for Fidesz.

[16] Similarly, the roles of the European Union and the Council of Europe's European Commission for Democracy through Law, better known as the Venice Commission, while almost but not *entirely* irrelevant to the story, are by and large omitted, as the focus is on how domestic changes produced domestic outcomes.

4.2.1 Why 2010?

As (if not more) important for the story as Fidesz's performance in the 2010 elections is the performance of the rival Hungarian Socialist Party.[17] In the 2006 elections, its 43% of the votes translated into 190 of the 386 parliamentary seats. Its performance in the subsequent elections, however, illustrates the degree to which the electoral environment in Hungary went from being one of two major parties in close competition to something entirely else: in 2010 the MSZP won less than 20% of the popular vote and only fifty-nine seats in parliament (its coalition partner did not even cross the 5% threshold to make it into parliament). In one election, its popular support was less than half the previous election, and its parliamentary representation less than a third. The utter collapse of support for the Hungarian Socialists and the resulting implosion of a competitive electoral environment in Hungary is attributable to two key factors that occurred during the previous government's tenure in office, the first economic and the second political.

The 2008 economic crisis hit Hungary particularly hard. Hungarian GDP growth in 2009 was less than –4%, lower than in Portugal, Ireland, or Spain, and barely better than Greece, all four countries whose economic problems captured the attention of European leaders for years. Its recovery by the next parliamentary elections in April 2010, in addition, was on par or weaker than all but Greece's.[18] Compounding this was the fact that, being outside the Eurozone, inflation in Hungary was far higher than in these other countries. In other words, economic conditions under the incumbent governments were far from rosy, with the expectations for electoral performance that go along with such a situation.

Compounding this general economic problem, however, was a phenomenon that became widespread in the countries of Central and Eastern Europe in the mid-2000s, which was loans denominated in foreign currency (Bozóki 2015).[19] This phenomenon was most prevalent in Hungary and Poland, but for a variety of reasons its effects were far more pernicious in the former. In Hungary, it became common for housing, vehicle, and personal loans to be denominated in foreign currency, predominantly the Swiss franc, because interest rates on the Hungarian forint were far higher. The result was these loans reaching more than 10% of Hungarian GDP (Buszko & Krupa 2015).[20] This intensified the effects of

[17] Fidesz, it should be noted, gained votes in 2010, but not even half the percentage of votes that MSZP lost.

[18] Data on growth rates are from http://www.tradingeconomics.com and data on inflation from http://inflation.eu; both compile reports of national statistical offices.

[19] It was widely assumed that both countries would become part of the eurozone in 2009 or 2010, which would mean that borrowers would be exposed to the risks associate with fluctuating exchange rates for only a handful of years on, for example, a twenty-five-year mortgage (Norris 2014).

[20] The problem was less in Poland because the euro (the exchange rate of which worsened to a lesser degree for borrowers) was the predominant foreign currency, loans went to high income rather than all individuals, repayment was often possible in zloty, and loans were restricted to housing and a smaller

the economic crisis in Hungary after 2008, as the exchange rate between the forint and the franc moved rapidly against Hungarian borrowers (after moving in their favor for a few years), who were left with loans denominated in Swiss francs but income streams in Hungarian forints. In 2007 and 2008 (the peak years of foreign exchange loans being taken out in Hungary), one franc could buy 153 and 159 forints, respectively. In 2009 and 2010, however, the exchange rate had jumped to 186 and 200 forints, with catastrophic effects on the ability of Hungarian citizens and businesses to repay their loans denominated in francs. Thus, not only were Hungarian citizens witnessing increased inflation and unemployment as well as low growth when they went to the polls in 2010, but many were on top of this facing mortgage or auto payments whose cost has increased by a third and the expectation that these costs would only continue to rise.[21]

The second factor leading to the collapse of the Hungarian electoral arena was the behavior of the previous government, irrespective of the difficult economic times it faced. After eight years in power, the Socialist Party was widely seen as corrupt and ineffective, and one event highlights the degree to which this was the case. In May 2006, one month after winning elections, Prime Minister Ferenc Gyurcsány gave a private speech to parliamentary members of his party, which naturally was recorded and later broadcast by Hungarian state radio. After laying out the plans for the coming government, Gyurcsány offered a brutally honest and profanity-laced post-mortem on the four previous years of Socialist government and political life in Hungary, which began with:

> We did what we could in the past month. We did whatever was possible to do in secret in the preceding months, making sure that papers on what we were preparing for would not surface in the last weeks of the election campaign.
>
> ... we have fucked it up. Not a little but a lot. No country in Europe has screwed up as much as we have. It can be explained. We have obviously lied throughout the past 18 to 24 months. It was perfectly clear that what we were saying was not true.
>
> We are beyond the country's possibilities to such an extent that we could not conceive earlier that a joint government of the Socialists and the liberals would ever do. And in the meantime we did not actually do anything for four years. Nothing.
>
> You cannot mention any significant government measures that we can be proud of, apart from the fact that in the end we managed to get governance out of the shit. Nothing. If we have to give an account to the country of what we have done in four years, what are we going to say?

portion of GDP. This was further augmented by the fact that Poland was far more insulated from the 2008 crisis, avoiding even mild recession.

[21] On this, borrowers were correct. The exchange rates only continued to rise (for the past few years they have hovered not too far below 300:1), and in 2014 the Hungarian government passed legislation allowing borrowers to convert loans from francs into forints, but at the then market exchange rate of approximately 250 forints to one franc (Forint Exchange 2014).

The results included the first sustained protest in Hungary since the collapse of communism, riots, cratering poll numbers for the government, and refusal on the part of the Prime Minister to resign. His resignation did, however, arrive a year and a half later, and the result was a caretaker government appointed by the President of Hungary, László Sólyom. These political problems were only amplified by widespread corruption, which caught a number of members of parliament in investigations and prosecutions, and which a government report issued under the caretaker (but still Socialist) government concluded accounted for a full quarter of the cost of public works projects (Hodgson 2009). These political crises, coupled with the economic quagmire in Hungary precipitated by the 2008 financial crisis and a falling forint, meant that the main left-wing party was decimated in the 2010 parliamentary elections (as well as 2014 and 2018). The result of these events and their outcomes is an electoral environment in Hungary that for almost a decade has been uncompetitive, with the ruling Fidesz party in some sense more worried about shoring up its right flank against the far-right Jobbik party than worrying about what is left of the opposition in the center and on the left.

In the 2010 election campaign, which given the collapse of the MSZP all were considering Fidesz to be assured to win, Fidesz was asked what plans it had were it to secure the 2/3 majority in parliament that would allow it the ability to revise the constitution wholesale. Fidesz, it should be noted, did not campaign on a platform of constitutional change (Scheppele 2015), and the response prior to the election to the specific question was that no plans existed (Bánkuti, Halmai, & Scheppele 2012*b*, 253). Despite this, after securing a 2/3 majority, Prime Minister Victor Orbán called the result an "electoral revolution," promising and delivering on what has since been called, if nothing else, a constitutional revolution (Rupnik 2012). What, precisely, was Fidesz—a party that had governed from 1998 to 2002—engaging in revolutionary actions against?

4.2.2 From Communism's Collapse to the Collapse of Competition

Not only had Fidesz governed and Victor Orbán been Prime Minister before, but Fiatal Demokraták Szövetsége—Fidesz, the Alliance of Young Democrats,[22] which began as classical liberal party—had been one of seven opposition parties (or proto-parties) to push the Communist Party to negotiate a regime transition as part of the 1989 Round Table talks.[23] These talks, inspired by the Polish experience, were similar to other Central and Eastern European countries, and involved the nascent opposition organizations hammering out the details of elections in which opposition parties could run, as well as numerous other institutional details

[22] Its requirement that all members had to be under the age of 35 was removed in 1993.
[23] These talks were technically trilateral, as two non-party organizations were also involved.

that together painted the picture of the Hungarian state that was to succeed its previous state socialist incarnation.

The end product of this negotiated transition was a new state, but *not* a new constitution. Unlike any other post-communist state, the Hungarian constitutional order after communism's collapse was, formally, the same as before: Act XX of 1949, the Stalinist-era communist constitution. The degree to which this was true in practice, however, is very different. The Round Table talks involved over 100 amendments to this constitution, agreed on by the Communist Party and the umbrella organization of opposition groups, the Opposition Round Table (Bánkuti, Halmai & Scheppele 2012*b*). These significant changes were followed by even more amendments after free and fair elections in 1990, with the MSZP—the legal successor to the Hungarian Socialist Workers' Party, or MSzMP—winning only 10% of the votes and coming in fourth place behind three constituent parties of the Opposition Round Table. As political theorist and leader of the party to take second place in the 1990 elections János Kis argues, the large number of amendments and lack of transitory provisions means that "it is not misleading to call it the 1989 Constitution" (Kis 2012, 5).

While there were widespread expectations that a new, post-communist constitution would be adopted, such an event never occurred, with political parties of both the right and left failing to come together to reach the two-thirds consensus required to change the constitution. This was even the case during the coalition government of 1994–98, in which the Socialists and liberals who together possessed a two-thirds majority were unable to concur on the process of constitutional change; the most significant result of the first government with a two-thirds majority was an amendment to the constitution increasing the supermajority required to draft a new constitution to a four-fifths majority (Uitz 2015). The point that, regardless of what one calls it, the Hungarian constitution fully met democratic norms and expectations is made persuasively by another member of the Opposition Round Table and Chairman of the Committee on Constitutional and Judicial Affairs in the Hungarian parliament from 1994 to 1998, who contends that one must

> remember that the previous constitution, what they [Fidesz] name a "Communist constitution," was very closely supervised by the EU institutions before the joining of the EU around the turn of the century... everybody who investigated the Hungarian constitutional system was satisfied and said that the Hungarian constitutional system was in harmony with the Copenhagen criteria of the EU. (Péter Hack, personal communication, May 15, 2013)

The state that was created by the old/new constitution of 1948/1989 borrowed heavily from the experience of Hungary's neighbors to the West, and a parliamentary system was adopted over the presidential system desired by the Communist Party (Arato & Miklósi 2010). The fused legislative and executive functions are empowered even more strongly by the fact that power in the Hungarian state is centralized rather than federalized, the legislature features only one house, and the President of the Republic is elected by parliament and has mainly ceremonial powers. This institutional arrangement meant the only real veto point in the system to control the government was the Constitutional Court, which was designed as one of the most powerful examples of such a body in the world (Scheppele 1999).

The Court was created in October 1989 as a result of the Round Table Talks, with its first five judges being elected by the then existing parliament, with the agreement that the Court's remaining judges (for a total of eleven members of the court) would be elected by the subsequent parliament after democratic elections. While these judges would be elected by a 2/3 vote in parliament, seemingly making them highly dependent on one or two parties (and potentially just the government on those occasions it controlled a 2/3 majority), the *nomination* procedures under the 1989 constitutional rules strongly empowered the parliamentary opposition, resulting in a justices that were consensus choices (Bánkuti, Halmai, & Scheppele 2012*b*). The parliamentary committee tasked with the nomination of individuals to the Constitutional Court consisted of one representative from each parliamentary party, regardless of the number of parliamentary seats controlled by the party. During the government in power from 1990 to 1994, this meant the committee was balanced, with the three members each representing a party in the government coalition counterbalanced by representatives from the three parties in opposition. The 1994–98 parliament underlines even more clearly how minoritarian this nomination procedure in fact was: the government, with 72% of seats in parliament, controlled only two of the six seats in the committee, with an equal number controlled by two parties who each received only 7% of the vote and combined held only 11% of the parliamentary seats.[24] Melton & Ginsburg (2014) make a persuasive argument that having multiple institutional actors involved in the process of appointing judges to apex courts is critical, as this minimizes nakedly political appointments and decreases the dependence of those appointed on any one actor. While the Hungarian system did not use multiple institutional actors, its procedures for nomination distributed power among multiple political actors in such a way that the result was consensus picks whose credentials and independence were very high (Péter Kovács, personal communication, May 10, 2013).

The Hungarian Constitutional Court was not commonly referred to as the strongest in the world because of its independence-enhancing selection procedures, however, but rather because of the powers the court wielded, specifically its power of *actio popularis* (Kovács & Tóth 2011, Kelemen 2014). Hans Kelsen considered this form of constitutional review as the most powerful (Gárdos-Orosz

[24] One of these parties, notably, was Fidesz, who removed this minoritarian nomination procedure in 2010, as we will see.

2012), and the reason is obvious: *actio popularis* allows any individual the right to challenge the constitutionality of any law, provision, or regulation and request its annulment. Given that increased avenues of access to a court are widely seen as increasing a court's power and influence (Ginsburg 2003, Dallara, & Vauchez 2012, Robertson 2014), one can see that *actio popularis* should be associated with quite powerful constitutional courts. The specific Hungarian implementation of this further expanded the scope of the court's jurisdiction, however, by allowing individuals to challenge the unconstitutionality of an omission; that is, the lack of a law required to ensure the protection of a constitutionally enumerated right (Act XXXII of 1989, Act on the Constitutional Court Para. 21). This in turn was further expanded by the jurisprudence of the Court, which defined those as eligible to include not just natural but also legal persons, and not just Hungarian citizens but foreign citizens and stateless individuals (Gárdos-Orosz 2012). This *actio popularis* thus massively expanded access to the court, empowering the court with ex post review based on the petition of a single individual or organization. László Sólyom, first President of the Constitutional Court and later President of the Republic, argues that *actio popularis* was critical in establishing the significant role played by the court in Hungarian political and constitutional life, noting that not only were approximately 90% of applications from citizens rather than state actors, but also that "the large part of the laws challenged would never have been brought to court by ministers or parliamentarians because that would have contradicted governmental interests" (Sólyom 2003, 151).

The developments of 1989 follow the logic of the de jure insurance theory remarkably well, as scholars have noted (Halmai 2002, Lembcke, & Boulanger 2012). As Arato & Miklósi (2010, 360) explain, "the outcome of any popular elections, either presidential or legislative, was vastly unpredictable, especially for the legislature." In fact, Arato & Miklósi (2010, 368) go on to contend that the biggest institutional example of the practical effects of this uncertainty were the formal powers of the new Constitutional Court: "For Hungary's 1989–90 constitution, both the creation and the judicial practice of the Constitutional Court to a large extent reflect the circumstances of negotiated transitions." None of the actors involved in the decision-making process of the Round Table Talks had any clear expectations about the distribution of power after the first elections, due to the fluid and changing nature of the political environment, which was furthered by the general lack of popular connections among the newly established, elite-driven member organizations of the Opposition Round Table (this is in large contrast to Poland, where Solidarity was a unified organization with significant linkages between the leadership and the population). There were eight actors involved in the talks, only one of which—the Communist Party—existed two years before the talks began. While two of the opposition groups were formally reformed from parties existing during the inter-war era, like the other five they were effectively brand new organizations.

This uncertainty observed in the moment of constitution-drafting (or more appropriately, constitution-amending) coalesced into an electoral system with significantly high levels of competition and volatility. In the first election, no party obtained more than one quarter of the popular vote, and in the second not only did no party receive more than a third, but the largest vote-getter had placed fourth in the previous election. The second government, consisting of a Socialist–liberal coalition, was then followed by a center-right coalition where the largest government party controlled less than 40% of parliamentary seats. By this third election the electoral arena had settled into an arena possessing one each of large center-right and center-left parties along with a number of smaller parties. These parties alternated in government, and in the fourth and fifth post-communist elections (2002 and 2006) had almost equal and consistent levels of popular support. This highly competitive electoral environment is further evidenced by the levels of electoral volatility observed: according to the version of the Pedersen Index modified for the high levels of party entry and exit observed in Eastern Europe (Birch 2003, Epperly 2011), the mean level of electoral volatility in the first two post-communist decades was nearly 30, and the only time it dropped below 20 was the 2006 election where results among the two main parties repeated the previous contest.

Thus, from the era of constitutional adoption to the 2010 elections, the Hungarian electoral arena was one highly supportive of judicial independence. The uncertainty and fragmentation of parties during constitution drafting produced a constitutional tribunal with significant power and almost unprecedented access, and for twenty years a highly competitive political environment sustained high levels of de jure and de facto judicial independence. The collapse of this environment, hinted at before and confirmed by the results of the 2010 elections, however, radically changed the status of the Constitutional Court.

4.2.3 2010–2011: Constant Constitutional Revision

Having presented the political and institutional context that the 2010 elections overthrew, I can now examine the policies enacted by Fidesz in the aftermath of their supermajority victory. Fidesz engaged in a wholesale revision of both the legal and institutional order after securing a constitutional majority, actions that were self-described by Victor Orbań as both a "constitutional revolution" and "legislative storm." This storm required significant changes to the Constitution: in its first year of office, Fidesz amended the constitution a dozen times, and these amendments involved modifying over fifty constitutional provisions (Kovács & Tóth 2011, Bánkuti, Halmai, & Scheppele 2012*a*). These changes naturally brought the Hungarian Constitutional Court's role into sharp focus, as the court existed as the only veto point in the unicameral, non-federal Hungarian political system. The revolution pursued by Fidesz can be easily divided into two eras, demarcated by the date the new constitution (or Basic Law) came into force, January 1, 2012.[25] In this section I will address the government's actions towards the Constitutional Court in this first period before the institutional landscape was revised by the new constitution.[26]

Three specific changes that took place at the beginning of Fidesz's constitutional revolution are critical to understand the attack on the de jure independence of the court after 2010. The first of these was a constitutional amendment introduced within weeks of Fidesz assuming office, passing soon after. Because the composition of the parliamentary committee that nominated judges to the Court consisted of one representative from each parliamentary party, on occasion the court did not have its full complement of eleven members, in part because it was much easier to fill members of the court if there were two vacancies, which according to one former justice allowed compromise and the nomination of two candidates acceptable to all, one by the left and one by the right, ensuring that the court remained "more or less in equilibrium where half belonged to the political right, and the other to the left" (Péter Kovács, personal communication, May 10, 2013). This informal institution was self-enforcing, providing there was an at least as many parties in opposition as in government, which was all but assured due to Hungary's mixed-member proportional electoral system. Arguing that the then existing committee rules did "not provide for the continuous and uninterrupted functioning of the institution," Fidesz MP Márta Mátrai introduced legislation that would shift the composition of this nominating committee so that rather than one member from each parliamentary party it would have eight seats, distributed in accordance with each party's seats in parliament more broadly (Balogh 2010).

The implications of this de jure change for the independence of the Hungarian Constitutional Court are clear. Instead of a nomination process involving the equal input of a half dozen actors from competing political parties, the nomination process became by definition the decision of the government, as they are assured to have a majority in the nominating committee. While the 2/3 majority vote in parliament to appoint a nominee did not change, which might constrain governments that—unlike Fidesz in 2010—lack a supermajority from unilaterally placing their nominated justice on the court, it blocks any opposition input during the nomination stage, meaning the justices to the court are appointed by a single actor, rather than the multiplicity of actors that better ensures an independent judiciary. Two important institutional aspects of the Hungarian system must be

[25] Technically the name of the new constitution is the Basic (or Fundamental, depending on the preferred translation) Law, to differentiate it from the "historical constitution" of Hungary. In general I employ the term constitution.

[26] As noted, Fidesz pursued a host of policies, laws, and constitutional amendments affecting other institutions beyond the Constitutional Court. Though of vital importance, these are largely ignored here so the focus can remain on the issue of judicial independence.

kept in mind when considering the implications of this change, which might seem benign to those more accustomed to political appointments of judges.[27] First, the fact that until 2010, balance was seen as an important goal in both the process of nomination and the role of the court. This is illustrated not only by the comments above of one of the former judges of the Court, but also by the distribution of justices: when Fidesz took power in 2010, despite eight years of Socialist governments the court was split equally between four judges of the left and four of the right, with the remaining member being seen as a consensual centrist candidate (Szente 2016). Second, the nature of the separation of powers in the institutional arrangement of the Hungarian state is such that the Court is the only meaningful check on the fused legislative and executive. Absent any devolved powers to sub-national governments, a second legislative house, an independent executive, or ordinary courts with the ability to rule on the constitutionality of government laws and regulations, the Constitutional Court's independence from the executive was critical to maintaining the separation of powers.

The second important change for the Constitutional Court that occurred after Fidesz acquired a constitutional majority in parliament exacerbated the ways in which the first undermined the independence of the Court. Not long after changing the nomination rules, Fidesz amended the constitution to expand the size of the court from eleven to fifteen justices. This classic example of court-packing meant that, after filling the two seats on the Court that were empty when assuming power, Fidesz was able to quickly place another four judges on the Court (Uitz 2015). In other words, in one year it had appointed six justices, who, if able to convince two of the four conservative justices already on the court when Fidesz was elected in 2010, would have a majority on the only institution capable of checking the actions of the government. Within half a decade, the result was a court consisting solely of justices nominated by Fidesz with no support from opposition parties (or, in the case of a handful of justices nominated after February of 2015 but before the 2018 elections, with the support of one opposition MP). The unilateral expansion of the size of the court's effects on the independent functioning of the Constitutional Court are obvious, and widely condemned by the domestic opposition and international actors.

The third and most straightforward attack on the de jure independence of the Hungarian Constitutional Court during the first year of Fidesz's constitutional majority occurred via a further amendment to the constitution. This amendment explicitly limited the Court's powers of judicial review of certain types of legislation based on their content, and was passed in the wake of the first Court ruling against legislation passed by the new government (Kovács & Tóth 2011). After

[27] The fact that justices to the Supreme Court of the United States are nominated by the executive with only majority advise and consent input by the Senate was not lost on Fidesz, who referenced this in justifications of the change.

changing the nomination process of the court, Fidesz passed an amendment to the constitution that would allow for retroactive taxes on funds received from the state, "if the income was given contrary to good morals" (Constitution of Hungary, Art. 70/I(2), 2010). After passing this amendment, Fidesz enacted legislation taxing public sector severance pay above a specific threshold at the rate of 98%, retroactive to all severance paid after January 1, 2010. In line with the new amendment, the Constitutional Court ruled that the 98% tax did not affect solely state payments made contrary to good morals (such as golden parachutes paid to certain high-ranking state employees connected with the previous government), but also payments made according to existing statute, which could not be considered to be in violation and thus could not be taxed retroactively (Decision 184/2010, Hungarian Constitutional Court).

The government's response was two-pronged. The day after the decision, State Secretary Mihály Varga commented publicly that the constitution, not government policy, required change (Lembcke & Boulanger 2012). As such, it passed another amendment that tracked the logic of the Court's decision precisely, allowing any state incomes, not just those given contrary to good morals, to be taxed retroactively and granting the government a five-year window in which to do so. Second, and more important for the Court, it proposed a constitutional amendment that forbid the Court from reviewing any government actions that were not subject to popular referendum, substantially restricting the court's jurisdiction (Kovács & Tóth 2011). The Hungarian Constitutional Court, normally circumspect with regard to public pronouncements, responded by issuing a press release defending its right to review government policy without restriction by area.[28] This opinion was echoed by opposition parties, civil society, and international actors, resulting in the government shelving the amendment and instead proposing, and passing, an amendment restricting the jurisdiction of the Court on matters relating to the budget, central government taxes, duties, and any central state requirements affecting local taxes to those instances where the petition to the court is made with exclusive reference to the following rights: citizenship; life; dignity; protection of personal data; or freedom of thought, conscience, or religion. That is, rights that budgetary and tax matters by and large do not effect. Notably missing from the list were the right to property, non-discrimination, or proportionality of burden sharing, all of which budgets and taxes can easily violate (Bánkuti, Halmai, & Scheppele 2012b, Kovács & Tóth 2011). Indeed, it was precisely the prohibition of discrimination and the right to property that the Court had in the previous

[28] István Stumpf, the first judge nominated by Fidesz in 2010, who has received a reputation of uniquely not towing the government line, suggests (echoing Jeff Staton) that the Court's self-imposed disconnect from the public that has characterized the Court since its creation is a key contributing factor to the lack of public understanding of and support for it's role in Hungarian politics (István Stumpf, personal communication, May 30, 2013).

decades used to declare tax measures and other state actions unconstitutional (Lembcke & Boulanger 2012).[29]

That this change of the Court's jurisdiction, making it impossible to exercise its powers over large swathes of legislation, is a significant constriction of the court's powers and attack on its de jure independence is obvious, and further illustrated by the fact that this decision made the Hungarian Constitutional Court the only constitutional court in the world whose powers were constrained by the area of governmental policy being examined (Halmai 2012). These three entirely legal changes to the de jure powers of the court—formal constitutional changes in the selection procedures, size, and jurisdiction—combined to produce a court that by the close of Fidesz's first year in power was far weaker in a de jure sense than it had been before, and were achieved without engaging in any measures exerting undue influence over the judiciary (Péter Kovács, personal communication, May 10, 2013). As Bánkuti, Halmai, & Scheppele (2012*a*, 138) explain, describing the events to occur after the 2010 election, "What happened next was a mistake of constitutional design." Democracy, the rule of law, and judicial independence in Hungary were indeed all compromised in the first year due to a mistake of constitutional design. But constitutional the moves were, nonetheless. And that was only the first year.

4.2.4 A New Constitution

Concurrent with its amendment to change the process of nominating justices to the Constitutional Court, Fidesz passed another amendment with even more far-reaching ramifications. As noted, the Socialist–liberal coalition in power from 1994 to 1998 possessed a 2/3 constitutional majority, but due in no small part to the nature of coalitional politics was unable to establish a new constitutional order; it was, however, able to pass a constitutional amendment enshrining that any future constitution drafting would require a 4/5 majority of parliament. As such a 4/5 supermajority requirement would prevent Fidesz from drafting a new constitution, one of the party's earlier actions after assuming office was to pass a constitutional amendment removing this 4/5 requirement.[30]

With the 4/5 requirement out of the way, Fidesz quickly began the process of crafting a new constitution while simultaneously revising the existing constitution

[29] Without this constraint, the government's later compulsory nationalization of private pension funds, "one of the major instruments of the government coalition's financial recovery programme," would doubtless have been declared unconstitutional (Sztompka 1998, 133).

[30] The removal of an amendment mandating a 4/5 requirement to draft a new constitution via the means of a 2/3 majority was technically legal, as the 4/5 amendment did not specifically denote that it was exempted from the standard constitutional requirement of a 2/3 majority for change. Regardless, many argue that the action violated the law nonetheless (Kis 2012).

as necessary. One month after taking office, Fidesz issued a proclamation of "national cooperation," which among other things declared:

> In spring 2010, the Hungarian nation gathered its strength once again, and brought about a successful revolution in the polling booth. Parliament declares that it recognizes and will respect this constitutional revolution.
>
> Parliament declares that a new social contract was born in April by which the Hungarians decided to establish a new system of National Cooperation. This historic act of the Hungarian nation obliged the Parliament and the emerging new government to deliberately, unmoving and unscrupulously direct the work by which Hungary will build the system of National Cooperation (Parliament of Hungary 2010).

To achieve this goal, Fidesz established a parliamentary committee tasked with determining the outline of the new constitutional order. When it became clear that the government's plan was a Constitutional Court with severely limited powers, however, the opposition withdrew its membership from the committee (Lembcke & Boulanger 2012). This committee published its plan by the end of 2010, but by early 2011 Fidesz decided that the work of the committee would be advisory at best, and tasked a committee of three to write the new constitution. This committee, rather than being directed by an agent of the Hungarian parliament or government, was an extraparliamentary committee consisting of three Fidesz politicians and led by a Member of the European Parliament (Bánkuti, Halmai, & Scheppele 2012*a*). While the committee was drafting the constitution, a National Consultation Body was established, which issued a survey to citizens asking about twelve general issues. This survey included no questions about the architecture of government, the role of institutional actors, or the separation of powers. Instead, it asked for public thoughts on the role of the family, the need for mothers to possess proxy votes for their children, and the possible need for including life imprisonment in the new constitution. Before the results were fully tabulated (Kovács & Tóth 2011), the committee of three individuals completed their draft of the constitution—famously claimed to have been written on an iPad—and it was submitted to parliament. Notably, the proposed new constitution was submitted not as governmental legislation, but as a "private member's bill," a maneuver that avoids requirements for governmental legislation to consult opposition and civil society organizations. After the draft text was submitted to parliament and publicized, the government scheduled five days of parliamentary debate about the general concept of the proposed constitution, followed by four concerning specific details. By the end of these sessions, the opposition has abandoned any involvement in the process, refusing to legitimize it by casting votes against the document (Bánkuti, Halmai, & Scheppele 2012*b*). The new constitution was officially promulgated on April 25, 2011, the first anniversary of the election in which Fidesz won a constitutional majority, and would take effect at the beginning of 2012; in one year the party had amended the existing constitution a dozen times before replacing it with an entirely new document which had no effective input from other political actors or the public.[31]

The "Fidesz constitution" that came into effect on January 1, 2012, was a further attack on the de jure independence of the Hungarian Constitutional Court. It enshrined the three constitutional amendments discussed into the new document; despite the third change being justified as a temporary measure to handle the budgetary mess Fidesz inherited in 2010, it was made permanent by inclusion in Article 37 (Section 4) of the Public Finances section, not Article 24, covering the Constitutional Court. As a result, whenever "state debt exceeds half of the Gross Domestic Product," the Hungarian Constitutional Court has no ability to review government policy relating to the "central budget, the implementation of the central budget, central taxes, duties and contributions, customs duties and the central conditions for local taxes" except in matters related to "rights to life and human dignity, to the protection of personal data, to freedom of thought, conscience and religion, or the rights related to Hungarian citizenship" (Constitution of Hungary, 2012). Given first that these are not the rights directly effected by the listed matters, and second that Hungarian debt was 80% of GDP when Fidesz took power, 90% when the constitution was drafted, and according to the World Bank surpassed 97% in 2016, this means practically that the Court has been for the foreseeable future stripped of much of its competencies.[32] In case the economic future were to be bright, and the Court would thus be able to review the Fidesz-era policies concerning budgetary and fiscal matters, Section 5 of Article 37 codifies that even if state debt does not exceed 50% of GDP, none of these policies enacted when it did exceed 50% would become reviewable by the Court.

The new constitution also introduced another significant development. While the three amendments enacted in 2010–2011 undermined de jure independence with regards to selection procedures, size, and jurisdiction, the constitution restricted access to the court.[33] Specifically, it removed the ex post *actio popularis* powers of the court that had been so critical to its development of the post-communist rule of law and its role as an active player in Hungarian politics (Sólyom 2003).[34] While the new constitution did introduce German-style concrete

[31] Though not discussed here for reasons of brevity, by early 2013 the new Hungarian constitution was already on its 4th major amendment.

[32] This point is all the more clear once one considers that Hungarian debt has never been below 50% of GDP in the post-communist era.

[33] One de jure change that would be considered positive for the independence of the judiciary is the extension of tenure length from nine years to twelve years. Given the two vacant seats, the addition of four new seats, and the ability to appoint two additional judges before the next election, however, what this in practice did was ensure that the majority of judges on the court for over a decade would be appointed by Fidesz, with no input from opposition parties.

[34] According to another justice of the Constitutional Court, *actio popularis* was also of vital importance because it provided a link between the citizens and the Court, and is one of the reasons why the Court was widely respected among Hungarian citizens (Miklós Lévay, personal communication, May 30, 2013).

constitutional complaints, few consider this to offset the significant restriction of access that the removal of *actio popularis* signifies (Bánkuti, Dombos, Fleck, Halmai, Rozgonyi, Majtényi, Majtényi, Polgári, Lane, Scheppele, et al. 2012, Bánkuti, Halmai, & Scheppele 2012*a*, Gárdos-Orosz 2012, Lembcke & Boulanger 2012, Trajectory of Democracy 2013, Kelemen 2014, Bozóki 2015, Uitz 2015, Szente 2016). The restriction on access is beyond contestation when one recognizes that the substitute of complaints where rights are directly violated offers fewer avenues for judicial review of laws than a system of access in which all persons natural or legal have the right to submit a complaint against the constitutionality of any law regardless of whether it effects them.

As a result of this change, the only actors in Hungary who possess the ability to submit abstract complaints against the constitutionality of laws are the government, the President (for preliminary review), the ombudsman (who like the President is appointed by the government), or one quarter of parliament (Kovács & Tóth 2011). As Kelemen (2014) notes, this 25% requirement is comparably high for European democracies, with only two possessing a higher threshold of parliamentarians necessary for review of laws, and the only other country with the same threshold being Germany. Beyond 25% of the members of the Bundestag, however, Article 93 of the German constitution extends significant complaint powers to both the governments and constitutional courts of the *Länder*.[35] Practically, in contemporary Hungarian politics this has meant there have been few challenges to Fidesz policies by these actors: Fidesz appointed both the President and the ombudsman, and the distribution of political forces within parliament would require coordination between the Socialists and the far-right nationalist party Jobbik, and such cooperation has been predictably almost non-existent.[36] As such, the ability of the Hungarian Constitutional Court to weigh in on the constitutionality of government policy has been restricted primarily to individual constitutional complaints, and even here, fiscal and budgetary policies remain beyond review.

4.2.5 The Ordinary Courts

While the focus of this book is the independence of primarily constitutional and high courts, two changes to the de jure independence of ordinary courts in Hungary are nonetheless worthy of brief comment, as they are significant and

[35] If it has not become increasingly clear, one of the key lessons from the Hungarian experience for the development of the rule of law is that the implications of specific institutional arrangements or powers cannot be examined in isolation, but rather must be considered as part of a broader constellation of rules and actors.

[36] Even those sympathetic to the government and the new constitution point out that this "gives the impression that the right to make a petition is tailored to the voting proportions of the present legislative cycle, so the constitutive majority can impede the submission of petitions" (Jakab & Sonnevend 2013, 123).

received much attention. The first of these is the restructuring of the judicial administration, conducted via a 2/3 cardinal law weeks before the new constitution was to take effect. From 1997 until this change, the Hungarian judiciary had been self-administering, with committees of judges choosing who would serve on the lower courts. The transitional laws included the creation of a National Office for the Judiciary (NOJ), and the appointment of a President of the Office with significant, and significantly unchecked, powers. The President of the NOJ was given the ability to appoint, promote, and begin disciplinary proceedings of judges, and new judges are in their post for a three-year probationary term, after which they are retained or let go by the NOJ (Scheppele 2012*a*).[37] In addition, the President has the power to transfer cases from one court to another in an almost unchecked manner (Bánkuti, Halmai, & Scheppele 2012*a*). This latter power has been justified due to the disparate caseloads facing judges in different parts of the country (with judges in Budapest particularly overloaded); however, the lack of clearly defined procedures or justifications for the transfer affords the President of the NOJ significant discretion over what cases are transferred where.[38]

The concern here for the independence of the judiciary is not only the concentration of power over the administration of the ordinary courts in a single individual (Halmai 2017), but the fact that this person is appointed directly by the Prime Minister and afterwards faces no effective oversight of their administration of the judiciary. Two factors increase this concern. First, not only that the tenure of the President of the NOJ is nine years, and thus the government will be effective in exerting dead-hand control over the entire normal judiciary well into the future, but also because staffing the position requires a 2/3 vote of parliament. If parliament cannot appoint a new head of the NOJ, the previous head will remain in the position until parliament is able to muster the requisite 2/3 agreement. This means that even if Fidesz were to lose future elections, as long as it retains at least a third of parliament it is able to keep its agent in the position indefinitely. Second, the nature of the individual chosen has caused particular consternation among domestic and foreign critics (Rozenberg 2012). The first (and to date only) President is Tünde Handó, who although previously a judge, is also a long-time personal friend of the Prime Minister and wife of the Fidesz MEP in charge of the extraparliamentary committee that was tasked with drafting the constitution.

[37] Although for appointment of judges the candidates are given scores on numerous aspects of qualification, the only check on the President of the NOJ's discretion for appointment is the requirement to provide a written explanation for why they did not choose the top candidate (Tünde Handó, personal communication, May 15, 2013).

[38] When pressed on the specific rules and ex ante conditions guiding the transfer of cases and the constraints on the powers of the President of the National Office of the Judiciary to transfer cases, the President justified the powers by stating that control of transfer only applies to new cases and stressing that judges are independent due to constitutional provisions (Tünde Handó, personal communication, May 15, 2013). Notably, this was only weeks after the draft report by the European Parliament (the Tavares report, named after the MEP serving as the rapporteur) made headlines by among other things explicitly directing Hungary to establish objective criteria for the transfer of cases.

The second significant manner in which the independence of the ordinary judiciary was undermined was by lowering the retirement age of judges, which without warning compelled a significant portion of the upper echelons of the Hungarian judiciary to retire. This action forced almost 300 judges into retirement, among them 40% of the court presidents at the county level (the most important sub-national jurisdiction in Hungary), 40% of the court presidents at the appellate level, and 25% of the judges of the Supreme Court (Bánkuti, Halmai, & Scheppele 2012*b*).[39] Less than two months later, the government suspended the then existing appointment procedures by which the judiciary staffed vacant positions, holding all appointments in abeyance until the subsequent year and the creation of the National Office of the Judiciary (Halmai 2017). The result was the ability for Fidesz's chosen individual to oversee the appointment of a wide swathe of the Hungarian judiciary; when the President of the NOJ appointed 129 judges on one day only two months after taking office, less than 20% had prior judicial experience (Scheppele 2012*a*).

This move's potential long-term implications for the judicial hierarchy and its alignment with one party are clear, and received significant condemnation from the usual sources of the European Union and Council of Europe. Even when both the Hungarian Constitutional Court and the Court of Justice for the European Union ruled against the government in a suit brought by a number of judges who were dismissed for being older than the new retirement age, the government still in effect won. This is because while the rulings by the Court of Justice required the re-employment of judges, the specific senior positions held by most of the judges in question had already been filled, and the President of the NOJ had made it clear those who had replaced them would not be removed from their positions (Halmai 2017). As a result, the overwhelmingly majority of judges did not return to the judiciary, as they would have had to assume junior positions, and only a handful of judges ended up returning to their previous senior positions (András Kádár, personal communication, May 29, 2013).

4.2.6 The Public Response

Fidesz's undermining of the formal independence of the Constitutional Court and ordinary judiciary was by and large met with indifference on the part of the public. The two key reasons for this are, first, the general hostility felt towards the Socialist Party for its corruption and ineptitude when in power from 2002 to 2010, and second the nature of the de jure attacks carried out by the Orbán

[39] While this move was opposed by many members of the judiciary, it was unsurprisingly supported by many of those whose careers would advance more rapidly due to the removal of a significant portion of judges at the higher levels (Zoltán Fleck, personal communication, May 6, 2013).

government. The former highlights the important role of political competition, and the latter the degree to which transparency and a popular understanding of the issue is vital for sustaining public backlash. This is not to suggest there was no public opposition to the government's policies. In fact, there was a significant protest (observers say between 50,000–100,000 people) against the government's January 2, 2012 gala at the Budapest opera house celebrating their new constitution coming into force. This protest, however, underscores the degree to which public apathy and opposition unpopularity made the government's continued assault possible: twenty months after the landslide elections, and eighteen months after the process of constant constitutional revision began, these protests against the party celebrating the constitution coming into effect "was the first time that opposition groups, from political parties to civil organizations, joined forces to rally against the new Constitution" (Karasz & Eddy 2012).

This is in no small part because the opposition to the Fidesz government was discredited, unpopular, and in disarray (Mudde & Jenne 2012). The main center-left party had presided over years of corruption, poor economic performance even before the 2008 global financial crisis, and was exposed as entirely cynical by Gyurcsány's leaked secret speech; the other party in coalition with the Socialists during the previous governments had failed to reach even the 5% threshold. Of the two other parties that had made it into parliament, Jobbik was a far-right nationalist party that no other party would associate with, while the other was a new Green-ish party, the LMP (Politics Can Be Different), whose leadership spent a significant amount of time before and after the 2010 election criticizing the MSZP. That the opposition had not come together to oppose the government *before* the constitution went into effect is telling, and so too is the fact that it was not until the end of 2012 that the opposition groups (minus Jobbik) established an umbrella organization, Together 2014, to work together to oppose the constitutional revolution at that point already two and a half years old (Bozóki 2015). Unfortunately, the very next month LMP's decision at its party congress not to join this organization fractured the party, and by the beginning of 2013 its parliamentary leader and others had abandoned LMP to form a new organization (MTI 2012). Internal discord and jockeying for position within the opposition ensured further delay of any coordinated efforts to offer the Hungarian voters a credible alternative to Fidesz, which finally occurred when "in January 2014, a leftist electoral alliance was created, just three months before the April 2014 elections. It was far too late." (Bozóki 2015, 29) This electoral coalition, Unity, consisted of four parties (but not LMP), two led by former Socialist Prime Ministers: Ferenc Gyurcsány, who refused to step down after his speech admitting to ineffective governance and systematic deception was leaked, but who later resigned, and Gordon Bajnai, who succeeded Gyurcsány and instituted significant austerity policies before refusing to run in the 2010 elections (a third was led by the Socialist prime ministerial candidate in the 2010 elections). That this gallery of politicians associated with the era of Socialist corruption did not inspire Hungarian voters is unsurprising (Csipke 2014),[40] and the alliance faced a crushing defeat in the 2014 elections, capturing less than 20% of the seats, barely more than the far-right Jobbik.

The above illustrates clearly the importance of a credible opposition in both restraining the party in power according to the insurance as well as the public backlash logic. While Fidesz did take a heavy hit to its popularity in the polls in its first year in office, this is widely attributable to the economic calamity facing Hungary, and once this was checked it saw its popularity rise again (Bozóki 2015). At no point was the opposition able to offer any credible threat to Fidesz, who rather saw only continued chaos among the left, center-left, and centrist opposition. Almost a decade later, the opposition remains in disarray, with multiple competing groups, some still led by those, like Gyurcsány, associated with past failures. Public opinion polls in July 2017 of citizens in Budapest—less conservative than the country as a whole, historically the heart of opposition to Fidesz, and one of the few places that Unity did well in 2014—showed that support for Fidesz remained double that of the second place Socialists, who themselves performed only marginally better than Jobbik (Adam 2017*a*). The continued unpopularity of the opposition and their inability to offer a credible electoral threat to Fidesz further ensured that any potential unpopularity of its moves would not face public backlash, and that it had little reason to fear losing power.

Scholars routinely point to the fractured state of center and left political actors since 2010 as an explanation for Fidesz's continued dominance of politics and free hand with remaking the constitutional order (Mudde & Jenne 2012, Mudde 2014, Bozóki 2015); when it comes to Fidesz's changes to the Constitutional and ordinary courts specifically, legal experts in Hungary and members of the Constitutional Court almost universally reference the lack of public outcry or interest in the policies that have significantly constrained the de jure independence of the court. This is not to say that *other* Fidesz's policies did not rouse public interest, and that interest did not constrain the government: there were large protests and significant public opposition to Fidesz's policies that would require Hungarians to remain in Hungary for two years for each year they studied at university or pay a significant tax (Péter Kovács, personal communication, May 10, 2013). This policy, like many others, was easily understood by citizens and, directly affecting them, inspired opposition.

The precise role of the court and the specific rules concerning selection and jurisdiction, however, are neither easily understood nor directly relevant to

[40] It is worth quoting Mudde (2014) at length: "The euphemistically named Unity coalition was doomed from the beginning. The internal situation within the coalition is the literal opposite of its name: Although ideologically close, all five parties are almost more divided by personality clashes than united in their opposition to Orbán. It took months for the various leaders, virtually all stalwarts of the last unpopular MSZP government, to agree to one electoral list. The many centrist voters looking for a credible center-left alternative largely ignored or rejected the coalition."

citizens. This indifference and lack of understanding is noted by Hungarian legal experts from both the right and the left, and with regards to both the ordinary judiciary and the Constitutional Court.[41] The sentiment expressed by many legal scholars that the matter was too complicated to rouse public interest or understanding was echoed by both left-leaning and conservative justices of the Constitutional Court. Justice Lévay suggests that, "average Hungarians more or less cannot understand what's going on in our court," a sentiment echoed by his colleague Justice Kovács, who thinks that, "concerning the problem of constitution versus Basic Law or competencies with the Constitutional Court and the changes, probably it is too abstract." (Miklós Lévay, personal communication, May 30, 2013, Péter Kovács, personal communication, May 10, 2013). There is certainly reason to think that such sentiments are accurate: the government did not, after all, simply sack all the judges appointed by the Socialist government, and instead changed the specific composition of a parliamentary committee and the Court's jurisdiction on certain matters, considering certain rights, under certain economic conditions. The increase in the size of the court might have been the one issue easily understood and able to capture public attention, but even here the government was successful in framing the issue as one of efficiency, given the overwhelming number of petitions created by *actio popularis*.

Given the complexity of jurisdictional issues and the specifics of the composition of parliamentary committees, it is likely the case that absent popular opposition parties able to mobilize citizens these issues are simply too removed from people's lives to be of interest (András Kádár, personal communication, May 29, 2013). If this is the case, then it further cements the role of political competition, not only for its ability to induce respect for fear of what happens after losing power, but also for its importance in linking government actions that undermine judicial independence and the rule of law to the public backlash that might constrain such behavior. This has implications not only for my argument regarding the de jure/de facto split, but also for existing theories about the role that public pressure and coordination play in maintaining judicial independence and the rule of law more broadly (Weingast 1997, Vanberg 2001).

4.2.7 De Jure not De Facto

For fear of being misunderstood, I feel compelled to state explicitly that I in no way mean to offer an apologia for the Fidesz government's undermining of the

[41] Examples from the right and left are, respectively, Pál Sonnevend (personal communication, May 13, 2013) and Péter Hack (personal communication, May 15, 2013). The latter went as far as to suggest that "in Hungary if you stop anybody in the street they would know much more about the American judicial system than about the Hungarian system because they are watching the American films and very few people are appearing before courts."

independence of the Hungarian Constitutional Court and ordinary judiciary; one can be normatively opposed to such changes while still recognizing that most all of them were entirely legal, following the constitutional rules in place.[42] The question as to whether these changes were bad for independence of the judiciary are different from whether they were illegal, and the fact that these and other actions have together substantially weakened the rule of law does not detract from their formal characteristics. Although what occurred was indeed a failure of constitutional design, that does not make it any less constitutional. Similarly, while it would likely have been far better for the rule of law in Hungary had the Constitutional Court decided previously that it had the ability to consider the constitutionality of constitutional amendments, it explicitly absolved itself of such a role in decisions in 1994 and 1998, and the majority on the Court adhered to this precedent in cases considering Fidesz amendments (Halmai 2017).[43]

First and foremost, the jurisprudence of the Hungarian Constitutional Court established that the institution—like the overwhelming majority of such institutions around the globe—lacks the explicit ability to rule on the constitutionality of constitutional amendments,[44] and while some might consider that this lack of explicit power does not constrain the Hungarian Court from doing so, like in the American case they remain in the minority (Wright 1990, Halmai 2017). Regardless, however, of whether such constitutionality is in theory possessed by a constitutional tribunal either abstractly or in the specifics of the Hungarian case, it remains that the Court did not exert that power, even when petitions were submitted against the amendments to the 1989 and 2012 constitutions, challenging the constitutionality of these amendments. Given the overwhelming focus of the study of de jure independence has been and remains the formal constitutional provisions concerning the independence of the judiciary (Ginsburg 2003, Finkel 2005, Tate & Keith 2007, Ríos-Figueroa & Staton 2012, Melton & Ginsburg 2014), these constitutional changes are a textbook case of attacks on the de jure independence of the judiciary.

At the conceptual level, if one considers changes to the constitutional provisions affecting the judiciary that occurred according to proscribed procedures as de facto attacks on judicial independence, then one has entirely obscured the differentiation between de jure and de facto attacks on the court.[45] Those on the

[42] Most is not all, of course, and there were a handful of attacks that might be considered attacks on the de facto rather than de jure independence of the judiciary, most notably the removal of the President of the Supreme Court, András Baka, via a legal maneuver that the European Court of Human Rights deemed a violation. The vast majority of and most meaningful attacks, however, were de jure, and even the removal of Baka was done via the legal process, even if the specifics of the process were later ruled illegal.

[43] Hungarian Constitutional Court rulings 23/1994. (IV. 29.) and 1260/B/1997.

[44] Specifically, it lacks the ability to rule on the substantive constitutionality of amendments, while reserving the right to rule on the procedural constitutionality.

[45] And there is a compelling argument to be made that in obscuring the difference one would be applying the double standards about which Fidesz politicians so regularly declaim: it is not rare for the

Court are well aware of the difference, and note that while competencies have been restricted there has not been any development of the court's behavioral independence being curtailed (András Bragyova, personal communication, May 15, 2013). In fact, many of those who sounded the alarm about the changes to the de jure independence of the court have pointed out that the Court remained significantly more of a check than predicted, exerting de facto independence (Uitz 2013):

> Even though the government had cut the jurisdiction of the Constitutional Court, changed the system for electing judges, expanded the bench and packed it with party loyalists, Court President Péter Paczolay has been able to skillfully mobilize bare majorities to hand setbacks to the government. These strong decisions have honored basic rights and defended important constitutional principles, often agreeing with petitions sent to the Court by the surprisingly active Ombudsman Máté Szabó. (Scheppele 2013)

One potential response to the statement that the Court's de facto independence has remained strong despite the changes to its de jure independence is that Paczolay is no longer the Court President, and the bare majority he was able to cobble together in the first years of Fidesz power after 2010 has been replaced by judges hand-picked by the current government. Both are true, as is the fact that the majority of the judges appointed after 2010 are of a different stripe, far more aligned with the parliament than those appointed before (Pál Sonnevend, personal communication, May 13, 2013). Such is clear from the published views of some, like Justice Pokol, who have long advocated for a unitary state and Court far more deferential to parliamentary power (Balogh 2011). Indeed, both conservative and leftist Constitutional Court judges appointed before 2010 concur that the main divide after 2010 was not the previous left/right split, but rather a split on judicial philosophies and conception of the court's proper role as a constraint on parliamentary action (Péter Kovács, personal communication, May 10, 2013, and Miklós Lévay, personal communication, May 30, 2013). The exception to this has been the judicial philosophy of István Stumpf, appointed two months after Fidesz took power in 2010, whose appointment Justice Bragyova likened to President Eisenhower's "biggest mistake" of nominating Earl Warren, a mistake Fidesz would not repeat (András Bragyova, personal communication, May 15, 2013). It would be highly problematic, however, to consider the appointment of judges with philosophies of restraint to be an attack on the de facto independence of the court, or at least an attack unique to Fidesz and not found in democracies

French Constitutional Council to engage in a back and forth with parliament over the constitutionality of proposed legislation, after all (Stone Sweet 2000), and as previously noted, the rules for the selection of federal judges in the United States have changed twice in the past half decade. If one were to consider changes at the sub-national level, the de jure independence of American state courts have been in regular flux (Pilatovsky 2016).

(and autocracies) across the world; the new judges' (broadly similar) judicial philosophy has, in fact, been commonly compared to "strict constructionists" in the American sense, and many consider their decisions motivated more by politics than by law. If judicial decisions being motivated by personal attitudes is a signal of de facto dependent courts, however, then de facto independence as a concept becomes effectively meaningless.

The Hungarian experience after Fidesz achieved a constitutional majority as a result of the nigh-total collapse of support for the Socialists in the 2010 elections demonstrates the ways in which judicial independence is effected in a democracy when the competitiveness of the electoral system changes. It does so by tracing the role of competition and public opposition—or rather lack thereof—in Fidesz's changes to the de jure powers of the Hungarian Constitutional Court, illustrating the theoretical argument developed in Section 4.1. It does not, however, truly test this argument, as it was devised thinking explicitly about the Hungarian case. It is to testing it "out-of-sample" that I now briefly turn.

4.3 Testing De Jure vs. De Facto Independence beyond Hungary

To examine the relationship between changes in the competitiveness of the electoral system in democracies and autocracies and changes in de jure vs. de facto independence, I rely on much of the same data and methods discussed in Chapter 3, making the task here comparably quick and painless. Beyond introducing a measure of de jure independence, the key difference in this analysis is that rather than look at the level of judicial independence across dictatorships and democracies, I specifically look at changes to this level to ascertain whether the logic articulated in Section 4.1. That is, whether increases or decreases in competition should have differential effects depending on regime type, with democracies evidencing far more de jure changes than de facto, and autocracies the opposite.

To operationalize the changing competitiveness of electoral politics, I take the difference in the measure of political competition used in Chapter 3 in a given country-year compared to the value in the year prior, providing an obvious and direct account of the changing competitiveness of the electoral arena. In operationalizing de jure independence, I rely on the measure of de jure independence developed by Keith (2002) and Tate & Keith (2009), widely used in empirical studies of de jure independence (Keith, Tate, & Poe 2009, Conrad & Ritter 2013, Hill & Jones 2014). The conceptualization for the measure is based on the United Nations *Principles on the Independence of the Judiciary*, and it is operationalized via the first principal component score of seven constitutional provisions deemed relevant by the UN principles. These provisions are: (1) a guarantee of judicial terms and tenure; (2) a statement that judicial decisions are final; (3) a statement that courts have the exclusive authority to decide on their own competencies as defined by law; (4) whether the constitution provides for the separation of powers; (5) that judges should be selected on enumerated qualifications; (6) the existence of judicial or constitutional review of legislation; and (7) whether the judiciary is arranged hierarchically with the apex court (rather than some other actor) exercising final review of lower court decisions. Each provision is coded in an ordinal manner. For example, the provision for judicial review has four categories, noting whether the constitution gives the power of review to a different branch, fails to provide review, provides for it in a limited fashion, or provides for it fully.[46]

As I am interested in whether a change in competition (i.e. between t and t_{-1}) produces a change in the level of de jure independence, I assess whether such a one-year change in political competition is associated with a decreased value in de jure independence compared to before the change in competition occurred (i.e. between t and t_{-2}). The same procedure is conducted for the value of the Linzer & Staton (2015) measure of de facto independence discussed at length in the Chapter 1. I also include a covariate to account for the one obvious factor that might be related to changes in both de jure independence and competition, whether a regime transition has occurred during this time.[47] Like the models in Chapter 3, each is a linear model with country fixed effects (unreported), with robust standard errors clustered by country. Unlike the model reported in Chapter 3, the models here are fit to a substantially reduced number of observations, due to temporal availability of the de jure independence measure.[48]

Table 4.2 presents four linear models of judicial independence. As the object here is not to assess a conditional effect, but rather the lack of effect for competition depending on the combination of regime type and form of independence, models are fit individually by regime type and form of independence. The results in Table 4.2 provide significant support for the relationship theorized in Section 4.1 and traced in the case study of Hungary. In Models 1 and 2, fit to changes in de jure independence, changes in the competitiveness of the electoral arena in

[46] An alternative is to use the six items analyzed by Melton & Ginsburg (2014). I refrain from analyzing these, however, because the authors dichotomize each provision, restricting the amount of information available on how the constitution states these provisions. The unfortunate drawback is thus that I do not have information on tenure length or selection procedures, which are important. Although these are included in the Melton & Ginsburg analysis, the authors treat all non-life tenure as identical, running against theoretical arguments offered elsewhere (including, for example, Ginsburg 2003); similarly, their analysis of selection procedures is limited due to their exclusive focus on institutional rather than political actors, as discussed above.

[47] As the analysis here is exclusively on proximate change, the logged level of economic development, used to assess overall levels of independence in Chapter 3, no longer has the potential to confound. Regardless, its inclusion does not change the results presented.

[48] The data are fit to the 1992–2004 time span, and the Cheibub, Gandhi, & Vreeland (2009) measure of democracy is employed due to the fact that for the restricted years analyzed it has up to 28% more coverage, and models of de facto independence are restricted to this same sample for comparability. The substantive results concerning the relationship between changes in competition and independence in democratic contexts remains the same if using the Boix, Miller, & Rosato (2013) measure, with the only difference being that the substantially smaller number of observations means that the coefficient for change in competition just fails to reach the $p < 0.05$ level of statistical significance in Model 1.

Table 4.2 De jure and de facto independence. Coefficient estimates of four linear models of the two-year change in the listed form of judicial independence by regime type, with country fixed effects (not reported) and robust standard errors clustered by country.

	Δ de jure		Δ de facto	
	Model 1 Democracy	Model 2 Autocracy	Model 3 Democracy	Model 4 Autocracy
Intercept	0.16	0.03	0.02**	−0.00
	(0.21)	(0.02)	(0.01)	(0.00)
Δ Political competition	0.62*	0.26	0.02	0.05***
	(0.27)	(0.22)	(0.01)	(0.02)
Democratic breakdown	0.02	−0.29	−0.01	−0.03***
	(0.18)	(0.19)	(0.01)	(0.01)
Democratic transition	0.40*	0.14	0.02	0.04
	(0.19)	(0.37)	(0.01)	(0.02)
AIC	855.91	1358.84	−4732.42	−3934.48
BIC	1325.23	1771.17	−4262.92	−3522.15
Num. obs.	1033	893	1035	893

$^{***}p < 0.001$, $^{**}p < 0.01$, $^{*}p < 0.05$

democracies are associated with changes in the first principal components score of de jure provisions for independence: increases in competition are associated with better de jure provisions (either in number of the robustness of the measure), decreases with the opposite. In autocracies, however, the estimated coefficient is less than half the value in democracies, and does not come close to reaching conventional levels of significance. This is visualized in plot (a) of Figure 4.2, which plots the expected change in de jure independence as change in competition is allowed to vary from its observed minimum to maximum by regime type. The solid black line shows democracies, the dashed black non-democracies, with gray shaded 95% confidence intervals around each. Not only is the substantive effect of competition on de jure independence far greater in democracies, but it can also be differentiated from zero.

The exact opposite is observed in Models 3 and 4, fit to de facto changes. Here, it is only in autocracies that changes in competition are associated with significant changes in independence; in democracies, however, the effect is far smaller and not statistically significant, corroborating the results of the models in Chapter 3. Plot (b) in Figure 4.2 illustrates this graphically, with the same differences as previous plots: solid black lines represent democracies, dashed black lines non-democracies. Here, we see that changes in competition is far more salient in non-democratic regimes than in democratic.

Combined, the results of the four models presented in Table 4.2 help answer the question raised by the discordant findings of case studies in the existing literature (strongly supporting a relationship between competition and judicial

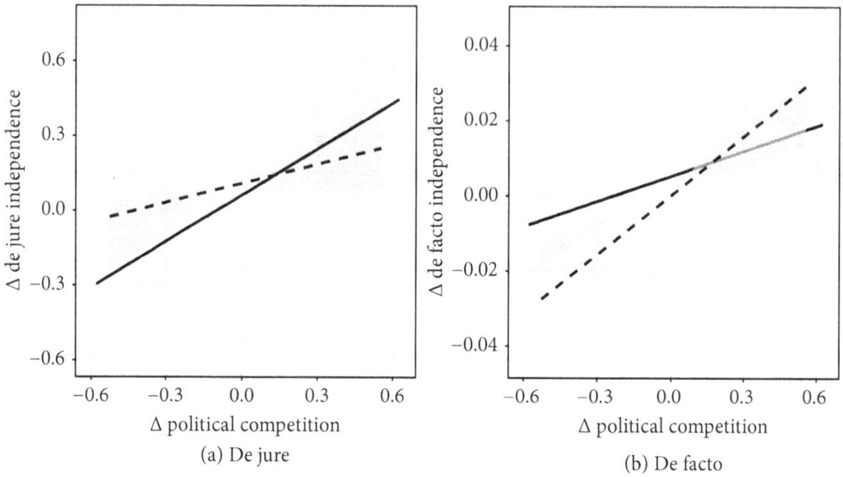

Figure 4.2 Competition, regime type, and form of independence. The expected value of latent judicial independence from the four models in Table 4.2 when change in competition is allowed to vary from its observed minimum to maximum by regime type. The solid black line reports the expected change for democracies, while the dashed black line reports non-democracies, with 95% confidence intervals shaded around each.

independence in democracies) and the analyses presented in Chapter 3. Given that many of these case studies, such as those of Ginsburg (2003) and Finkel (2008), either focus exclusively or overwhelmingly on the more easily measured de jure provisions for courts, this is more readily understood. The result is strong support for the idea that democratic leaders, when able to pursue a policy of shifting toleration of the judiciary due to changes in electoral competition, do so by increasing or decreasing the formal provisions for judicial independence.

4.4 Conclusion

The analysis presented in the case study of the Hungarian experience after the 2010 landslide victory of the right-wing Fidesz party and the cross-national analysis illustrates that the "anomalous" results in Chapter 3 for democratic regimes are not anomalous if one considers the relationship between competition and independence as one that is not only variable by regime type but also by form of judicial independence. Beyond resolving the apparent contradiction between the careful empirical results and instrumental variables analysis from Chapter 3 and the significant case study work in the existing literature, this chapter makes three important contributions to the study of law and courts. The first of these is that it offers a careful examination of how changes in competition produce changes in

Table 4.3 Competition, independence, and regime type in the literature. Examples from the comparative law and courts literature showing how existing work addresses the combination of regime type and form of independence.

	Democracy	Non-democracy
De facto	Ramseyer (1994), Aydin (2013)	Popova (2012), Epperly (2017)
De jure	Ginsburg (2003), Ramos (2006)	Moustafa (2007), Ginsburg, & Versteeg (2013)

the de jure independence of the judiciary, both by way of an in-depth case study and a cross-national corroboration of the explanation offered. Second, this chapter complicates and develops the exogenous, public backlash account of judicial independence. I show both theoretically and empirically in the Hungarian case that the public holding democratic governments to account requires integrating the endogenous insurance explanation, as without a credible opposition threat public backlash does not offer a serious enough threat to incumbents when the competitiveness of the electoral arena is in flux.

Third, and most important, it presents a development of the insurance framework that enables a far broader understanding of the relationship between competition and judicial independence than any previous approach. In the existing literature, there is little in the way of empirics and even less in the way of well-developed theorizing about how we should understand the relationship between competition, regime type, and the form of independence. To date, research has focused on one of the four potential combinations of regime type and form of judicial independence. Table 4.3 shows this by way of a two-by-two table, placing form of independence in rows and regime type in columns. Each of the four cells lists two examples of existing work that address competition's effects in the context of that specific combination of factors. The theory and empirics in previous chapters advanced our understanding by addressing both columns in the first row, looking at how competition related to de facto independence in both democracies and non-democracies. Section 4.1 presented a theoretical account of both columns in the second row, arguing that competition's effects should be concentrated in the first cell; that is, that the effects of competition for de jure independence are found primarily in democratic regimes. For this reason, I conduct an in-depth case study of an example from this cell, Hungary after 2010. Combining the theoretical arguments offered in this chapter and in Chapter 1, along with the case study and cross-national analyses presented in Section 4.2, this chapter finalizes the preliminary details of a "complete" account of competition, independence, and regime type. With reference to Table 4.2, the synthesis presented here offers a coherent way of understanding all four cells: competition matters across regime type, but how it matters differs, depending on whether the regime is democratic or autocratic. In doing so it highlights the benefits of theorizing within and beyond certain scope conditions, and hopefully sets the stage for significant further research into the conditional relationship between competition, regime type, and form of independence.

5
Conclusion

The previous four chapters have offered a new explanation for one key determinant of judicial independence, both across regime type and form of independence. Taking as a starting point the fundamental logic of insurance models of judicial independence developed in democratic contexts, I present an argument about the differential importance of electoral competition in dictatorship and democracy that I hope offers a comprehensive explanation for changes in judicial independence across regime type. In doing so I marshal various methods and forms of data, relying on cross-national statistical models and expert interviews with Constitutional Court judges and leading legal scholars in Hungary. This chapter reviews the argument I forward and speaks to some of its important implications for understanding judicial independence, the rule of law, and democracy. While I am not certain if a picture is worth a thousand words, I am sure that the visualization of arguments is of great utility, and a handful of key figures from the previous chapters are presented here again to aid in summarizing the argument.

5.1 Summary of the Argument

Before presenting my argument of judicial independence as both autocratic and democratic insurance in Chapter 1, I first had to revisit the core logic of the insurance argument as developed in democratic regimes as well as the existing explanations for insurance in autocracies. Given that few if any political actors like to bind their own hands absent some benefit of doing so, insurance accounts look at the potential benefits an independent judiciary can provide, and how this might induce the preferences of leaders towards establishing, maintaining, or deepening judicial independence. At its heart, the insurance model is an argument about an expected utility calculation made by leaders, with the outcome choice being the product of the perceived likelihood of losing office and the costs if this were to occur. In existing research focusing on democracies, this calculation is rarely formalized, and the latter half of the equation—what happens if a leader loses office—is assumed constant. As minoritarian institutions capable of providing a brake on governments revising and instituting policy, independent judiciaries serve as a

The Political Foundations of Judicial Independence in Dictatorship and Democracy. Brad Epperly, Oxford University Press (2019). © Brad Epperly
DOI: 10.1093/oso/9780198845027.001.0001

form of insurance to political actors who expect to be out of office in the future; this insurance is usually viewed as the continuation of the policies they enacted while in power, and occasionally as well the protection of minority political rights. This being held constant, the variation in the need for insurance is therefore treated purely as a function of the probability of losing office, typically conceived of as the competitiveness of the electoral environment and operationalized in some manner of varying appropriateness.

The crux of my argument is the contention that the risks associated with losing power in autocratic regimes are greater than in democracies, and therefore competition should be more salient in dictatorships than democracies. This is not, of course, to say either that competition is typically more present in autocracies, or that we should expect higher levels of judicial independence in such regimes; I do not doubt that judicial independence is, like nearly all political phenomena, far from monocausal. It is rather to suggest that competition—when it is present or develops—should have greater effect on the likelihood of independence in autocratic regimes because the stakes are higher. The reason the stakes are higher is both because autocratic power means access to wealth and state resources in a way rarely equaled in democratic regimes, and also because the likelihood of being punished after leaving office is greater for former autocrats.

Judiciaries exercising greater independence, however, can minimize the risks of being a former leader in both democratic and autocratic regimes, and I leverage this effect to create a simple expected utility model that allows me to consider both components of the logic of insurance. Using the predicted probability of being unpunished after leaving office depending on regime type and degree of judicial independence, I show the expected utility for democrats and autocrats of either choosing to pay the price for insurance or forgoing this cost. This is presented visually in Figure 5.1, which reproduces Figures 1.3 and 1.4. The fact that competition plays a greater role in autocratic rather than democratic insurance is illustrated by the relationship between the gray and black lines across the figures: in autocratic regimes the expected utility of choosing insurance is greater at lower levels of risk, whereas in democracies it requires far more certainty about losing office. This is, of course, a stylized account: the risks associated with being out of office no doubt vary across time and space both within and across regime type. This model, however, illustrates by its simplicity that the greater risks associated with being out of office in autocratic regimes should make competition, when present, far more salient. Finally, it provides by way of this clear empirical implication a distinctly different story than the strategic pressure explanation of judicial independence in electoral autocracies forwarded by Popova (2012). Rather than the insurance logic being reversed in autocratic regimes as she theorizes, my model suggests that competition's effects are even more salient.

In Chapter 2 I aim to convince the reader of the descriptive accuracy of some key mechanisms of the insurance framework—mechanisms that to date have been

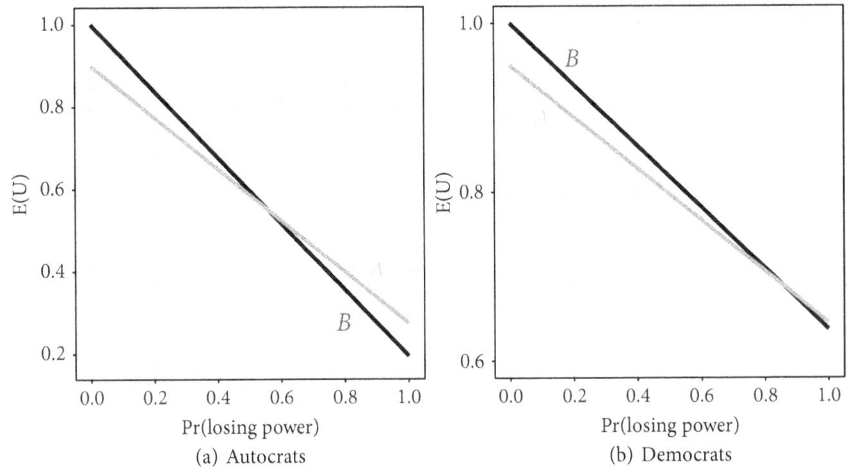

Figure 5.1 The expected utility of insurance for autocrats and democrats. The expected utility of an independent or dependent judiciary as the parameter capturing the probability of losing office is allowed to vary from 0 to 1 across autocratic and democratic regimess. The gray line is the expected utility of option *A*, buying insurance; that is, paying the costs associated with higher judicial independence to reap the decreased likelihood of punishment if one loses office. The black line is the expected utility of *B*, low levels of judicial independence

assumed rather than examined. This lack of examination has left much doubt as to the accuracy of the insurance framework, even in democratic regimes. This doubt stems from the fact that for the insurance logic to hold, those who assume power must not run roughshod over the judiciary after taking office. If they do, the insurance logic falls apart: no leader—be they democrat or autocrat—would want to pay insurance's premiums if they had no expectation of being able to cash in on its benefits when things go south. In other words, if new leaders violate judicial independence, then the insurance function it offers fails to hold, and therefore we should not expect competition to incentivize judicial independence since its costs would outweigh its benefits. To let evidence rather than intuition determine one's perspective on the likelihood that new leaders, all else being equal, respect existing levels of judicial independence, I present data on four measures of infringements against the judiciary. Through a variety of models and specifications, I show that new leaders are not more likely to attack the integrity of the judiciary or refuse to comply with unfavorable rulings, and are not associated with lower levels of de facto judicial independence. All the evidence points to those newly in power respecting the existing levels of judicial independence, and against the skeptical take that insurance cannot obtain because new leaders would undermine a judiciary protecting the policies or persons associated with those previously in power.

An obvious response to this argument and the evidence offered to support it is that the reason new leaders are not associated with bad outcomes for courts is precisely because independent courts do not in fact provide insurance, as they know that if they did their independence would be undermined. To address this concern and show fully that the foundational mechanisms of the insurance logic hold, I look to data on the post-tenure fate of leaders to determine whether independent courts provide insurance. I show that more independent judiciaries are strongly associated with lower probabilities of punishment for those formerly in power, and that this result holds regardless of whether the former leader was a democrat or dictator. To better ascertain that this relationship is a function of the insurance logic rather than some competing explanation, I look to two further empirical implications, showing that how a leader leaves office and who they are replaced by each condition the beneficial effects of independence: the results show that the benefits of insurance obtain under conditions of "normal," electoral turnover, and that the results are far stronger when a leader is replaced by an opposition figure rather than a co-partisan. Not only can courts provide insurance, they do.

Chapter 3 consists of direct tests of the empirical implications of the theoretical model forwarded in Chapter 1. I begin by revisiting the logic of insurance—specifically, what it is about the electoral environment that should induce leaders to maintain or further judicial independence. Arguing for a clear connection between concept and measure, I review how existing quantitative work on insurance operationalizes electoral competition. I contend that an ideal measure captures both the distribution of power within the legislature both politically and institutionally. If the inducement to independence is a function of the credibility of opposition replacement, then a unified opposition should have greater weight than a fragmented opposition even if each controls the same percentage of seats. Furthermore, if one key function of insurance is the protection of minority rights and policy continuity, then considering the distribution of power across legislative houses is necessary.

After presenting just such a measure, I show that the degree of competition is strongly associated with the level of de facto judicial independence in autocratic regimes, and far less so in democratic. These results hold up not only accounting for potential confounding variables, but also against competing explanations, including the existing argument that it is only during times of autocratic twilight that increasing de facto independence should be observed. Rather, I show that even the most conservative conceptualizations of autocratic twilight do not affect the substantive results, and that competition's effects hold irrespective of whether autocrats see the writing on the wall and regime change looms. Recognizing that these analyses are purely observational, I argue for the appropriateness of two instruments of competition. Drawing on research looking at how economic performance and non-tax revenue bolster support for both autocratic and democratic incumbents, I contend that inflation and a state's oil reserves are effective instruments. This is because both should affect the security of those in office—inflation decreasing support for incumbents, and oil reserves allowing for the non-tax spending that increases support—without having any effect on the judiciary except by way of how each affects the likelihood of replacement. I show via two-stage least squares models that these are effective instruments of competition, and offer the first attempt to assess the relationship between competition and independence in a causal manner. The results are strongly supportive of the theory of autocratic insurance, but far less so for democratic: the relationship between competition and independence in democracies, weak already in the linear models, becomes non-existent in the instrumental variables analysis.

Chapter 4 addresses the disconnect between these empirical results about how competition affects de facto independence in democracies and the many case studies in the literature. I present the argument that in democracies, changes in the competitiveness of the electoral arena should primarily be associated changes in the formal, de jure provisions for courts. This is because the costs and benefits of infringing on de jure vs. de facto insurance vary across regime type. In democracies, the stronger effects of constitutionalism mean that flouting the rules has a greater likelihood of producing the public backlash that scholars such as Vanberg (2005) contend is important. This factor is amplified in democracies by the greater degree of media freedom, which means that the transparency of attacks should be more visible and courts more able to rely on public support (Staton 2010).

The main test of this argument comes by way of an in-depth case study of the de jure attacks on the independence of the judiciary, especially the Constitutional Court, in Hungary after the 2010 election in which the right-wing party Fidesz won a 2/3 majority of parliamentary seats. This "historical" case study draws on the work of the many scholars who have publicized the ways in which Fidesz has changed constitutional provisions affecting the selection, size, and jurisdiction of the Hungarian Constitutional Court. It additionally draws on extensive expert interviews with leading legal scholars, government officials, and sitting justices of the Hungarian Constitutional Court, expert interviews that were conducted not long after the events in question but during debates over the validity of many of these constitutional changes. I show that the manner in which Fidesz went about dismantling the independence of the court was entirely de jure, and that the complicated nature of institutional rules and jurisdictional debates dampened public attention to and support for the Court's formal independence.

Recognizing that theories should be tested "out-of-sample" whenever possible, I again turn to time-series cross-sectional models, and demonstrate that it is precisely de jure independence that is associated with changing levels of electoral competition in democracies. These relationships are presented visually in the two plots in Figure 5.2, which reproduces Figure 4.2. Increases in competition are associated with increases in independence across regime type and form of

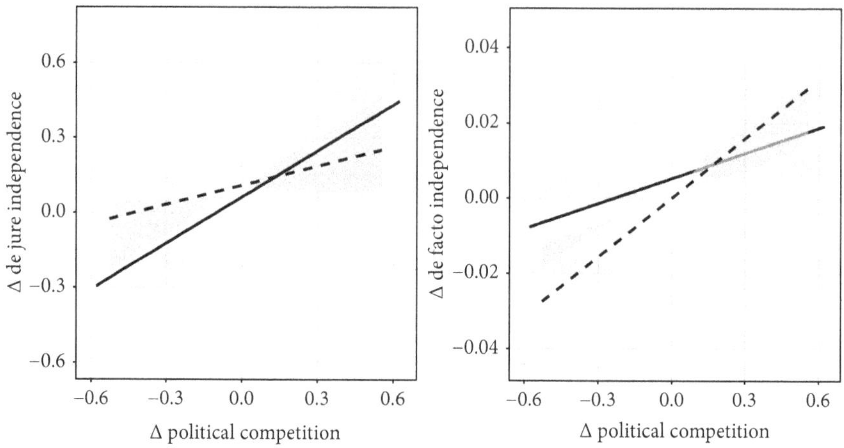

(a) De jure independence (b) De facto independence

Figure 5.2 Competition, regime type, and form of independence. The expected value of latent judicial independence from the when change in competition is allowed to vary from its observed minimum to maximum by regime type. The solid black line reports the expected change for democracies, while the dashed black line reports non-democracies, with 95% confidence intervals shaded around each.

independence. In democracies, however, the relationship is statistically significant only for de jure independence, where it is highly substantively significant. The reverse is the case for autocracies: there, a statistically significant effect is found only for de facto independence, where the effect is substantively very important. These results suggest that while competition is important across regime type, how it is important varies, and provides significant support for the autocratic insurance argument forwarded throughout the book.

5.2 Implications

This book has important implications for the study of judicial independence, the building and maintenance of the rule of law, and democratization. When it comes to the study of judicial independence, I make both fundamental theoretical and empirical contributions to our understanding of the relationship between competition and independence and how independence varies across regime type.

5.2.1 Theoretical contributions

At the theoretical level I offer two pairs of contributions that advance the insurance framework. First, I show that the logic of the insurance account, considered the foremost explanation for independence (VonDoepp & Ellet 2011, Vanberg 2015), should obtain outside the democratic contexts in which it has been developed.

I further show that, when present, electoral competition should be more salient in non-democratic regimes. I do this via the second contribution, which is the incorporation of varying risks into the insurance logic. Despite being a popular account for understanding variation in democratic regimes for two decades, little attention has been paid to the second half of the equation, with scholars implicitly holding this parameter constant. Deriving these risks by way of an empirical model, I show through formalizing the expected utility calculation that this is an important parameter, and that taking it into account allows for a deeper understanding of both the insurance logic and the empirical regularities observed. This is, of course, only a first step. Future research should focus on far more nuanced variations in the risks associated with losing office, both within and across regime type. Such research would provide us with more detailed answers to not whether competition is important in explaining judicial independence, but rather to the specific conditions under which it is, or is not, important.

To resolve the apparent contradiction between the results that instrument for competition and existing case study research, in Chapter 4 I develop an argument concerning how changing levels of competition should be associated with de jure rather than de facto changes in democracies. The process of doing so produces the second pair of theoretical contributions to the study of independence. My explanation synthesizes public backlash and electoral insurance accounts, suggesting that when levels of competition are changing, the potential for backlash should induce democratic leaders to play by the rules, here meaning changing them according to prescribed procedures. This integration of what Vanberg (2015) refers to as "exogenous" explanations of independence into "endogenous" explanations is the third contribution. As I show in Chapter 4, the distinction between these two types of explanation is in fact unclear, because it is only under certain conditions, namely when the endogenous explanations obtain, that the exogenous explanations do or do not have purchase. Fourth, by integrating these two types of explanation I am able to offer the first holistic account of competition and independence across regime type. Whereas existing theories focus on either de jure or de facto independence in either democracies or dictatorships, I present an overarching account of how competition should matter that applies across regime type and form of independence.

In concert, these four contributions shift substantially the approach by comparative law and courts scholars to not only the study of the insurance framework specifically but judicial independence more broadly. In doing so it both complicates and simplifies our framework for explaining independence. It complicates because it forces us to include in our theoretical apparatus not just the likelihood of losing office, but also the risks associated with such an outcome. It simplifies because rather than offer disparate ways of approaching the form of independence across the type of regime, it instead shows that competition is an effective explanatory factor in dictatorships and democracies, both for de jure and de facto independence. This is, I should stress, not to say there is a single cause of judicial independence and that it obtains at all times and all places. There are no doubt other factors—systematic or otherwise—that affect the level of judicial independence within and across states. Rather, this contribution identifies one significant factor theorized as *an* important answer to the fundamental question of comparative judicial politics. Future research should continue to search for other answers, and in making strides forward will first identify them (and ideally examine them outside of the contexts in which they were first identified, a step too often not taken in comparative courts research), and second, integrate them with insurance-based answers. That future research integrates other causal factors with electoral explanation is critical, for if I am correct that competition interacts with regime type, it likely also interacts with other structural, institutional, or political factors.

5.2.2 Empirical contributions

Chapters 2, 3, and 4 each make empirical contributions, and combined offer the most thorough account of the insurance model to date. Chapter 2 offers one of the first analyses of the mechanisms underlying the insurance model to date; to my knowledge, there has been no research demonstrating the descriptive accuracy of the assumed mechanisms that are fundamental to the insurance logic.[1] In Chapter 2 I present an exhaustive account of the effect new leaders (do not) have on the independence of the judiciary. I show that regardless of the measure one uses or how one models leader turnover there is no evidence for the skeptical position that insurance is impossible because new leaders will run roughshod over the judiciary. Importantly, I focus not only on statistical insignificance as is common, but rather follow best practices to show that there is a negligible relationship between leader turnover and infringements on the judiciary (Rainey 2014). This contribution replaces intuition about this relationship with evidence, and going forward it is incumbent on those who suspect that courts cannot or do not provide insurance to bolster their skepticism with analysis.

The second empirical contribution offered is the bringing to bear of methods of causal inference on the relationship between competition and judicial independence. While there has been an increase in the number and sophistication of statistical studies of this relationship (Aydın 2013, Ginsburg & Versteeg 2013, Randazzo, Gibler, & Reid 2016, Epperly 2017), to date none have attempted to address the question casually. There are good reasons for this: field experiments tackling such matters are nigh impossible, natural experiments rare, and good instruments difficult to find. I hope, of course, that I have offered a convincing account for why the chosen instruments meet the exclusion restriction, and that

[1] The one exception being my earlier work (Epperly 2013).

as a result the reader finds my use of instrumental variables estimation compelling. Even if not, however, I hope that the attempt provides other scholars the impetus to propose and defend alternative instruments for the relationship between competition and independence, as we all are committed to better understanding this vitally important phenomenon.

The final important empirical contribution to the study of judicial independence is the bringing of broadly comparative evidence to bear on alternative explanations of judicial independence. Here, the contribution is in what the analysis in the book does not find. In her influential study of Russia and Ukraine, Popova (2012) contends that in autocratic regimes with competition, such competition disincentivizes judicial independence, because dependent courts provide greater benefits.[2] The empirical implications of this strategic pressure account—if one extends it beyond its intended scope condition of electoral autocratic regimes—are opposite the implications of my model of autocratic insurance, and the cross-national results are strikingly in favor of the latter. In his important study of Egypt, Moustafa (2007) argues not for competition but for the incentivizing effects of the need to attract foreign investment, monitor state agents, and bolster regime legitimacy. The results presented in Chapter 3 offer little in the way of support for such arguments, however, and suggest that these factors—ubiquitous across democracy and dictatorship—are not consistently associated with higher levels of de facto independence.

5.2.3 Implications beyond independence

When it comes to the broader study of comparative constitutional law, the book contributes another brick to the—by now quite impressive—edifice; that is, positive explanations for constitutional policies driven by fundamentally political factors (Ginsburg 2008, Hirschl 2014). The theoretical and empirical arguments I forward argue strongly against ideational explanations of constitutional provisions and institutions securing rights protections; rather, it is domestic political factors that provide the most convincing account for variation in both the scope and behavior of independent courts. I stress *domestic* political factors because it is clear that while there is certainly an international element to constitutional content (Elkins 2010), the role of outside actors in constitutional practice is severely limited. This is perhaps most obvious by what I do not discuss in Chapter 4: the role of foreign governments or supranational actors in effectively constraining the Fidesz government's attacks on the formal powers of the Hungarian Constitutional Court.

[2] Although Popova prefers the term 'emerging democracy', I am wary to adopt terminology that implies either that these regimes were or are are a form of democracy (Collier & Levitsky 1997), or are transitioning to some endpoint of democracy, as transition is neither guaranteed nor a form of regime type.

This is not because these actors did not attempt to play a role, nor because there is not much to be said about the steps taken by the European Parliament or the Venice Commission. Rather, it is because these actors were unable to exert any meaningful constraint on the Orbán government. The feebleness of European institutions has been widely recognized by scholars, and was echoed by every Hungarian legal expert and Constitutional Court justice with whom I spoke. The most memorable articulation of this was offered by Péter Hack (personal communication, May 15, 2013), a founding leader of the liberal Alliance of Free Democrats (SZDSZ) and former Chairman of the Constitution and Judicial Committee in the Hungarian parliament. In describing the (un)constraining role of European institutions, he analogized the situation as being akin to "if you got an invitation that says let's go to this black tie and at the gate everyone is checking whether you have black tie, and when you get inside everybody is in their swimming suits because nobody cares what's happening inside, just in the door... that's happening in the Copenhagen area." The implication of this story and this book for comparative constitutional scholarship echoes similar work in a positive vein: politics matters, and creating or maintaining institutions and institutional rules conducive to the rule of law requires such to be in the interest of powerful domestic actors. Absent such interest, the provisions and behavior necessary for the constitutional order to be more than "constitutions without constitutionalism" are tenuous at best. Put in more pithy terms, if Ambrose Bierce's cynicism is warranted and politics is "a strife of interests masquerading as a contest of principles," then Madison was undoubtedly correct in Federalist No. 51 and "Ambition must be made to counteract ambition." Correct, but incomplete: without sustained competition, an institutional arrangement is unlikely to be self-enforcing. Absent such competition, neither the normative appeal of the rule of law nor external attempts to support it can ensure the rule of law continues free from threat.

Research studying the nature and dynamics of autocratic regimes has made significant strides in recent years, with scholars moving beyond black box explanations that treat autocracies as monolithic, in the sense of either as individual states or as a type of state. Some of this research has been typological, focusing on how different forms of autocracy operate differently, while some has instead focused on interactions either within the elite or between elites and societal actors. This book contributes to this welcome trend in two ways. First, it identifies clearly the risks facing autocrats, offering one avenue for how they might mitigate these risks under conditions, and why they might do so under conditions of electoral competition. Second, it provides new evidence for the important insight that we ought not treat autocratic regimes as wholly different than their democratic counterparts. Instead, we need to identify specific institutional features or political incentives that may or may not be present in both democracies and dictatorships, and if present how these incentives might be more (or less) salient given institutional differences. Just as previous comparative politics research largely dismissed any role for legislatures in autocratic contexts, existing comparative courts work treats elections as irrelevant in these contexts. Like recent comparative politics work on legislatures, in this book I show that it is not the case that electoral dynamics are unimportant in autocracies, but rather that their salience differs.

With regards to explicitly policy recommendations, the arguments developed and insights drawn from this book are threefold. The first is the clarity by which Chapter 4 illustrates the importance of multiple veto points for the stability of a constitutional order. While this contribution is neither theoretical nor novel, as the previous reference to Federalist No. 51 makes obvious, the case study of constitutional change in Hungary and the subsequent cross-national examination of the argument offer a forceful rejoinder to those who would argue for legislative supremacy or the normative appeal of constitutions free from the dead-hand control of past generations. The Hungarian experience thoroughly demonstrates the danger of unconstrained legislative power. The lack of a second, explicitly political institution able to make some claim to democratic legitimacy doomed a Constitutional Court facing a parliamentary majority with the requisite 2/3 majority for constitutional change as sure as the lack of a temporal, popular, or institutional check to constitutional revision or replacement doomed the constitution facing such an actor. In other words, while institutional arrangements cannot ensure that those in power are constrained and that the rule of law flourishes absent the balance of interest against interest, they can make evading constraint more or less difficult. While much political science research has taken the implicit normative position that a multiplicity of veto points are undesirable because such an arrangement bogs down policy change, the Hungarian experience illustrates the dangers implicit in constitutional orders that allow for rapid, unilateral policy change. As today even many of the most long-standing and well-consolidated democratic regimes witness parties that question the legitimacy of liberal democratic norms and the rule of law, the danger of institutional arrangements whereby single electoral victories secured with bare majorities can mean governments able to revise institutions wholesale becomes clear.

The Hungary case specifically and the results in Chapter 4 more broadly also provide the second policy implication, which, much like the first, also deals with constitutional architecture. Put simply, there are acute perils that arise from setting a low bar to constitutional change.[3] What Fidesz might have done were there temporal or popular requirements for constitutional change, even in the absence of

[3] See, for example, David Cameron's government deciding to allow for two referenda (Scottish independence and Brexit) regarding the fundamental arrangement of the British state, each requiring only a simple majority to pass.

another veto point with popular legitimacy, is a counterfactual without an answer. Nonetheless, it is probably safe to say that the results would have been no worse than what has been observed in the post-2010 Hungarian polity, and likely far better. Even if no domestic factors changed, the European and international outcry against the constitutional revisions pursued by the Orbán government might have had the potential to be effective in moderating, if not constraining, the dismantling of the rule of law had the conclusions of the Venice Commission or Tavares Report (for example) come between two rounds of voting on constitutional revisions, rather than long after the new constitutional rules were put in place. The perils of easily revising constitutional orders are further exacerbated by the dangers of unicameral parliaments, a reminder that the Hungarian case demonstrates that the effect of institutional rules cannot be examined in isolation.

The third, overarching policy implication of the argument forwarded can be summarized glibly as, "Putin was right." That is, fears of foreign support for organizations and parties opposing autocratic rule were well-founded not because such support was instrumental in the Color Revolutions that toppled governments in Georgia, Ukraine, and Kyrgyzstan, but rather because such opposition can have meaningful effects. A competitive electoral environment is of huge importance not only for its role in incentivizing leaders to establish, maintain, and further an independent judiciary, but also because it constrains state exploitation by partisan actors (Gryzmala-Busse 2007), supports economic development (Frye 2010), and deepens governmental accountability (Berliner & Erlich 2015). As such, policies aimed at supporting the competitiveness of the electoral arena are called for, and those able to do so successfully are of great value. This is true with regard to both domestic and foreign policy, regardless of the actor in question. The corollary to this is that those policies that inhibit the competitiveness of the electoral arena or whose benefits accrue overwhelmingly to incumbents should be considered suspect. To the degree that foreign aid, for example, does so (Yuichi Kono & Montinola 2009, Jablonski 2014, Cruz & Schneider 2017), this increasing consensus suggests that aid's benefits might be tempered by undermining the political competition critical to many normatively desirable outcomes, of which judicial independence is but one. Unfortunately, of course, encouraging a more competitive electoral arena—be it abroad or domestically—is easier said than done, as, much like the rule of law, the interests of those in power are more often than not in direct opposition to a competitive electoral environment. When it comes to policies encouraging competitiveness abroad, policymakers, be they states or multilateral institutions, face incumbents that do not welcome such endeavors. Putin's repeated claims regarding American meddling in post-communist elections is an obvious example. Less obvious, but far more effective, are policies regulating foreign support for non-governmental organizations, as developments in Russia, Hungary, and Poland make evident.

5.3 Conclusion

At the beginning of this book I noted that its impetus was twofold. First, the normatively critical role that an independent judiciary can play in a polity, made so clear by the tragedy of the post-2010 Hungarian experience. Second, three unanswered questions concerning judicial independence. To what degree does political competition affect independence in autocratic and not just democratic contexts? Are new leaders bound by existing institutions, and as such are courts able to offer insurance to outgoing leaders? Why the disconnect between the results answering the first question and what we know from existing case studies of judicial independence around the world?

The rest of this book has been an attempt to better understand and explain events in autocratic and democratic regimes around the world, and to offer a theoretical account that better links what we know about electoral competition and both de jure and de facto independence. The result is an argument for an expanded insurance framework to better understand judicial independence, and a thorough analysis of the descriptive accuracy of the mechanisms foundational to the insurance model. Critical to expanding the insurance framework so that it is able to offer a comprehensive account of judicial independence across all combinations of regime type and form of independence are two of my arguments: the first concerning the role of autocratic insurance, captured succinctly in Figure 5.1, and second the importance of thinking about the form of independence, itself visualized by Figure 5.2.

The arguments are fairly simple. For the latter, the form of independence that is affected by changing levels of competition should be related to the nature of the regime, with democratic leaders far more likely to play by the rules, changing the de jure powers and prerogatives of the court as opposed to engaging in extra-legal attacks on the de facto independence of the judiciary. For the former, the downside risk for autocrats overwhelms that of democrats, and as a result even lower levels of competition can be highly salient in non-democratic regimes. The result of this simplicity, however, is an insurance model that takes into account both the likelihood of losing office and the risks associated with this outcome. This inclusion of the risks is an important step forward for explanations of judicial independence, but it is a first step. If going forward, scholars of comparative law and courts take seriously and treat carefully variation in the risks that leaders—both dictators and democrats—face from losing office, then this argument will have achieved its objective, and its insights will no doubt quickly be surpassed.

Bibliography

Acemoglu, Daron & James A. Robinson. 2006. *Economic Origins of Dictatorship and Democracy*. New York: Cambridge University Press.

Adam, Christopher. 2017*a*. "Budapest Voters Reject Fidesz, Prefer Left-Liberal Government in 2018." Retrived from http://hungarianfreepress.com/2017/07/18/budapest-voters-reject-fidesz-prefer-left-liberal-government-in-2018/

Adam, Christopher. 2017*b*. "Fidesz on Track to Win Three-Fourths Majority in 2018 Elections." http://hungarianfreepress.com/2017/10/26/fidesz-on-track-to-win-three-fourths-majority-in-2018-elections/.

Adsera, Alicia, Carles Boix, & Mark Payne. 2003. "Are you Being Served? Political Accountability and Quality of Government." *Journal of Law, Economics, and Organization* 19(2):445–90.

Agrast, Mark D., Juan Carlos Botero, & Alejandro Ponce. 2011. *The World Justice Project Rule of Law Index*. Washington, DC: The World Justice Project.

Akhmedov, Akhmed & Ekaterina Zhuravskaya. 2004. "Opportunistic Political Cycles: Test in a Young Democracy Setting." *Quarterly Journal of Economics* 119(4):1301–38.

Albertus, Michael & Victor Menaldo. 2012. "If You're Against Them You're With Us: The Effect of Expropriation on Autocratic Survival." *Comparative Political Studies* 45(8): 973–1003.

Alvarez, Michael, Jose A. Cheibub, Fernando Limongi, & Adam Przeworski. 1996. "Classifying Political Regimes." *Studies in Comparative International Development* 31(2):3–36.

Andersen, Jørgen Juel, & Silje Aslaksen. 2013. "Oil and Political Survival." *Journal of Development Economics* 100(1):89–106.

Arato, Andrew & Zoltan Miklósi. 2010. Constitution Making in Hungary 1989–1996. In *Framing the State in Times of Transition: Case Studies in Constitution Making*, ed. L. E. Miller & L. Aucoin. Washington, DC: United States Institute for Peace.

Aydın, Aylin. 2013. "Judicial Independence Across Democratic Regimes: Understanding the Varying Impact of Political Competition." *Law & Society Review* 47(1):105–34.

Balli, Hatice Ozer & Bent E Sørensen. 2013. "Interaction Effects in Econometrics." *Empirical Economics* 45:583–603.

Balogh, Eva S. 2010. "A Legislative Proposal That Would Change the Composition of the Constitutional Court." http://hungarianspectrum.org/2010/06/10/a-legislative-proposal-that-would-change-the-composition-of-the-constitutional-court/.

Balogh, Eva S. 2011. "How Qualified Will the New Judges in the Hungarian Constitutional Be: the Case of Béla Pokol." http://hungarianspectrum.org/2011/06/20/how-qualified-will-be-the-new-judges-in-the-hungarian-constitutional-court-the-case-of-bela-pokol/.

Balogh, Eva S. 2017. "The Latest Opinion Polls on the Chances of the Opposition." http://hungarianspectrum.org/2017/10/12/the-latest-opinion-polls-on-the-chances-of-the-opposition-parties/

Bánkuti, Miklós, Gábor Halmai, & Kim Lane Scheppele. 2012*a*. "Disabling the Constitution." *Journal of Democracy* 23(3):138–146.

Bánkuti, Miklós, Gábor Halmai, & Kim Lane Scheppele. 2012*b*. From Separation of Powers to a Government without Checks: Hungary's Old and New Constitution. In *Constitution for a Disunited Nation*, ed. Gábor Attila Tóth. Budapest: Central European University Press.

Bánkuti, Miklós, Tamás Dombos, Zoltán Fleck, Gábor Halmai, Krisztina Rozgonyi, Balázs Majtényi, László Majtényi, Eszter Polgári, Kim Lane, Bernadette Somody Scheppele, et al. 2012. "Opinion on Hungary's New Constitutional Order:." Amicus Brief for the Venice Commission on the Transitional Provisions of the Fundamental Law and the Key Cardinal Laws.

Barros, Robert. 2002. *Constitutionalism and Dictatorship: Pinochet, the Junta, and the 1980 Constitution*. New York: Cambridge University Press.

Beck, Thorsten, George R. G. Clarke, Alberto Groff, Philip Keefer, & Patrich Walsh. 2001. "New Tools and New Tests in Comparative Political Economy: the Database of Political Institutions." *World Bank Paper*.

Bentele, Keith G. & Erin E. O'Brien. 2013. "Jim Crow 2.0? Why States Consider and Adopt Restrictive Voter Access Policies." *Perspectives on Politics* 11(4):1088–1116.

Berger, Roger L. & Jason C. Hsu. 1996. "Bioequivalence Trials, Intersection-Union Tests and Equivalence Confidence Sets." *Statistical Science* 11(4):283–319.

Berliner, Daniel & Aaron Erlich. 2015. "Competing for Transparency: Political Competition and Institutional Reform in Mexican States." *American Political Science Review* 109(1):110–128.

Birch, Sarah. 2003. *Electoral Systems and Political Transformation in Post-Communist Europe*. Basingstoke: Palgrave MacMillan.

Bogaards, Matthijs. 2010. "Measures of Democratization: From Degree to Type to War." *Political Research Quarterly* 63(2):475–88.

Boix, Carles, Michael Miller, & Sebastian Rosato. 2013. "A Complete Data Set of Political Regimes, 1800–2007." *Comparative Political Studies* 46(12):1523–54.

Boix, Carles & Milan W Svolik. 2013. "The Foundations of Limited Authoritarian Government: Institutions, Commitment, and Power-Sharing in Dictatorships." *Journal of Politics* 75(2):300–16.

Bound, John, David A. Jaeger & Regina Baker. 1993. "The Cure Can be Worse than the Disease: A Cautionary Tale Regarding Instrumental Variables." *National Bureau of Economic Research Working Papers*.

Bound, John, David A. Jaeger & Regina M. Baker. 1995. "Problems with Instrumental Variables Estimation when the Correlation between the Instruments and the Endogenous Explanatory Variable is Weak." *Journal of the American Statistical Association* 90(430):443–50.

Boylan, Delia M. 2001. *Defusing Democracy: Central Bank Autonomy and the Transition from Authoritarian Rule*. Ann Arbor: University of Michican Press.

Bozóki, András. 2015. Broken Democracy, Predatory State, and Nationalist Populism. In *The Hungarian Patient: Social Opposition to an Illiberal Democracy*, ed. Péter Krasztev & Jon Van Til. Budapest: Central European University Press.

Brownlee, Jason. 2009. Harbinger of Democracy: Competitive Elections before the End of Authoritarianism. In *Democratization By Elections*, ed. Staffan Lindberg. Baltimore: Johns Hopkins University Press.

Burbank, Sstephen B. & Barry Friedman. 2002. *Judicial Independence at the Crossroads: An Interdisciplinary Approach*. Thousand Oaks: Sage Publications.

Buszko, Michal & Dorota Krupa. 2015. "Foreign Currency Loans in Poland and Hungary—A Comparative Analysis." *Procedia Economics and Finance* 30:124–36.

Byrne, Andrew. 2016. "Orbán Tightens Grip on Hungary's Media." *Financial Times*, August 16.

Carrubba, Clifford J., Matthew Gabel, Gretchen Helmke, Jeffrey K. Staton, & Andrew D. Martin. 2015. "When Parchment Barriers Matter: De Jure Judicial Independence and the Concentration of Power." Unpublished manuscript.

Carrubba, Clifford J, & Matthew J, Gabel. 2014. *International Courts and the Performance of International Agreements: A General Theory with Evidence from the European Union*. New York: Cambridge University Press.

Carrubba, Clifford James. 2009. "A Model of the Endogenous Development of Judicial Institutions in Federal and International Systems." *Journal of Politics* 71(1):55–69.

Carrubba, Clifford, Matthew Gabel, Gretchen Helmke, Andrew Martin & Jeffery Staton. 2012. "An Introduction to the CompLaw Database." Unpublished Manuscript, Emory University. http://perma.cc/MMA6-UBVR.

Case, William. 2006. Manipulative Skills: How Do Rulers Control the Electoral Arena? In *Electoral Authoritarianism: The Dynamics of Unfree Competition*, ed. Andreas Schedler. Boulder: Lynne Rienner Publishers.

Chappell Jr., Henry W & Linda Goncalves Veiga. 2000. "Economics and Elections in Western Europe: 1960–1997." *Electoral Studies* 19(2):183–197.

Chavez, Rebecca Bill. 2004. *The Rule of Law in Nascent Democracies: Judicial Politics in Argentina*. Palo Alto: Stanford University Press.

Cheibub, Jose A., Jennifer Gandhi & James R. Vreeland. 2009. "Democracy and Dictatorship Revisited Codebook." Data codebook.

Cheibub, Jose A., Jennifer Gandhi & James R. Vreeland. 2010. "Democracy and Dictatorship Revisted." *Public Choice* 143(1):67–101.

Cienski, Jan. 2007. "Judge Curbs Polish Informers Law." *Financial Times*, May 12, http://www.ft.com/cms/917b1c82-0026-11dc-8c98-000b5df10621.html.

Cingranelli, David L. & David L. Richards. 2010. "The Cingranelli Richards (CIRI) Human Rights Database Coding Manual." http://ciri.binghamton.edu/documentation.asp

Clague, Christopher, Philip Keefer, Stephen Knack, & Mancur Olson. 1999. "Contract-Intensive Money: Contract Enforcement, Property Rights, and Economic Performance." *Journal of Economic Growth* 4(2):185–211.

Clark, William Roberts & Matt Golder. 2006. "Rehabilitating Duverger's Theory: Testing the Mechanical and Strategic Modifying Effects of Electoral Laws." *Comparative Political Studies* 39(6):679–708.

Clarke, Kevin A, & Randall W, Stone. 2008. "Democracy and the Logic of Political Survival." *American Political Science Review* 102(3):387–92.

Clarke, Vivienne. 2016. "Register for Judges Needed." https://www.irishtimes.com/news/crime-and-law/register-for-judges-needed-as-they-might-forget-their-oath-says-shane-ross-1.2867171

Collier, David & Robert Adcock. 1999. "Democracy and Dichotomies: A Pragmatic Approach to Choices about Concepts." *Annual Review of Political Science* 2:537–55.

Collier, David & Steven Levitsky. 1997. "Democracy with Adjectives: Strategies to Avoid Conceptual Stretching." *World Politics* 49(3):430–51.

Colton, Timothy J. & Michael McFaul. 2003. *Popular Choice and Managed Democracy: The Russian Elections of 1999 and 2000*. Washington, DC: Brookings Institution Press.

Conrad, Courtenay R. & Emily Hencken Ritter. 2013. "Treaties, Tenure, and Torture: The Conflicting Domestic Effects of International Law." *Journal of Politics* 75(2):397–409.

Coolidge, Jacqueline & Susan Rose-Ackerman. 1997. "High-Level Rent-Seeking and Corruption in African Regimes: Theory and Cases." *Policy Research Working Paper Series*.

Coppedge, Michael, John Gerring, Staffan I. Lindberg, Svend-Erik Skaaning, Jan Teorell, Frida Andersson, Kyle L Marquardt, Valeriya Mechkova, Farhad Miri, Daniel Pemstein, et al. 2016*a*. "V-Dem Dataset v6."

Coppedge, Michael, John Gerring, Staffan I. Lindberg, Svend-Erik Skaaning, Jan Teorell, Frida Andersson, Kyle L Marquardt, Valeriya Mechkova, Farhad Miri, Daniel Pemstein, et al. 2016*b*. "V-Dem Methodology v6."

Cruz, Cesi & Christina J. Schneider. 2017. "Foreign Aid and Undeserved Credit Claiming." *American Journal of Political Science* 61(2):396–408.

Csipke, Zoltán. 2014. "Forget Rigged Elections, Fidesz Will Win Because There is No Viable Alternative." http://www.politics.hu/20140405/forget-eigged-elections-fidesz-will-win-because-of-there-is-no-viable-alternative/.

Dahl, Robert A. 1971. *Polyarchy: Participation and Opposition*. New Haven: Yale University Press.

Dallara, Cristina & Antoine Vauchez. 2012. "Courts, Social Changes and Judicial Independence." Technical report, European University Institute Global Governance Programme.

Danilova, Maria. 2013. "Yulia Tymoshenko Murder Case: Former Ukrainian Prime Minister Suspected of Killing Business Rival." http://www.huffingtonpost.com/2013/01/19/yulia-tymoshenko-murder-case-suspectn22511241.html.

Dawisha, Karen. 2014. *Putin's Kleptocracy: Who Owns Russia?* New York: Simon and Schuster.

Dimovski, Sase. 2012. "Macedonia Court Scraps Lustration Verdicts." *Balkan Insight*, May 16. http://www.balkaninsight.com/en/article/macedonia-court-scraps-lustration-findings.

Dixon, Rosalind & Tom Ginsburg. 2017. "The Forms and Limits of Constitutions as Political Insurance." *International Journal of Constitutional Law* 15(4):988–1012.

Elder, Mirriam. 2010. "Day of Judgment for Vladimir Putin's Billionaire Rival Mikhail Khodorkovsky." https://www.theguardian.com/world/2010/dec/14/judgment-day-putins-billionaire-rival.

Elkins, Zachary. 2000. "Gradations of Democracy? Empirical Tests of Alternative Conceptualizations." *American Journal of Political Science* 44(2):293–300.

Elkins, Zachary. 2010. "Diffusion and the Constitutionalization of Europe." *Comparative Political Studies* 43(8):969–99.

Elman, Colin & Colleen Dougherty Burton. 2016. "Research Cycles: Adding More Substance to the Spin." *Perspectives on Politics* 14(4):1067–70.

Elster, Jon. 2004. *Closing the Books: Transitional Justice in Historical Perspective*. New York: Cambridge University Press.

Epperly, Brad. 2011. "Institutions and Legacies: Electoral Volatility in the Postcommunist World." *Comparative Political Studies* 44(8):829–53.

Epperly, Brad. 2013. "The Provision of Insurance? Judicial Independence and the Post-tenure Fate of Leaders." *Journal of Law and Courts* 1(2):247–78.

Epperly, Brad. 2017. "Political Competition and De Facto Judicial Independence in Non-Democracies." *European Journal of Political Research* 56(2):279–300.

Epperly, Brad. 2018. "(Re)examining the Insurance Model of Judicial Independence across Democracies." *Journal of Law and Courts* 6(2):405–19.

Epperly, Brad & Jacqueline Sievert. 2018. "Conflict and Courts: Civil War and Judicial Independence across Democracies." *Political Research Quarterly*.

Epperly, Brad & Monica Lineberger. 2017. Strategic Behavior of Comparative Courts. In *Routledge Handbook of Judicial Behavior*, ed. Robert M. Howard & Kirk A. Randazzo. New York: Routledge.

Epstein, Lee, Jack Knight, & Olga Shvetsova. 2001*a*. "Comparing Judicial Selection Systems." *William & Mary Bill of Rights Journal* 10:7–36.

Epstein, Lee, Jack Knight, & Olga Shvetsova. 2001*b*. "The Role of Constitutional Courts in the Establishment and Maintenance of Democratic Systems of Government." *Law & Society Review* 35(1):117–64.

Escribà-Folch, Abel & Joseph Wright. 2015. "Human Rights Prosecutions and Autocratic Survival." *International Organization* 69(2):343–73.

European Court of Human Rights. 2011. "European Court Decides to Fast Track Complaints About Detention of Former Ukrainian Prime Minister Tymoshenko." *Press Release issued by the Registrar of the Rourt*, ECHR 292.

Feld, Lars P. & Stefan Voigt. 2003. "Economic Growth and Judicial Independence: Cross-Country Evidence Using a New Set of Indicators." *European Journal of Political Economy* 19(3):497–527.

Finkel, Evgeny & Yitzhak M. Brudny. 2012. "No More Colour! Authoritarian Regimes and Colour Revolutions in Eurasia." *Democratization* 19(1):1–14.

Finkel, Jodi. 2005. "Judicial Reform as Insurance Policy: Mexico in the 1990s." *Latin American Politics and Society* 47(1):87–113.

Finkel, Jodi. 2008. *Judicial Reform as Political Insurance: Argentina, Peru, and Mexico in the 1990s*. Notre Dame: University of Notre Dame Press.

Finkel, S. E., A. Pérez-Liñán, M. A. Seligson, & C. N. Tate. 2008. "Deepening Our Understanding of the Effects of US Foreign Assistance on Democracy Building, Final Report." Washington, DC: USAID.

Forint Exchange. 2014. "Hungary's Government Gives Struggling Borrowers a Break." *Economist*, November 15.

Franco, Annie, Neil Malhotra, & Gabor Simonovits. 2014. "Publication Bias in the Social Sciences: Unlocking the File Drawer." *Science* 345(6203):1502–05.

Freedom House. 2011. "Freedom In the World 2011." http://www.freedomhouse.org/report/freedom-world/2011/ukraine.

Freedom House. 2012. "Freedom In the World 2012." http://www.freedomhouse.org/report/freedom-world/2012/ukraine-0.

Friedheim, Daniel V. 1993. "Bringing Society Back into Democratic Transition Theory After 1989: Pact Making and Regime Collapse." *East European Politics and Societies* 7(3): 482–512.

Frye, Timothy. 2010. *Building States and Markets After Communism: The Perils of Polarized Democracy*. New York: Cambridge University Press.

Futey, Bohdan A. 2011. "The Suppression of an Independent Judiciary in Ukraine." http://www.kyivpost.com/opinion/op-ed/the-suppression-of-an-independent-judiciary-in-ukr-119708.html.

Gallagher, Mary E. & Jonathan K. Hanson. 2015. "Power Tool or Dull Blade? Selectorate Theory for Autocracies." *Annual Review of Political Science* 18:367–85.

Gandhi, Jennifer & Ellen Lust-Okar. 2009. "Elections Under Authoritarianism." *Annual Review of Political Science* 12:403–22.

Gárdos-Orosz, Fruzsina. 2012. "The Hungarian Constitutional Court in Transition—From Actio Popularis to Constitutional Complaint." *Acta Juridica Hungarica* 53(4): 302–15.

Geddes, Barbara. 1994. *Politician's Dilemma: Building State Capacity in Latin America*. Berkeley: University of California Press.

Geddes, Barbara. 1999. "What Do We Know about Democratization After 20 Years?" *Annual Review of Political Science* 2:115–44.

Geddes, Barbara, Joseph Wright, & Erica Frantz. 2014. "Autocratic Breakdown and Regime Transitions: A New Data Set." *Perspectives on Politics* 12(2):313–31.

Gelman, Andrew. 2011. "Descriptive Statistics, Causal Inference, and Story Time." http://andrewgelman.com/2011/07/07/descriptive_sta/.

Gessen, Masha. 2012. "The Wrath of Putin." https://www.vanityfair.com/news/politics/2012/04/vladimir-putin-mikhail-khodorkovsky-russia.

Getty, J Arch. 1991. "State and Society Under Stalin: Constitutions and Elections in the 1930s." *Slavic Review* 50(1):18–35.

Gibson, James L. Gregory A. Caldeira & Vanessa A. Baird. 1998. "On the Legitimacy of National High Courts." *American Political Science Review* 92(2):343–58.

Gill, Jeff. 1999. "The Insignificance of Null Hypothesis Significance Testing." *Political Research Quarterly* 52(3):647–74.

Ginsburg, Tom. 2003. *Judicial Review in New Democracies: Constitutional Courts in Asian Cases*. New York: Cambridge University Press.

Ginsburg, Tom. 2008. The Global Spread of Constitutional Review. In *Oxford Handbook of Law and Politics*, ed. Keith E. Whittington & Daniel Keleman. New York: Oxford University Press.

Ginsburg, Tom & Alberto Simpser. 2013. *Constitutions in Authoritarian Regimes*. New York: Cambridge University Press.

Ginsburg, Tom, James Melton, & Zachary Elkins. 2013. The Content of Authoritarian Constitutions. In *Constitutions in Authoritarian Regimes*, ed. Tom Ginsburg & Alberto Simpser. New York: Cambridge University Press.

Ginsburg, Tom & Mila Versteeg. 2013. "Why do Countries Adopt Constitutional Review?" *Journal of Law, Economics, & Organization* 30(3):587–622.

Ginsburg, Tom & Tamir Moustafa. 2008. *Rule by Law: The Politics of Courts in Authoritarian Regimes*. New York: Cambridge University Press.

Glaeser, Edward L. & Andrei Shleifer. 2002. "Legal Origins." *Quarterly Journal of Economics* 117(4):1193–1229.

Gleditsch, Kristian S. & Michael D. Ward. 1997. "Double Take A Reexamination of Democracy and Autocracy in Modern Polities." *Journal of Conflict Resolution* 41(3): 361–83.

Goemans, Hein, Kristian S. Gleditsch, & Giacomo Chiozza. 2006. "Archigos: A Data Set of Leaders 1875–2004." Data codebook.

Goemans, Hein, Kristian S. Gleditsch, & Giacomo Chiozza. 2009. "Introducing Archigos: A Data Set of Political Leaders." *Journal of Peace Research* 46(2):269–83.

Goldman, Marshall I. 2004. "Putin and the Oligarchs." *Foreign Affairs* 83:33–44.

Group, Political Risk Services. 2012. "International Country Risk Guide." http://www.prsgroup.com/ICRG_Methodology.aspx.

Gryzmala-Busse, Anna. 2007. *Rebuilding Leviathan: Party Competition and State Exploitation in Post-Communist Democracies*. New York: Cambridge University Press.

Gwartney, James & Robert Lawson. 2007. "Economic Freedom of the World Annual Report." http://freetheworld.com/2007/EFW2007BOOK2.pdf.

Haber, Stephen & Victor Menaldo. 2011. "Do Natural Resources Fuel Authoritarianism? A Reappraisal of the Resource Curse." *American Political Science Review* 105(01):1–26.

Haggard, Stephan, Andrew MacIntyre, & Lydia Tiede. 2008. "The Rule of Law and Economic Development." *Annual Review of Political Science* 11:205–34.

Hall, Melinda Gann. 2001. "State Supreme Courts in American Democracy: Probing the Myths of Judicial Reform." *American Political Science Review* 95(2):315–30.

Halmai, Gábor. 2002. The Hungarian Approach of Constitutional Review. In *Constitutional Justice, East and West: Democratic Legitimacy and Constitutional Courts in*

Post-Communist Europe in a Comparative Perspective, ed. Wojciech Sadurski. Springer Netherlands.

Halmai, Gábor. 2012. "Unconstitutional Constitutional Amendments: Constitutional Courts as Guardians of the Constitution?" *Constellations* 19(2):182–203.

Halmai, Gábor. 2017. The Early Retirement Age of the Hungarian Judges. In *EU Law Stories: Contextual and Critical Histories of European Jurisprudence*, ed. Fernanda Nicola & Bill Davies. New York: Cambridge University Press.

Helmke, Gretchen. 2002. "The Logic of Strategic Defection: Court-Executive Relations in Argentina under Dictatorship and Democracy." *American Political Science Review* 96(2):291–303.

Helmke, Gretchen. 2005. *Courts Under Constraints: Judges, Generals, and Presidents in Argentina*. New York: Cambridge University Press.

Helmke, Gretchen & Frances McCall Rosenbluth. 2009. "Regimes and the Rule of Law: Judicial Independence in Comparative Perspective." *Annual Review of Political Science* 12:345–66.

Helmke, Gretchen & Steven Levitsky. 2006. *Informal Institutions and Democracy: Lessons from Latin America*. Baltimore: Johns Hopkins University Press.

Hendley, Kathryn. 2009. " 'Telephone Law' and the 'Rule of Law': The Russian Case." *Hague Journal on the Rule of Law* 1(2):241–62.

Hendrix, Cullen, Stephan Haggard, & Beatriz Magaloni. 2009. "Grievance and Opportunity: Food Prices, Political Regime, and Protest." Paper presented at the annual meeting of the International Studies Association.

Henisz, Witold J. 2000. "The Institutional Environment for Economic Growth." *Economics and Politics* 12(1):1–31.

Henisz, Witold J. 2002. "The Institutional Environment for Infrastructure Investment." *Industrial and Corporate Change* 11(2):355–89.

Herron, Erik S. & Kirk A. Randazzo. 2003. "The Relationship Between Independence and Judicial Review in Post-Communist Courts." *Journal of Politics* 62(2):422–38.

Herszenhorn, David M. 2013. "Putin Critic Gets 5-Year Jail Term, Setting Off Protests." http://www.nytimes.com/2013/07/19/world/europe/russian-court-convicts-opposition-leader-aleksei-navalny.html.

Hill, Daniel W. & Zachary M. Jones. 2014. "An Empirical Evaluation of Explanations for State Repression." *American Political Science Review* 108(3):661–87.

Hirschl, Ran. 2000. "The Political Origins of Judicial Empowerment through Constitutionalization: Lessons from Four Constitutional Revolutions." *Law & Social Inquiry* 25(1): 91–149.

Hirschl, Ran. 2004. *Towards Juristocracy: The Origins and Consequences of the New Constitutionalism*. Cambridge: Harvard University Press.

Hirschl, Ran. 2008. "The Judicialization of Mega-Politics and the Rise of Political Courts." *Annual Review of Political Science* 11:93–118.

Hirschl, Ran. 2013. "From Comparative Constitutional Law to Comparative Constitutional Studies." *International Journal of Constitutional Law* 11(1):1–12.

Hirschl, Ran. 2014. *Comparative Matters: The Renaissance of Comparative Constitutional Law*. New York: Oxford University Press.

Hodgson, Robert. 2009. "Corruption Hangs Heavy Over Hungary." *Budapest Times*, November 3.

Horn, Murray J. 1995. *The Political Economy of Public Administration: Institutional Choice in the Public Sector*. New York: Cambridge University Press.

Horne, Cynthia M. 2009. "Late Lustration Programmes in Romania and Poland: Supporting or Undermining Democratic Transitions?" *Democratization* 16(2):344–76.

Howard, Robert M. & Henry F. Carey. 2004. "Is an Independent Judiciary Necessary for Democracy?" *Judicature* 87(6):284–90.

Interfax-Ukraine. 2009. "Poll: Ukraine President's Chances of Re-election Slim." http://www.kyivpost.com/content/ukraine/poll-ukraine-presidents-chances-of-re-election-sli-50997.html.

Interfax-Ukraine. 2012. "EU leaders: Ratification of Association Agreement and DCFTA depends on settlement of Tymoshenko-Lutsenko issue." http://www.kyivpost.com/content/politics/eu-leaders-ratification-of-association-agreement-a-310272.html.

Interfax-Ukraine. 2014. "Vlasenko: Gas Case Against Tymoshenko Put to Rest." https://www.kyivpost.com/article/content/yulia-tymoshenko/vlasenko-gas-case-against-tymoshenko-put-to-rest-2-353193.html.

Jablonski, Ryan S. 2014. "How Aid Targets Votes: The Impact of Electoral Incentives on Foreign Aid Distribution." *World Politics* 66(2):293–330.

Jakab, András & Pál Sonnevend. 2013. "Continuity with Deficiencies: The New Basic Law of Hungary." *European Constitutional Law Review* 9(1):102–38.

Karasz, Palko & Melissa Eddy. 2012. "Opposition Protests Constitution in Hungary." *New York Times*, January 2. http://www.nytimes.com/2012/01/03/world/europe/rare-opposition-protests-in-hungary.html.

Keith, Linda Camp. 2002. "Judicial Independence and Human Rights Protection Around the World." *Judicature* 85(4):195–200.

Keith, Linda Camp. 2012. *Political Repression: Courts and the Law*. Philadelphia: University of Pennsylvania Press.

Keith, Linda Camp, C. Neal Tate, & Steven C. Poe. 2009. "Is the Law a Mere Parchment Barrier to Human Rights Abuse?" *Journal of Politics* 71(2):644–60.

Kelemen, Roland. 2014. Posterior Norm Control in Hungary After the Abolition of Actio Popularis. In *Legal Studies on the Contemporary Hungarian Legal System*, ed. János Kálmán. Győr: Batthyány Lajos Szakkollégium Universitas.

Kennedy, Ryan. 2009. "Survival and Accountability: An Analysis of the Empirical Support for Selectorate Theory." *International Studies Quarterly* 53(3):695–714.

King, Gary, Robert O. Keohane, & Sidney Verba. 1994. *Designing Social Inquiry: Scientific Inference in Qualitative Research*. Princeton: Princeton University Press.

Kirby, Michael. 1998. Attacks on Judges: A Universal Phenomenon. In *Speeches by The Hon. Michael Kirby*. High Court of Australia. http://www.hcourt.gov.au/publications/speeches/former/speeches-by-the-hon-michael-kirby.

Kis, János. 2012. From the 1989 Constitution to the 2011 Fundamental Law. In *Constitution for a Disunited Nation*, ed. Gábor Attila Tóth. Budapest: Central European University Press.

Kocher, Matthew A. & Nuno P. Monteiro. 2016. "Lines of Demarcation: Causation, Design-Based Inference, and Historical Research." *Perspectives on Politics* 14(4): 952–75.

Kornhauser, Lewis A. 2002. Is Judicial Independence a Useful Concept? In *Judicial Independence at the Crossroads: An Interdisciplinary Approach*, ed. Stephen E. Burbank & Barry E. Friedman. Thousand Oaks: Sage.

Kovács, Kriszta & Gábor Attila Tóth. 2011. "Hungary's Constitutional Transformation." *European Constitutional Law Review* 7(2):183–203.

Krehbiel, Jay N. 2016. "Public Awareness and the Behavior of Unpopular Courts." Paper presented at the annual meeting of the American Political Science Association.

La Porta, Rafael, Florencio Lopez-de Silanes, Cristian Pop-Eleches, & Andrei Shleifer. 2004. "Judicial Checks and Balances." *Journal of Political Economy* 112(2):445–70.

Landes, William M. & Richard A. Posner. 1975. "The Independent Judiciary in an Interest-Group Perspective." *Journal of Law and Economics* 18(3):875–901.

Law, David S. & Mila Versteeg. 2013. "Sham Constitutions." *California Law Review* 101(4):863–952.

Ledeneva, Alena. 2008. "Telephone Justice in Russia." *Post-Soviet Affairs* 24(4):324–50.

Leeson, Peter T. 2008. "Media Freedom, Political Knowledge, and Participation." *Journal of Economic Perspectives* 22(2):155–69.

Lehman-Wilzig, Sam & Meyer Ungar. 1985. "The Economic and Political Determinants of Public Protest Frequency and Magnitude: The Israeli Experience." *International Review of Modern Sociology* 15(1-2):63–80.

Leigh, Andrew & Justin Wolfers. 2006. "Competing Approaches to Forecasting Elections: Economic Models, Opinion Polling and Prediction Markets." *Economic Record* 82(258):325–40.

Lembcke, Oliver & Christian Boulanger. 2012. Between Revolution and Constitution: The Roles of the Hungarian Constitutional Court. In *Constitution for a Disunited Nation*, ed. Gábor Attila Tóth. Budapest: Central European University Press.

Levin, Mark & Georgy Satarov. 2000. "Corruption and Institutions in Russia." *European Journal of Political Economy* 16(11):111–32.

Levitsky, Steven & Lucan A. Way. 2002. "The Rise of Competitive Authoritarianism." *Journal Of Democracy* 13(2):51–65.

Levitsky, Steven & Lucan A. Way. 2010. *Competitive Authoritarianism: Hybrid Regimes After the Cold War*. New York: Cambridge University Press.

Levitt, Steven D. & James M. Snyder Jr. 1997. "The Impact of Federal Spending on House Election Outcomes." *Journal of Political Economy* 105(1):30–54.

Lewis-Beck, Michael S. 1990. *Economics and Elections: The Major Western Democracies*. Ann Arbor: University of Michican Press.

Lewis-Beck, Michael S. & Mary Stegmaier. 2000. "Economic Determinants of Electoral Outcomes." *Annual Review of Political Science* 3:183–219.

Lieberman, Evan S. 2016. "Can the Biomedical Research Cycle be a Model for Political Science?" *Perspectives on Politics* 14(4):1054–66.

Lieven, Anatol. 1994. *The Baltic Revolution: Estonia, Latvia, Lithuania and the Path to Independence*. New Haven: Yale University Press.

Lindberg, Staffan. 2009. A Theory of Elections as a Mode of Transition. In *Democratization By Elections*, ed. Staffan Lindberg. Baltimore: Johns Hopkins University Press.

Linzer, Drew & Jeffrey K. Staton. 2015. "A Global Measure of Judicial Independence, 1948–2012." *Journal of Law and Courts* 3(2):223–56.

Luong, Pauline Jones & Erika Weinthal. 2010. *Oil is Not a Curse: Ownership Structure and Institutions in Soviet Successor States*. New York: Cambridge University Press.

Lust-Okar, Ellen. 2009. Legislative Elections in Hegemonic Authoritarian Regimes: Competitive Clientelism and Resistance to Democratization. In *Democratization by Elections: A New Mode of Transition*, ed. Staffan Lindberg. Baltimore: Johns Hopkins University Press.

Lutz, Ellen L. & Caitlin Reiger. 2009. *Prosecuting Heads of State*. New York: Cambridge University Press.

Magalhaes, Pedro C. 1999. "The Politics of Judicial Reform in Eastern Europe." *Comparative Politics* 32(1):43–62.

Magaloni, Beatriz. 2006. *Voting for Autocracy: The Politics of Party Hegemony and its Demise*. New York: Cambridge University Press.

Magaloni, Beatriz. 2008. "Credible Power-Sharing and the Longevity of Authoritarian Rule." *Comparative Political Studies* 41(4-5):715–41.

Marshall, Monty G., Keith Jaggers, & Ted R. Gurr. 2012. "Polity IV Project: Political Regime Characteristics and Transitions, 1800–2011." Center for Systemic Peace.

Marshall, Monty G., Keith Jaggers, & Ted R. Gurr. 2015. "Polity IV Project: Political Regime Characteristics and Transitions, Political Regime Characteristics and Transitions, 1800–2015 Dataset Users' Manual."

Mazaheri, Nimah. 2016. *Oil Booms and Business Busts: Why Resource Wealth Hurts Entrepreneurs in the Developing World*. New York: Oxford University Press.

McCubbins, Mathew D. & Thomas Schwartz. 1984. "Congressional Oversight Overlooked: Police Patrols versus Fire Alarms." *American Journal of Political Science* 28(1): 165–79.

Melton, James & Tom Ginsburg. 2014. "Does De Jure Judicial Independence Really Matter? A Reevaluation of Explanations for Judicial Independence." *Journal of Law and Courts* 2(2):187–217.

Monroe, Kristen R. 1984. *Presidential Popularity and the Economy*. Westport: Praeger Publishers.

Montgomery, Jacob M. & Brendan Nyhan. 2010. "Bayesian Model Averaging: Theoretical Developments and Practical Applications." *Political Analysis* 18(2):245–70.

Morrison, Kevin M. 2009. "Oil, Nontax Revenue, and the Redistributional Foundations of Regime Stability." *International Organization* 63(1):107–38.

Morrison, Kevin M. 2014. *Nontaxation and Representation*. New York: Cambridge University Press.

Moustafa, Tamir. 2003. "Law versus the State: The Judicialization of Politics in Egypt." *Law & Social Inquiry* 28(4):883–930.

Moustafa, Tamir. 2007. *The Struggle for Constitutional Power: Law, Politics, and Economic Development in Egypt*. New York: Cambridge University Press.

Moustafa, Tamir. 2008. Law and Resistance in Authoritarian States: the Judicialization of Politics in Egypt. In *Rule by Law: the Politics of Courts in Authoritarian Regimes*, ed. Tom Ginsburg & Tamir Moustafa. New York: Cambridge University Press.

MTI. 2012. "LMP Fails to Elect New Parliamentary Group Leader as Split in Party Continues." http://www.politics.hu/20121126/lmp-fails-to-elect-new-parliamentary-group-leader-as-split-in-party-continues/.

Mudde, Cas. 2014. "The 2014 Hungarian Parliamentary Elections, or How to Craft a Constitutional Majority." *The Monkey Cage (Washington Post Blog), April 14*. https://www.washingtonpost.com/news/monkey-cage/wp/2014/04/14/the-2014-hungarian-parliamentary-elections-or-how-to-craft-a-constitutional-majority.

Mudde, Cas & Erin K Jenne. 2012. "Can Outsider's Help?" *Journal of Democracy* 23(3): 147–55.

Munck, Gerardo L. & Jay Verkuilen. 2002. "Conceptualizing and Measuring Democracy." *Comparative Political Studies* 35(1):5–34.

Myagkov, Mikhail, Peter C. Ordeshook, & Dmitry Shakin. 2005. "Fraud or Fairytales: Russia and Ukraine's Electoral Experience." *Post-Soviet Affairs* 21(2):91–131.

Myagkov, Misha & Peter C. Ordeshook. 2008. "Russian Elections: An Oxymoron of Democracy." *Caltech/MIT Voting Project Working Paper No. 63*.

Norris, Floyd. 2014. "Borrowers in Hungary Learn Tough Lessons." *New York Times*, November 13.

ODIHR. 2010. "Ukraine Presidential Election, OSCE/ODIHR Election Observation Mission Final Report." http://www.osce.org/odihr/elections/ukraine/67844.

Okoth-Ogendo, HWO. 1993. Constitutions Without Constitutionalism: An African Political Paradox. In *Constitutionalism and Democracy: Transitions in the Contemporary World*, ed. Douglas Greenberg, Stanley N. Katz, Steven C. Wheatley, & Melanie Beth Oliviero. Oxford: Oxford University Press.

Olszański, Tadeusz A. 2012. "The Language Issue in Ukraine: An Attempt at a New Perspective." *Centre for Eastern Studies Working Paper* 40.

Orbán, Viktor. 2014. "The End of Liberal Democracy." Speech at Baăile Tuşnad (Tusnádfürdő). Full text available at https://budapestbeacon.com/full-text-of-viktor-orbans-speech-at-baile-tusnad-tusnadfurdo-of-26-july-2014.

Pabriks, Artis & Aldis Purs. 2001. *Latvia: The Challenges of Change*. New York: Routledge.

Pacek, Alexander C. & Benjamin Radcliff. 1995. "Economic Voting and the Welfare State: A Cross-National Analysis." *Journal of Politics* 57(1):44–61.

Paler, Laura. 2013. "Keeping the Public Purse: An Experiment in Windfalls, Taxes, and the Incentives to Restrain Government." *American Political Science Review* 107(4):706–25.

Palmer, Harvey D. & Guy D. Whitten. 1999. "The Electoral Impact of Unexpected Inflation and Economic Growth." *British Journal of Political Science* 29(4):623–39.

Parliament of Hungary [Az Országgyűlés]. 2010. "Political Declaration on National Co-operation [politikai nyilatkozata a Nemzeti Együttműködésről], 1/2010. (VI. 16.) OGY." http://2010–2014.kormany.hu/download/d/56/00000/politikai_nyilatkozat.pdf.

Paul, Christopher & Miriam Matthews. 2016. The Russian "Firehose of Falsehood" Propaganda Model. Technical report RAND Corporation.

Pepys, Mary N. 2003. "Corruption in the Justice System." Sectoral Perspectives on Corruption, USAID, http://www.usaid.gov/our_work/democracy_and_governance/publications.

Pifer, Steven. 2012. "Ukraine: Digging in Deeper on Tymoshenko." http://www.brookings.edu/research/opinions/2012/12/20-tymoshenko-ukraine-pifer.

Pilatovsky, Kimberly. 2016. "De Jure Provisions for Judicial Independence in US States: 1776 to 2015." Paper presented at the annual meeting of the Southern Political Science Association.

Polese, Abel & Donnacha Ó Beacháin. 2011. "The Color Revolution Virus and Authoritarian Antidotes: Political Protest and Regime Counterattacks in Post-Communist Spaces." *Demokratizatsiya* 19(2):111–33.

Polityuk, Pavel. 2012. "Ukraine Seethes After Russian Language Law Voted In." Reuters News Service, July 4, http://www.reuters.com/article/2012/07/04/us-ukraine-language-idUSBRE86309120120704.

Pop-Eleches, Grigore. 2010. "Throwing Out the Bums: Protest Voting and Unorthodox Parties After Communism." *World Politics* 62(2):221–60.

Popova, Maria. 2010. "Political Competition as an Obstacle to Judicial Independence: Evidence From Russia and Ukraine." *Comparative Political Studies* 43(10): 1202–29.

Popova, Maria. 2012. *Politicized Justice in Emerging Democracies: A Study of Courts in Russia and Ukraine*. New York: Cambridge University Press.

Przeworski, Adam, Michael Alvarez, Jose A. Cheibub, & Fernando Limongi. 2000. *Democracy and Development: Political Institutions and Well-Being in the World, 1950–1990*. New York: Cambridge University Press.

Puddington, Arch. 2017. "Breaking Down Democracy: Goals, Strategies, and Methods of Modern Authoritarians." Freedom House.

Rainey, Carlisle. 2014. "Arguing for a Negligible Effect." *American Journal of Political Science* 58(4):1083–91.

Ramos, Francisco. 2006. "The Establishment of Constitutional Courts: A Study of 128 Democratic Constitutions." *Review of Law and Economics* 1(2):1–33.

Ramseyer, J. Mark. 1994. "The Puzzling (in)Dependence of Courts: A Comparative Approach." *Journal of Legal Studies* 23(2):721–47.

Randazzo, Kirk, Douglas Gibler, & Rebecca Reid. 2016. "Examining the Development of Judicial Independence." *Political Research Quarterly* 69(3):583–93.

Remmer, Karen L. 1991. "The Political Impact of Economic Crisis in Latin America in the 1980s." *American Political Science Review* 85(3):777–800.

Reuter, Ora John & Jennifer Gandhi. 2011. "Economic Performance and Elite Defection from Hegemonic Parties." *British Journal of Political Science* 41(1):83–110.

Reuters. 2013. "Hillary Clinton To Yulia Tymoshenko: Secretary Of State Sends Jailed Ex-PM Of Ukraine Message Of Support." http://www.huffingtonpost.com/2013/01/22/hillary-clinton-yulia-tymoshenko-pm-ukraine-murder$_{n2}$526781.html.

Ríos-Figueroa, Julio. 2006. The Determinants of Judicial Independence and Constitutional Adjudication A Study of Latin America, 1950–2002. In *Global Fellows Forum*, New York University School of Law.

Ríos-Figueroa, Julio. 2007. "Fragmentation of Power and the Emergence of an Effective Judiciary in Mexico, 1994–2002." *Latin American Politics and Society* 49(1):31–57.

Ríos-Figueroa, Julio & Jeffrey K. Staton. 2012. "An Evaluation of Cross-National Measures of Judicial Independence." *Journal of Law, Economics and Organization* 30(1):104–37.

Roberts, Kenneth M. & Erik Wibbels. 1999. "Party Systems and Electoral Volatility in Latin America: A Test of Economic, Institutional, and Structural Explanations." *American Political Science Review* 93(3):575–90.

Robertson, Geoffrey. 2014. "Judicial Independence: Some Recent Problems." *International Bar Association Human Rights Institute Working Papers* 4.

Robison, Richard. 1988. "Authoritarian States, Capital-Owning Classes, and the Politics of Newly Industrializing Countries." *World Politics* 41(1):52–74.

Roessler, Philip & Marc M. Howard. 2009. Post-Cold War Political Regimes: When Do Elections Matter? In *Democratization By Elections*, ed. Staffan I. Lindberg. Baltimore: Johns Hopkins University Press.

Rogeberg, Ole & Hans Olav Melberg. 2011. "Acceptance of Unsupported Claims About Reality: A Blind Spot in Economics." *Journal of Economic Methodology* 18(01):29–52.

Rogers, James R. 2001. "Information and Judicial Review: A Signaling Game of Legislative–Judicial Interaction." *American Journal of Political Science*, 45(1):84–99.

Rosenn, Keith S. 1987. "The Protection of Judicial Independence in Latin America." *The University of Miami Inter-American Law Review* 19(1):1–35.

Rozenberg, Joshua. 2012. "Meet Tünde Handó." *Guardian*, March 20. http://www.theguardian.com/law/2012/mar/20/tunde-handoff-hungarian-judges

Rundlett, Ashlea & Milan W. Svolik. 2016. "Deliver the Vote! Micromotives and Macrobehavior in Electoral Fraud." *American Political Science Review* 110(1):180–97.

Rupnik, Jacques. 2012. "How Things Went Wrong." *Journal of Democracy* 23(3):132–7.

Sartori, Giovanni. 1987. *The Theory of Democracy Revisited*. Chatham: Chatham House.

Schedler, Andreas. 2002. "The Menu of Manipulation." *Journal of Democracy* 13(2):36–50.

Schedler, Andreas. 2006. *Electoral Authoritarianism: The Dynamics of Unfree Competition*. Boulder: Lynne Rienner.

Scheppele, Kim Lane. 1999. "The New Hungarian Constitutional Court." *East European Constitutional Review* 8(4):81–87.

Scheppele, Kim Lane. 2012*a*. "First Let's Pick All the Judges." *New York Times*, March 10.

Scheppele, Kim Lane. 2012*b*. "Hungary's Free Media." *New York Times*, March 14.

Scheppele, Kim Lane. 2013. "Constitutional Revenge." http://verfassungsblog.de/constitutional-revenge-2.

Scheppele, Kim Lane. 2015. Understanding Hungary's Constitutional Revolution. In *Constitutional Crisis in the European Constitutional Area,* ed. Armin von Bogdandy & Pal Sonnevend. London: Hart.

Schumpeter, Joseph A. 1950. *Capitalism, Socialism and Democracy.* New York: Harper & Bros. (Originally published 1942).

Simpser, Alberto. 2013. *Why Governments and Parties Manipulate Elections: Theory, Practice, and Implications.* New York: Cambridge University Press.

Smith, Benjamin. 2004. "Oil Wealth and Regime Survival in the Developing World, 1960–1999." *American Journal of Political Science* 48(2):232–46.

Smith, David J. 2001. *Estonia: Independence and European Integration.* New York: Routledge.

Smithey, Shannon Ishiyama & John Ishiyama. 2002. "Judicial Activism in Post-Communist Politics." *Law & Society Review* 36(4):719.

Snyder Jr., James M. & David Strömberg. 2010. "Press Coverage and Political Accountability." *Journal of Political Economy* 118(2):355–408.

Sobel, Russell S. 1998. "The Political Costs of Tax Increases and Expenditure Reductions: Evidence from State Legislative Turnover." *Public Choice* 96(1):61–79.

Sólyom, László. 2003. "The Role of Constitutional Courts in the Transition to Democracy: With Special Reference to Hungary." *International Sociology* 18(1):133–61.

Spillius, Alex. 2012. "Ukraine Minister Insists Yulia Tymoshenko Broke the Law." *Telegraph* August 29. http://www.telegraph.co.uk/news/worldnews/europe/ukraine/9507147/Ukraine-minister-insists-Yulia-Tymoshenko-broke-the-law.html.

Staton, Jeffrey K. 2010. *Judicial Power and Strategic Communication in Mexico.* New York: Cambridge University Press.

Staton, Jeffrey K. 2017. Judical Independence Research Beyond the Crossroads. In *The Routledge Handbook of Judicial Behavior,* ed. Robert M. Howard & Kirk A. Randazzo. New York: Routledge.

Stephenson, Matthew C. 2003. "'When the Devil Turns...': The Political Foundations of Independent Judicial Review." *Journal of Legal Studies* 32(1):59–89.

Stephenson, Matthew C. 2004. "Court of Public Opinion: Government Accountability and Judicial Independence." *Journal of Law, Economics, and Organization* 20(2):379–99.

Stokes, Susan C. 2001. *Mandates and Democracy: Neoliberalism by Surprise in Latin America.* New York: Cambridge University Press.

Stone Sweet, Alec. 2000. *Governing with Judges: Constitutional Politics in Europe.* New York: Oxford University Press.

Stroh, Alexander & Charlotte Heyl. 2015. "Institutional Diffusion, Strategic Insurance, and the Creation of West African Constitutional Courts." *Comparative Politics* 47(2):169–87.

Strzelecki, Marek. 2017. "Polish Ruling Party Attacks Top Judge in New Democracy Row." https://www.bloomberg.com/news/articles/2017-03-02/polish-ruling-party-moves-against-top-judge-in-new-democracy-row.

Svolik, Milan. 2012. *The Politics of Authoritarian Rule.* New York: Cambridge University Press.

Szente, Zoltán. 2016. "The Political Orientation of the Members of the Hungarian Constitutional Court between 2010 and 2014." *Constitutional Studies* 1(1):123–49.

Sztompka, Piotyr. 1998. "Trust, Distrust and Two Paradoxes of Democracy." *European Journal of Social Theory* 1(1):19–32.

Tate, C. Neal & Linda C. Keith. 2007. "Conceptualizing and Operationalizing Judicial Independence Globally." Paper presented at the annual meeting of the American Political Science.

Tate, C. Neal & Linda C. Keith. 2009. "Conceptualizing and Operationalizing Judicial Independence Globally." Unpublished manuscript.

Tate, C. Neal & Torbjorn Vallinder. 1995. *The Global Expansion of Judicial Power: The Judicialization of Politics*. New York: New York University Press.

Tavits, Margit. 2005. "The Development of Stable Party Support: Electoral Dynamics in Post-Communist Europe." *American Journal of Political Science* 49(2):283–98.

Tezcür, Güneş Murat. 2012. "Democracy Promotion, Authoritarian Resiliency, and Political Unrest in Iran." *Democratization* 19(1):120–40.

Than, Krisztina & Marton Dunai. 2012. "Insight: In Hungary, a Business Elite Thrives." http://www.reuters.com/article/us-hungary-idUSBRE83F0KG20120416.

Thomas, Daniel C. 1999. The Helsinki Accords and Political Change in Eastern Europe. In *The Power of Human Rights: International Norms and Domestic Change*, ed. Thomas Risse-Kappen, Stephen C. Ropp & Kathryn Sikkink. New York: Cambridge University Press.

Thompson, Mark & Philipp Kuntz. 2006. After Defeat: When do Rulers Steal Elections? In *Electoral Authoritarianism: The Dynamics of Unfree Competition*, ed. Andreas Schedler. Boulder: Lynne Rienner.

Trajectory of Democracy. 2013. "U.S. Commission on Security and Cooperation in Europe." (Testimony of Kim Lane Scheppele, March 19).

Trochev, Alexei. 2004. "Less Democracy, More Courts: A Puzzle of Judicial Review in Russia." *Law & Society Review* 38(3):513–48.

Tullock, Gordon. 1986. "Industrial Organization and Rent Seeking in Dictatorships." *Journal of Institutional and Theoretical Economics* 142(1):4–15.

Uitz, Renáta. 2013. "The Return of the Hungarian Constitutional Court." http://verfassungsblog.de/the-return-of-the-hungarian-constitutional-court.

Uitz, Renáta. 2015. "Can You Tell When an Illiberal Democracy is in the Making? An Appeal to Comparative Constitutional Scholarship from Hungary." *International Journal of Constitutional Law* 13(1):279–300.

Ulfelder, Jay. 2005. "Contentious Collective Action and the Breakdown of Authoritarian Regimes." *International Political Science Review* 26(3):311–34.

Urban, Michael E. 1997. *The Rebirth of Politics in Russia*. New York: Cambridge University Press.

Vanberg, Georg. 2000. "Establishing Judicial Independence in West Germany: The Impact of Opinion Leadership and the Separation of Powers." *Comparative Politics* 32(3):333–53.

Vanberg, Georg. 2001. "Legislative–Judicial Relations: A Game–Theoretic Approach to Constitutional Review." *American Journal of Political Science* 45(2):346–61.

Vanberg, Georg. 2005. *The Politics of Constitutional Review in Germany*. New York: Cambridge University Press.

Vanberg, Georg. 2011. "Substance vs. Procedure: Constitutional Enforcement and Constitutional Choice." *Journal of Economic Behavior & Organization* 80(2):309–18.

Vanberg, Georg. 2015. "Constitutional Courts in Comparative Perspective: A Theoretical Assessment." *Annual Review of Political Science* 18:167–85.

Vanhanen, Tatu. 2000. "A New Dataset for Measuring Democracy, 1810–1998." *Journal of Peace Research* 37(2):251–65.

Voigt, Stefan & Jerg Gutmann. 2013. "Turning Cheap Talk into Economic Growth: On the Relationship between Property Rights and Judicial Independence." *Journal of Comparative Economics* 41(1):66–73.

Voigt, Stefan, Jerg Gutmann, & Lars P. Feld. 2015. "Economic Growth and Judicial Independence, a Dozen Years On: Cross-Country Evidence Using an Updated Set of Indicators." *European Journal of Political Economy* 38:197–211.

VonDoepp, Peter. 2009. *Judicial Politics in New Democracies: Cases from Southern Africa*. Boulder: Lynne Rienner Publishers.

VonDoepp, Peter & Rachel Ellet. 2011. "Reworking Strategic Models of Executive–Judicial Relations: Insights from New African Democracies." *Comparative Politics* 43(2):147–65.

Ward, Michael D., Randolph M. Siverson, & Xun Cao. 2007. "Disputes, Democracies, and Dependencies: A Reexamination of the Kantian Peace." *American Journal of Political Science* 51(3):583–601.

Way, Lucan. 2008. "The Real Causes of the Color Revolution." *Journal of Democracy* 19(3):55–69.

Weingast, Barry R. 1997. "The Political Foundations of Democracy and the Rule of Law." *American Political Science Review* 91(2):245–63.

Wellek, Stefan. 2010. *Testing Statistical Hypotheses of Equivalence and Noninferiority*. Boca Raton: CRC Press.

Westlake, Wilfred J. 1979. "Statistical Aspects of Comparative Bioavailability Trials." *Biometrics* 35(1):273–80.

White, Allison C. 2016. "Electoral Fraud and Electoral Geography: United Russia Strongholds in the 2007 and 2011 Russian Parliamentary Elections." *Europe-Asia Studies* 68(7):1127–78.

Whitmore, Brian. 2007. "Russia: Uncertainty Over Putin Succession Fuels 'Siloviki War'." Radio Free Europe/Radio Liberty: The Power Vertical, November 9, /www.rferl.org/content/article/1079108.html.

Whitten-Woodring, Jenifer & Douglas A. Van Belle. 2017. "The Correlates of Media Freedom: An Introduction of the Global Media Freedom Dataset." *Political Science Research and Methods* 5(1):179–88.

Whittington, Keith E. 2003. "Legislative Sanctions and the Strategic Environment of Judicial Review." *International Journal of Constitutional Law* 1(3):446–74.

Whittington, Keith E. 2005. "'Interpose Your Friendly Hand': Political Supports for the Exercise of Judicial Review by the United States Supreme Court." *American Political Science Review* 99(4):583–96.

Wilson, Matthew C. 2014. "A Discreet Critique of Discrete Regime Type Data." *Comparative Political Studies* 47(5):689–714.

Wright, Joseph. 2008. "Do Authoritarian Institutions Constrain? How Legislatures Impact Economic Growth and Investment." *American Journal of Political Science* 52(2):322–43.

Wright, R. George. 1990. "Could a Constitutional Amendment Be Unconstitutional." *Loyolya University Chicago Law Journal* 22(4):741–64.

Yadav, Vineeta & Bumba Mukherjee. 2014. *Democracy, Electoral Systems, and Judicial Empowerment in Developing Countries*. Ann Arbor: University of Michigan Press.

Yuichi Kono, Daniel & Gabriella R. Montinola. 2009. "Does Foreign Aid Support Autocrats, Democrats, or Both?" *Journal of Politics* 71(2):704–18.

Zadorozhnii, Oleksandr. 2010. Separation of Powers in Russia and Ukraine. In *Separation of Powers in Russia and Ukraine: A Comparative Perspective*, ed. William E. Pomeranz & F. Joseph Dresen. Washington, DC: Woodrow Wilson International Center for Scholars.

Index

The manufacturer's authorised representative in the EU for product safety is Oxford University Press España S.A. of el Parque Empresarial San Fernando de Henares, Avenida de Castilla, 2 – 28830 Madrid (www.oup.es/en or product.safety@oup.com). OUP España S.A. also acts as importer into Spain of products made by the manufacturer.

www.ingramcontent.com/pod-product-compliance
Lightning Source LLC
LaVergne TN
LVHW011818200926
848484LV00005B/1236
* 9 7 8 0 1 9 8 8 4 5 0 2 7 *